Dissident Friendships

DISSIDENT FEMINISMS

A list of books in the series appears at the end of this book.

Dissident Friendships

Feminism, Imperialism, and
Transnational Solidarity

EDITED BY ELORA HALIM CHOWDHURY
AND LIZ PHILIPOSE

UNIVERSITY OF ILLINOIS PRESS
Urbana, Chicago, and Springfield

4. For Sister or State? Nationalism and the Indigenous
   and Bengali Women's Movements in Bangladesh   91

   Kabita Chakma and Glen Hill

5. Solidarity through Dissidence: Violence and Community
   in Indian Cinema   117

   Alka Kurian

PART THREE: NEOLIBERALISM, AGENCY, FRIENDSHIP

6. Kinship Drives, Friendly Affect: Difference and Dissidence
   in the New Indian Border Cinema   143

   Esha Niyogi De

7. *The Space Between Us*: Reading Umrigar and Sangari
   in the Quest for Female Friendship   160

   Elora Halim Chowdhury

8. Who Are "We" in the Novel?   182

   Shreerekha Subramanian

PART FOUR: FRIENDSHIP ACROSS BORDERS

9. A Spirit of Solidarity: Transatlantic Friendships among Early
   Twentieth-century Female Peace Activists (Wilpfers)   203

   Laurie R. Cohen

10. The Dissidence of Daily Life: Feminist Friendships
    and the Social Fabric of Democracy   221

    Lori E. Amy and Eglantina Gjermeni

Contributors   241

Index   247

Acknowledgments

As an intellectual, political, and affective project, the idea and praxis of "friendships across borders" inform our own friendship, politics, and the respective relationships we have in and beyond the academy. The two of us met at a Global Feminisms Summer Institute in 2005 at Cornell University. The institute was intended for feminist scholars at various stages of their careers to grapple with issues of identity, knowledge, pedagogy, and practice. The institute engendered a deep sense of community and solidarity among the fellows whose identities, histories, political, and scholarly trajectories seemed infinitely divergent. Dialogue, self-interrogation, and genuine interest and investment in one another's histories fostered a bond that helped us imagine friendship as a mode for social and political transformation. There is no small contribution here by our beloved mentors, Professors Chandra Talpade Mohanty and Beverly Guy-Sheftall, who created a rigorous and provocative syllabus and mentored and guided us through our (re)discoveries, re(affirmations), and commitments to social justice and activism. They also modeled genuine friendship in their dynamic with each other and with us. We are grateful for those idyllic yet emotionally and intellectually turbulent two weeks in Ithaca, to the Future of Minority Studies (FMS) scholars' vision, and for their commitment to support us who come to the academy for a political and transformative project. It has engendered lifelong friendships that continue to sustain and nourish our minds and souls.

Dawn Durante has been the most supportive, encouraging, and dedicated editor one could ever ask for. Inheriting the project at a time of transition, she shepherded it through and offered us critical and clear advice at every stage. We owe much to our former editor Larin McLaughlin, and series editor Piya Chatterjee who envisioned the Dissident Feminisms series, in which we found a fitting home for our volume, *Dissident Friendships*. Our brilliant contributors have engaged and extended the ideas inhering feminist solidarity in valuable and delightful ways. What a joy it has been to work and learn alongside them in this journey. The cross-disciplinary, cross-cultural conversations have been exciting and invigorating in what we believe is a burgeoning field. The anonymous reviewers of the volume provided sharp insights. Our work has been enriched by their thoughtful suggestions. We owe a great debt to Riva Pearson, our research assistant for her tireless editorial support. Our heartfelt appreciation to Ambreen Butt for her extraordinary art, which adorns the cover of this book. In her words, "The image and the title were made for each other." We are grateful for the grants from the Offices of the Dean and Provost at University of Massachusetts Boston, which enabled us to complete the project efficiently.

This project would not have been possible without the soul-sustaining love and unfailing encouragement I (Elora) received from my mother, Shamsun Nahar Chowdhury; Alok Kapoor, my friend and life partner; and my cheeky boys Zain and Zahin Aziz. Their loving confidence in me, with a healthy dose of pestering and humor, kept me grounded and appreciating the bigger picture! I also wish to thank my colleagues, students, and friends at UMass Boston for their amazing work—they inspire me every day!

I (Liz) am grateful for all of the relationships that come into my life and inspire me in all things—friends, mentors, colleagues, students, creators, clients, partners, teachers, playmates, fellow travelers, visionaries, lovers, and adventurers—and for the divine orchestration that makes all of it so.

Dissident Friendships

Introduction

ELORA HALIM CHOWDHURY AND LIZ PHILIPOSE

Several years ago, a number of U.S. feminists organized "hijab day," a day when women of all religions and ethnicities would don the hijab in a gesture of solidarity with believing women who wore the hijab on a daily basis. The intention was to deflect the negativity directed against Muslim women in the United States, and to diffuse attention by forming a much larger group. It was also a way of saying to "believing women" that we are with you and for your freedom of religion to be realized, and we stand together against the bigotry and violence directed against you since the recent and virulent revival of old Islamaphobia and colonial tropes in this new, precarious, and shifting global context.

Hijab day was a response to the racial and sexual violence directed against believing women who wore a veil as the visible marker of Islam. This, despite the many pronouncements made by presidents of the United States and preambles of recent antiterrorism legislation that claim that Islam is not the enemy and Muslims are not the target. Terrorism, however, is coded as Muslim and women wearing gendered markers in U.S. patriarchal society are racialized and reduced to a simple signifier of our collective loathing. In many ways, hijab day was conceived as an act of friendship, a counter to hatred, and even a dissident friendship given the context of the contemporary United States.

At once, however, a conundrum was at hand. The hijab, or "the veil," as it is often called, is a complex and shifting signifier that is not understood well by a broad audience. It may well be an affront to believing women who veil for nonbelievers to adopt the veil as a political statement. It may not be appropriate, given the sanctity of religion and the sensitivities of believers. It might not be interpreted as an act of solidarity because the translation between us and them may not be transparent. As some feminists took pause to reflect and consider the potential impacts of hijab day, they came to some important realizations about the distance between "us" and "them," between the U.S. non-Muslim feminists who were proposing hijab day and actual Muslim women in the United States who wore the veil on a daily basis. There were not already existing friendships between non-Muslim feminists and Muslim women to turn to for clarification and discussion about hijab day. It was rather sudden, in fact, that US feminists were turning their attention to Muslim women who veil as partners in solidarity.

The conversations around hijab day highlighted the absence of friendship between Muslim and non-Muslim women, and even between Muslim women who veil and those who do not. These conversations hinted that while there is a sincere desire to express solidarity with Muslim women who are increasingly targets of racism and violence, "we"—women who may be of different cultural, national, or religious backgrounds or who share those backgrounds yet inhabit/make different sartorial/political communities/choices—do not know how to do it in a way that communicates our intention because we do not know each other. The debate about the wisdom or folly of hijab day brings into sharp relief the importance of friendship to solidarity efforts. The potential of debates like this is to spark movements of dissident friendship: as a process of coming to know each others' stories and unlearning "an impulse that allows mythologies about each other to replace knowing about one another" (Alexander 2005, 269).

Friendship is to know someone, and to know them in particular. We can have friendly feelings and desires, but friendship itself is intimate, personal, caring, in particular, attached, and connected. To get to friendship, we would have to unravel our assumptions and clear the colonial and racial debris from our perceptual apparatus to see intimately and to become personal. In friendship is a sense of belonging. Political theory conversations about belonging and attachment take the nation-state as the unit in which friendship is possible. Yet, we know that friendship is not guaranteed between nationals and, in fact, a central concern of political theory is to find the mechanisms to catalyze fellow-feeling.

Friendship is significant to collective life. It highlights lived experience, emotions, love, intimacy, and caring, all of which are central to creating life-enhancing communities. The fact is, whatever is happening in the material world, "even the most egregious signatures of new empire are not the sole organizing nexus of subjectivity," and we have the capacity to think beyond power (Alexander 2005, 328). Friendship is an important impulse that counters fear and speaks truth to power in a unique way, by embodying and experiencing human and heart-centered connections with unlikely interlocutors. Our lived experiences deny the stories that structural power tells and demonstrate that the imperial imagination does not control our horizon of possibilities.

In friendship, then, is our resistance to the divisive and fragmenting lies of structural power; the seeds of global compassion, generosity, empathy and love; and the foundation of a world that works on behalf of life. The dissidence of which this volume speaks is in the friendships across political boundaries and structural power that demonstrate the power of affect and emotional bonding to counter divisions. National, racial, imperial, class, gender, and "enemy lines" fail to keep people from crossing lines in friendship. Hence, "all those invisible affective gestures that refuse alignment" that Leela Gandhi names "dissident friendships" are worthy of further exploration as they offer yet another site to observe that power does not monopolize our subjectivities (2006, 10). The border-crossing friendships under discussion in this volume demonstrate, repeatedly, that regardless of the social and material conditions, the "irremediable leaky boundaries of imperialism" give way to deep relationships of attachment and belonging (2). Dissident friendships, then, are potentially transformative, personally and socially transformative, and in many cases, subversive, as Gandhi says, "a breach ... in the fabric of imperial inhospitality" (189). The essays in this volume each express in different ways the forging of hospitality in the midst of divisive political structures, across spatial and temporal borders and, in doing so, contribute insight to the ways that we connect and are connected across constraints. The analytical contribution of these essays is an analytics of care and openness to the other, to be transformed by each other and our affective connections.

As several of the authors point out, the complexity of the potentially radical trope of friendship between women is that it can be and is often collapsed into the discourse of neoliberal transnationalism. Specifically, the motifs of individual motivation, women's empowerment, flexible connectivity, and multicultural development recur in various discourses of empire, globalization, and neoliberalism designed to maintain power structures as they are. Learning from theorists of feminism, alliance, and empire, we must note the propensity of such discourses of individuality and difference to contribute to flexible, neoliberal imperialism and approach the topic of dissident friendships with a critical eye. Set in historical and contemporary contexts of imperial, national, and global structures of inequalities, the ideas of dissident cross-cultural alliance and friendship in these chapters provide transformative visions of transnational solidarity and praxis. The essays grapple with the critical question, do unlikely alliances among associates of oppressor and oppressed communities trump, or get trumped by, other kinds of allegiances individuals and collectives might have, to family, community, or nation, in the pursuit of social justice? This volume is thus motivated by an interest in fostering a transnational analytic of care: one that does not play into the politics of accommodation; is not defensive, reactionary, or silencing; and is cognizant of "local" and "global" processes that create conditions of vulnerability for women (and men) and form the uneven and asymmetrical planes in which dissident, cross-cultural friendships, alliances, and solidarity practices—particularly within the interpersonal realm—are ever more urgent.

The ten essays are grouped into four themes. In the first section, Nicole Nguyen et al. and Azza Basarudin and Himika Bhattacharya discuss instances when they as feminists have confronted and negotiated the complicated, conflicted, and contradictory terrain of "Praxis of Friendship." In the Nguyen et al. piece, the authors meditate on collective knowledge making that expands the project of transnational feminist coalitions and action within and beyond the university. Designed as a project for the course Transnational Feminist Practices taught by Professor Chandra Talpade Mohanty at Syracuse University, the joint task was to create an undergraduate teaching module about the Israeli occupation of the Palestinian territories. Inspired by Jacqui Alexander's directive to imagine alternatives to hegemonic academic structures, the authors grapple with epistemic friendships that subvert narrowly defined agendas even while they reproduce inequality. The authors define epistemic friendship as not simply coalition or solidarity across difference, but rather the enactment of a community of support based on shared politics. As emerging feminist scholars, the process of decolonizing knowledge and creating emancipatory pedagogies highlights the value of multiple ways of learning (with the community) and being (practicing affection and kindness) within an exclusionary, alienating, and hierarchical academic culture.

Ruminating about the significance of friendship in enacting feminist ethnography, coauthors and friends Azza Basarudin and Himika Bhattacharya think through the often hidden role friendship plays in academic rituals. A reflection on their fieldwork in Malaysia and India, respectively, enable the shifting of locus from "self-reflexivity and legitimacy into transformative epistemological and methodological approaches to transnational feminist solidarities and systems of knowledge production." Complicated friendships with interlocutors inhere the praxis of feminist knowledge production even if they remain obscured or trivialized in the larger project of rigorous scholarship and "truth making." Emotional entanglements, love, and affection are often at the heart of ethnographic projects and are intricately involved in the creation of ethical and revolutionary knowledge. It is an introspective engagement with the question, "How do we as critical feminist ethnographers from the Global South, located in elite institutions in the Global North, negotiate our multiple and sometimes contradictory subjectivities within and beyond our field sites, while remaining respectful to the imagination, blood, and sweat of those who allow us into the intimate folds of their worlds?"

In "Gender, Nation, Solidarity," Yuangfang Dai, Kabita Chakma and Glen Hill, and Alka Kurian grapple with the historically uneasy relationship between feminism and nationalism and offer fresh perspectives on feminists' invested, reluctant, and selective use of the nation, even as it is a limiting framework. Grappling with both the epistemology and politics of solidarity, and foregrounding the conceptual frameworks of antiracist, third world, and transnational feminisms, Yuangfang Dai's essay develops the notion of a transcultural feminist solidarity in the context of globalization and in relation to Chinese feminism's position to the imperial U.S. center. How could feminists on either side foster fruitful dialogue around fraught issues such as "human rights" when the meaning and advocacy of it could be seen as irreconcilable given historical, geopolitical, and practical divides? Arguing that solidarity is an important vehicle for personal and collective transformation because of its grounding in a feeling of interdependence—whether confrontational or harmonious but nevertheless, mutually meaningful—it has the potential to create a self-conscious coalition based on group identity even as it is aware of gender difference and differential oppressions. Critiquing notions of "global sisterhood" and "common oppression," Dai settles on a radical antiracist and transnational feminist platform that deals directly with the "problem of difference" through a collective intentionality. She follows Maria Lugones's directive that feminists need to travel to each other's worlds and strive for plurality in the process of their political work. Such a worldview allows for a deeper cross-cultural understanding of women's realities and constrained choices, particularly of those "different" from our own.

Chakma and Hill provide a nuanced picture of the use of the glorious nationalist framework in the secular nationalist women's movement in Bangladesh as a matter of national pride and liberation, yet at the same time, the underside of this movement, which has yet to adequately acknowledge, integrate, and secure indigenous women's rights as a part of that same history. Furthermore, Bengali nationalism, even of the feminist kind, serves to silence indigenous women's complex struggle against state-sponsored militarism and patriarchy. In this context, the Bengali women's movement functions as a colonial power where nationalism becomes a dubious force that divides populations. Alka

Kurian's critique of cinematic representations of cross-caste, class, and faith-based dissident friendship and solidarity, in contrast to the prior essays, is a cautious, yet intimate portrayal of human connection at times of grave injustice. Kurian argues that Nandita Das' Firaaq (2009), Govind Nihalani's Hazaar Chaurasi Ki Ma (1998), and Sudhir Mishra's Hazaaron Khawishein Aisi (2001) are three instances in Indian cinema where we witness meaningful alliances of oppressor-oppressed communities and interrogation of positions of privilege with regard to Hindu nationalism, anti-Muslim sentiments, and Naxalite peasant insurgency—conflicts that are rife in postcolonial India. Women's resistance and solidarity is foregrounded through an examination of heteropatriarchal, bourgeois, and masculinist systems of power, which purport to liberate, yet serve to undermine women's participation and gendered experiences.

In "Neoliberalism, Agency, Friendship," the essays reflect on the contributions that contemporary film, fiction, and art make to conversations about feminism, dissent, resistance, and solidarity. Highlighting the instrumental role of literary imagination to articulate justice *contra* hegemonic power, these pieces complicate the enactment of cross-border solidarity. Through her engagement with contemporary Indian "border-crossing" cinema—both commercial, Veer Zaara, and critical feminist, Aparna Sen's Paromitar Ek Din (2000) and Mr. and Mrs. Iyer (2002)—Esha Niyogi De finds that the friendship trope serves a neoliberal imagination about individualism, family, and market-driven values. Yet, following Lugones, De argues that the friendship metaphor, especially when dissident, is useful because it identifies forms of institutional alliance and the potential therein of agency and transformation.

Both Elora Halim Chowdhury's and Shreerekha Subramanian's essays engage the fiction of novelist Thrity Umrigar as tools to interrogate the power dyadic of self-Other and dissident female friendships that attempt to dislodge it. The essay by Chowdhury is a deep investigation of ways in which middle-class femininity invests in social and economic security over gender-based solidarity, which leads, ultimately, to women's consensual and complicitous maintenance of patriarchy. Subramanian's essay tackles the vicissitudes of globalization and capital that are also and ultimately insurmountable in the quest for dissident friendships. Despite the failed dissident friendships in Umrigar's novels, Subramanian nevertheless argues that the readers of these texts are transnational subjects who are imagining "feminisms unbound" through their agentic readings of such texts that reenvision the self-Other in a renewed relationship.

"Friendship across Borders" contains two accounts of collective and individual transnational dissident friendships, which navigate the forces of nation, sexuality, and war. The essay by Laurie Cohen traces diverse friendships in the early twentieth century between committed German, Austrian-Hungarian, and British feminist peace activists, on one hand, and American counterparts on the other, all of whom were associated with the feminist organization, Women's International League for Peace and Freedom (WILPF). Based on an understanding of friendship as "essentially a kind of relationship grounded in a particular type of special concern each has for the other as the person she is" (Helm 2013), this chapter highlights the empowering connections these women had that allowed them to be vulnerable and authentic about their expectations and disappointments. These wartime transatlantic friendships were not devoid of politics and tensions, yet they were confronted through mutual concern and care for each other.

Finally, Lori Amy and Eglantina Gjermeni's coauthored piece is a dialogic rendition of a union between a U.S.-based researcher of trauma, identity, and war and an activist/practitioner in the field of gender and development who became politically active in Albania. While Gjermeni struggles with the seemingly hopeless quagmire of Albania's political sphere, Amy wants to understand the trajectory of Cold War cultures, the politics of transition, and contemporary war-on-terror agendas that shape the political and economic problems in Albania. The friendship is thus one in which emotional attachment and an empathic response to each other's lived experience help both women reenvision their possibilities for transformative intellectual, academic, and political engagement.

Together, the essays in this volume help us envision the kinds of solidarities—oppositional, dissident, complicit, failed, attempted, or realized—that we can envision at the intersections of the contradictory practices of neoliberalism, militarism, imperialism, and humanism and peace-building initiatives, which seem to implicate women as their primary agents.

Jacqui Alexander argues that all living beings share a profound and sacred connection with one another, which can only be realized through deep reflection and self-conscious practice. How do we imagine and strive for such connection and consciousness even as we are fractured by identity and geopolitics? This volume offers a range of insights about dissident feminist alliances and the possibilities for pluralist friendships that are meaningful, empathetic, reciprocal, and transformative.

References

Alexander, Jacqui M. 2005. *Pedagogies of Crossing*. Durham, N.C.: Duke University Press.
Gandhi, Leela. 2006. *Affective Communities*. Durham, N.C.: Duke University Press.
Helm, Bennett. 2013. "Friendship." *Stanford Encyclopedia of Philosophy*, June 21. Accessed August 2, 2015. http://plato.stanford.edu/entries/friendship.

PART ONE

Praxis of Friendship

CHAPTER 1

Epistemic Friendships

Collective Knowledge-Making through Transnational Feminist Praxis

NICOLE NGUYEN, A. WENDY NASTASI, ANGIE MEJIA, ANYA STANGER, MEREDITH MADDEN (POSTSCRIPT BY CHANDRA TALPADE MOHANTY)

Introduction

"Thinking justice, teaching for justice, and living justice means that we continually challenge each other to enunciate our vision of justice . . . we all have ownership in this new vision; no single one of us stands in a proprietary relationship to it, for it is to be collectively imagined, collectively guarded, collectively worked out" (Alexander 2005, 114). Drawing from a shared course-based experience, the coauthors of this chapter characterize transnational epistemic friendships that are produced through purposeful collective knowledge making. We describe our collaborative course assignment and project, providing an analysis of how the assignment, the process of developing our group project, and the act of sharing our group products with the entire class as a practice of shared meaning making led to the production of a radical feminist curriculum and a collective epistemic *process*. We further describe this process as illuminating both the dynamic possibilities of such "epistemic friendships" and their limitations. We argue that these epistemic friendships are essential to understanding emerging feminists' pathways to transnational feminist coalitions and action, and respatializing and relocating knowledge production beyond university space.

This chapter offers a description and analysis of a pedagogy project designed by Chandra Talpade Mohanty for a 2012 Transnational Feminist Practices graduate seminar at Syracuse University and produced by the coauthors. The course focused on transnational feminist theories, fostered a critical praxis of radical feminist cross-border solidarities, and nurtured epistemic friendships. For our pedagogy project, we (as a small collective) were tasked with creating an instructional plan and pedagogical approach to teaching the Israeli occupation of Palestine to undergraduate students while simultaneously reflecting on this collective epistemic process. In this chapter, we examine the steps that constituted this collaborative process, including building a unit plan geared toward undergraduates, researching appropriate topics of discussion, and creating assignments and learning objectives. After collaborating in our small groups on our respective syllabi, we came together as a whole class to present our work, solicit feedback, thoughtfully think through the process of the project, and plan on how we could continue this work outside the context of this seminar (in our own classes, communities, and departments).

Building off this collaborative process and following M. Jacqui Alexander's mandate that we must "imagine collectivities that can thrive outside of hegemony's death grip," we ask: How do we map dissident epistemic friendships in (and outside of) the academy? (2005, 8) How do we define these collectives? How do these friendships simultaneously subvert the status quo and reproduce capitalist, patriarchal processes and practices? How do they enable or limit a radical praxis? Importantly, what collaborative possibilities are available beyond that of the academy, and what contributions and limitations emerge from such friendships? These questions and our collaborative project frame our work in order to animate the complexities of such generative collective processes that foster solidarity, enable social action, and, also, reproduce inequality.

Transnational Feminism and Dissident Friendships

We approach this chapter using a transnational feminist theoretical framework as it "addresses the multiple and interlocking kinds of power relations that affect women's lives within and across national boundaries" (Stone-Mediatore 2003, 126). Transnational feminism challenges the relations of economic, heteropatriarchal, white supremacist, and ableist domination that shape women's lives across borders. Accordingly, in theorizing our coalition building, following Lugones (1995), we eschew the use of "sisterhood" to describe our efforts and insist on conceptualizing a type of "pluralist friendship" that recognizes how we are differentially located where "location is ... multiply constituted and traversed by different social formations" (Kaplan 1996, 182). It is the *common struggle* toward liberation and the recognition of common interests that unite women cross-culturally, rather than an assumption of shared oppression. Because coalitionary politics demand working together across difference(s), we offer that our individual and collective experiences of collaboration across social identities and politics can help us map pathways of resistance and struggle for feminist graduate students in the academy. We provide an account of how collaborative pedagogy projects that take seriously a politics of location can help us think through the promises, complexities, provocations, and limitations of such dissident friendships (Young 1995; Gandhi 2006; Blackmore 2005; hooks 1995).

We assert that given our common radical feminist struggle toward decolonizing pedagogies, resistance lies in the active and self-conscious contestation of dominant discourses, representations, and epistemologies in our classrooms and in the production of knowledge that disrupts these sedimented and violent ways of knowing. Although other feminist coalitions such as the Global Feminisms Project[1] chart how various women have "[come] of age politically" as feminist-activists in ways that have "made it possible for ... women to resist social structures in which they were also deeply embedded," we examine the opportunities and pathways available to emerging feminist graduate students (McGuire, Stewart, and Curtin 2010, 99). This chapter thinks through such pathways, our struggles, and their possibilities, particularly in what we will define as "epistemic friendships." Furthermore, as graduate students, instructors, and transnational feminists, we view our classrooms as "political and cultural sites that represent accommodations and contestations over knowledge by differently empowered social constituencies" where dissident theories and practices can be "grounded in definitions of difference, difference that attempts to resist incorporation and appropriation by providing a space for historically silenced peoples to construct knowledge" (Mohanty 2003, 194). We recognize classrooms as potential, complex, and contradictory sites of dissidence where teaching and learning can both reproduce and subvert the status quo. In this way, we situate teaching and learning in the academy as an epistemic project at once a source of domination and a site of radical possibility.

As such, while the academy rewards and privileges individual scholarly work, we trace the transformative process of becoming transnational feminists working in collective solidarity as knowledge producers. We map how this transformative process shifted our intellectual and activist principles, politics, and scholarship in ways that resist and refuse normative knowledge practices within and outside of the academy. As Alexander and Mohanty offer, if we are to "take seriously the mandate to do collaborative work ... the kind of work that would demystify the borders between inside and out . . . it is imperative that the academy *not* be the only location that determines our research and pedagogical work" (2010, 27). In considering the possibilities of transnational feminist pathways available to emerging feminists today, we outline explicit strategies for developing what we will conceptualize as "epistemic friendships," enacted and strengthened through collective knowledge production that make possible dissident epistemological contributions within and beyond the academy. In this way, epistemic friendships, in form and practice, challenge the traditional epistemological order of universities that continues to reward individual knowledge-production processes.

Epistemic friendships are a learning for social justice with and by others. In our understanding, epistemic friendship is a distinct notion: more political than standard notions of friendship, but also not simply coalitionary or in solidarity. It does not explicitly seek to reach across difference, but rather strives to provide a community of support attuned to, but regardless of, one's location. An epistemic friendship is based on shared politics, rather than shared identities, and is marked by a desire to push one another toward greater, more effective, more nuanced political work for radical justice. Epistemic friendships are multiple and overlapping; we can seamlessly "belong" to diverse groups. They are not confined to the academy, though that is where we, as graduate students, find them most commonly. Such dissident political and epistemic commitments require a decentering of self, collaboration across difference(s) that refuses to ignore such differences, and reflexive processes invested in our responsibility to each other as feminist academics and as activists.

Methodology

This chapter describes the authors' interpretations of the intellectual and social justice implications of a course-based collaborative pedagogy project. To fully animate the analytical process at work in this chapter, we provide an account of the assignment and a description of our product (see the appendix). Finally, we detail how the process of writing this chapter demonstrates epistemic friendships and trace activist-feminist pathways for emerging scholars invested in dissident feminist commitments with communities.

Making Friends: The Course Assignment

As students enrolled in Professor Mohanty's graduate-level course on Practices of Transnational Feminist Theory, the coauthors engaged with each other as classmates on readings central to both current and "classic" texts in transnational feminist theory. To extend this understanding of theory, Professor Mohanty built a collaborative pedagogical project into our course. We formed small groups (in our case, a group of four doctoral students) to collectively craft an undergraduate syllabus and unit plan on the Israeli occupation of Palestine. Consistent with other documented examples of social justice pedagogy (e.g., Case 2010; Zuniga et al. 2007), Professor Mohanty challenged us not only to apply theory to practice, but to do so as a collective, with other feminists, with the explicit purpose of producing a collaborative mode of knowledge production and transmission (i.e., designing the content and process of teaching/learning) (Adams, Bell, and Griffin 2010).

On Becoming Transnational Feminist Friends: The Course Product

Drawing from our individual disciplinary backgrounds (sociology, education, geography, and philosophy), we collectively selected the scope, content, assignments, and desired outcomes of our unit plan, which focused on teaching an undergraduate course about the carceral techniques of and embodied resistances to the Israeli occupation of Palestine. From our course readings to our teaching plan to our assignments, we each mobilized our disciplinary identities in the design of our collaborative pedagogy project. This process fostered a type of "transdisciplinarity" (Soja 1996, 6). Though we did not think about this at the time, the assignment also engaged us in a curricular process: We worked together in a way that connected us as emerging feminist scholars and as joint knowledge makers. Unusually, particularly at a private research university, we collaborated across differences in social identity, disciplinary location, and personal political investments to build a social justice curriculum that was meaningful and reflective of each of us, but also consistent with our readings and theorizing about transnational feminist practices (Sudbury and Okazawa-Rey 2009). This was, for us, an experience of epistemic friendship, of working with other women through an organic process where each of us was valued and yet unique. We entered a knowledge-making cocoon and were eager to share the fruits of our labors with others, particularly our classmates (Mernissi 1995).

In planning a teaching module that deeply contests students' perceptions and dominant knowledges about the Israeli occupation, this epistemic friendship provided the space to share texts, knowledges, cross-border personal experiences, and pedagogical resources. Furthermore, when we implemented this curriculum in our individual classrooms, we turned toward our epistemic friends for the encouragement and reflection needed to sustain ourselves in such dissident classroom encounters. When Nicole struggled with her students' frequent demand to "tell both sides" of the Israeli occupation, she relied on her epistemic friends for support and for pedagogical tools to dispel students' investment in the myth of two sides. For Nicole, her epistemic friends not only refortified her radical commitments, they also pushed her to critically rethink her pedagogy and analysis of the occupation as a conflict.

Additionally, in designing our pedagogy project, Wendy suggested a "gallery walk" where students walk into the classroom and define on posters hanging throughout the classroom key concepts such as occupation and colonialism based on required course readings. Students then come together as a class and collectively work together to define each term through the facilitation of the instructor. Such a pedagogical approach, Wendy taught us, contributes to the destabilization of what students know and to the collective meaning-making process radical classrooms strive for. As these two examples show, epistemic friendships enable meaning-making and pedagogical practices that would not otherwise be possible without this supportive and reflexive space. For each of us, this collective epistemic process that applied theory to practice proved to be a unique experience that helped to foster our identities not merely as feminist academics, but also as feminist teachers.

Epistemic Friendships: On Making Meaning as a Collective

Although our pedagogy project finalized our feminist collective, we arrived at Professor Mohanty's class with an academic history with each other: A few of us had taken classes with each other, conversed with one another at department gatherings, or shared our frustrations and strategies in the face of ongoing confrontations of racist and sexist microaggressions in the academy. Our resistance to the oppressive undercurrents in our respective disciplines initiated these early conversations whether in class, at social events, or at coffee shops that provided respite from the academic trenches.

In these early stages of our individual friendships with one another, we worked from a premise of dissidence: We relied on one another to make sense of and disrupt the epistemic and structural violence we witnessed and experienced in our daily academic lives. In class, we supported each other as dissident allies, defending our interventions that challenged hegemonic ways of knowing. Leading up to Professor Mohanty's class, we engaged in debates about our complicity in the injustices endemic to and sutured into academy. At a predominately white institution, we struggled to devise strategies to use our privilege to combat the structures of oppression we, and others, confronted daily. Most importantly, we learned we were not alone and found courage in one another.

In these early encounters, we recognized that although we were cisgender able-bodied women graduate students, there were many differences among us: white women, women of color, newly middle-class women, working-class women, Latina and white and biracial women, mothers, women with partners who help sustain our graduate studies, single women, first-generation graduate students, second-generation immigrants. Given our different social locations and relationality to each other, our initial friendships each included an unstated but agreed upon covenant that we would hold each other accountable. Holding each other accountable allowed us to better interrogate how power operated through our friendship, name each other's oppressive actions, and call out absences or erasures in our resistance. This process forced us to contend with pressing questions that would define the shape of our friendship: How could we synchronize our schedules in ways conducive to mothers? How could we address the various forms of cultural capital we brought to our friendships? How might we create the space for multiple cultural codes to structure our conversations, meetings, and friendship? How could we center the experiences and knowledges of women of color without alienating the white women in our growing collective? How could we disrupt U.S.-centric ways of interpreting the world in which we live? These, and other issues, required constant negotiation, dialogue, and respect.

Holding each other accountable made our epistemic friendships possible and enriched our activism. Taking our responsibilities to each other seriously meant we also needed to undertake the reflexive work necessary for our collective to thrive. We each made many mistakes, yet our collective allowed for these mistakes: Our epistemic friendships, imbued with a political commitment to resistance in the academy, created the space for us to grow from these mistakes and to sharpen our feminist praxis.

These previous interactions, political commitments, and accountability practices staged the foundation upon which we forged our dissident epistemic friendships in Professor Mohanty's class. As Professor Mohanty called upon us to engage in a radical decolonial praxis, our political alignment pushed us to work collectively to disrupt racist commentary, insist upon engaging Other ways of knowing, and resist the tendency to center the narratives of white women in this, and other, classes. As a group, we choreographed our dissident contributions to a larger epistemic project: How could we define the terms of the kind of talk, knowledges, and political commitments in which we would collectively engage as a class?

Our collective dissident epistemic work throughout the semester formalized as we collaborated on our pedagogy project. Forming our group required no conversation: Our political alignment and resistance in class drew us together.

As we developed our project, so too did our trust and, subsequently, epistemic friendships.

Although our epistemic friendships deepened through our continued dissidence within and outside of class, our commitment to epistemic justice compelled us to invite all of our classmates to write this chapter. Despite our solicitation for other contributors, only our pedagogy project group and our teaching assistant, Anya, responded. Two students expressed concern about what writing about Palestine might mean for the job market. Although we worried about the ever-intensifying pro-Israel climate in the United States, as an epistemic project we could not erase the radical politics that defined our classwork. We needed to incorporate our Israeli occupation pedagogy projects and the counterepistemologies upon which they relied into this chapter. Meanwhile, other graduate students politely declined or ignored our invitation. Had they accepted, another kind of story would have emerged.

The Possibilities of Epistemic Friendships

In reflecting together on our process as collaborators on our pedagogy project, we realized that "through a shared feminist politics and vision, a shared commitment to collective knowledge production, solidarity, and accountability," we came to mean something to each other (Mohanty 2006, x). The logic that positions knowledge making as always shared and always in connection to others has been well articulated (Mohanty 2003; Sudbury and Okazawa-Rey 2009). Yet, as women raised in the neoliberal intellectual system of *I*—what I know, what I argue, what I found—we experienced for the first time what it means to build knowledge with others and for others. Professor Mohanty asked each student as she presented in class, "What did you learn from this? What did it mean for you? How did you work with each other? What does this mean for the work you hope to do?" She then facilitated ongoing dialogue that kept us present in the assignment. We were not permitted to just "turn it in" and go on. Rather, by reflexively investigating our role in relation to each other, we were made critically conscious of the politics of knowledge making by our reciprocal and collective traversing of dominant epistemic convention. Drawing from Butler (2004), the architecture of this project forced us to consider how our lives—academic, activist, and everyday—are implicated and relational to the lives of others, drawing us to consider our collective responsibility to each other. Never before had we, as graduate students, been required to think about our responsibility to each other as peers, educators, and scholars, or to think less individually and more collectively about knowledge production. Indeed, this collectively authored chapter is itself a testament to how this project altered how we thought about what counted as scholarship and how that scholarship is produced.

Julia Sudbury writes of the benefits, the openness that can follow when unlearning and rethinking occur in the classroom. She argues that "openness has immense potential for transformative educational praxis that allows students to locate their own experience within systems of dominance and to imagine and begin to enact forms of resistance" (2009, 20). When coupled with collaborative process and reflexivity, this openness also creates a place where epistemic friendships can form and begin to develop. As a basis for learning, such a process distinctly challenges Western knowledge making. As we constructed knowledge together, we engaged in a politics of epistemic resistance. Our dissident friendship, while political, in fact vis-à-vis its nature as political, is necessarily epistemic.

Collaborating together on our pedagogy project not only disrupted traditional knowledges so often reproduced in the university by considering how to (re)shape our pedagogy in ways that radically contested this normative system of privilege, it also incited us to build these epistemic friendships. For the first time, we were required to construct knowledge collectively and to consider the implications of this epistemic process in relation to our own teaching and praxis beyond the university. For some of us, this process challenged how we thought about knowledge production and what kinds of scholarship are rewarded and privileged in the academy. For others, our project provided the support necessary to sustain such work that is so often devalued and marginalized. As we unlearned the hypervaluation of individual scholarship through this collaborative epistemic process, we reimagined our classrooms as sites to disrupt hegemonic epistemologies and as places to foster collective knowledge making among undergraduate students. We began to understand not only how universities reproduce capitalist, heteropatriarchal, ableist, and white supremacist knowledges and hierarchies, but also our role and responsibility in subverting and resisting this hegemonic formation.

Working together gave us the courage to take risks we might not otherwise consider taking alone in the classroom. Knitting together multiscalar examples of indefinite detention, confinement, and border checkpoints, we formulated lessons that highlighted how the occupation corporeally commits violences on and through bodies by drawing from specific stories of Palestinian hunger strikes. Together, we considered how students might resist these disruptions of hegemonic constructions of the occupation and engaged each other in how we might formatively respond to this student resistance. In doing so, we enter our classrooms as individual bodies with collective knowledge(s) and support invested in disrupting the hegemonic academy. Teaching, in this sense, is a radical act. Thus, while this epistemic process forced us to consider how we might create a more radical classroom within the colonized university, what endures nearly four years later are our commitments to radical teaching, (em)braced by our epistemic friendships, and the teaching approaches and reflexive practices necessary to make such decolonizing engagements possible.

The Limitations of Epistemic Friendships

This is not to idealize or valorize epistemic friendships. While they acknowledge and attend to power relations within and outside of the university, epistemic friendships cannot erase power differences between and among friends. This is a limitation.

We also recognize that epistemic friendships operate within university structures, which inherently strive to limit and foreclose radical praxis. We are reminded of Robin Wilson's (2011) *Chronicle of Higher Education* piece, "Syracuse Slide," which defined Syracuse University's commitment to inclusive work with and by local communities as a "slide," a degradation of academic pedigree. As problematic as we find Wilson's piece, such assertions dominated Syracuse University discussions about the future direction of the university's curricula, the composition of its student body, and its engagement with local communities. It renewed commitments to the university's role in reproducing inequality and in limiting activist work for more democratic and less violent futures.

As graduate students, our work has often been devalued by those who deny the epistemic credibility of such collaborations in order to reassert the value and legitimacy of traditional knowledge production within an ivory tower. We have been told our work with local public high schools, for instance, is not "real" scholarship. Department chairs classified these engagements as "service" that did not fulfill our responsibilities as graduate students and instructors. Thus, while epistemic friendships enable collaborations across difference in radical ways that resist and remake university spaces, they do not—and cannot—erase how universities privilege traditional knowledges and marginalize these radical engagements. Although epistemic friendships contribute to this dissidence, they are also constrained by the very conditions invested in reproducing the current hegemonic formation of the academy.

Despite these limitations, we suggest that such epistemic friendships make possible critical, collaborative knowledge-making processes that push back against and dismantle the myth that scholarship belongs to or is housed only within the university. The cartography of knowledge within today's academy too often includes the erection of epistemic (and real) borders between universities and local communities. It locates knowledge production solely within the halls of university offices and thus rewards singular knowledge-making processes. Epistemic friendships challenge us to extend the conceptual borders of how and with whom knowledge is produced and, in turn, where it is produced. One way to resist injustice and to transform practices that perpetuate oppression is to make knowledge in solidarity with others. We offer that epistemic friendships—while complex and contradictory, never fully eschewing power relations or difference(s)—make possible the opportunity, support, theoretical tools, and reflexive spaces necessary to challenge the traditional academy. They also work to sustain us as we continue to challenge and contest the hegemonic hold of the university dedicated to reproducing traditional forms of power along gendered, capitalist, and white supremacist lines.

Transformative Process of Becoming Transnational Feminists

As McGuire, Steward, and Curtin acknowledge, "only some women become feminists; of those, only a few become activists" (2010, 99). Given the transformative nature of our epistemic friendships, we consider how our investments as transnational feminist activists are made possible for us as emerging feminist graduate students. While many scholars and activists study transnational feminism, we are interested in how we arrive at and deepen our place of radical feminist practice while in school. Our experiences in Professor Mohanty's course provided an effective route toward this goal. For each of us, this was a project of epistemic possibility, of what can be even within the current political and social structures that bear down on each of us. Furthermore, we offer that for each of us to name ourselves a transnational feminist, a transformative process had to occur. Reflexively thinking through this *transformative process* can illuminate how we engage in transnational feminist praxis, how particular epistemic friendships can sustain us, and one way to work through and across difference(s).

On first consideration, let us consider the *transformative process* of "becoming" transnational feminists for members of the pedagogy project described in this chapter. We share similar foundational pillars. Through our course, each coauthor experienced a deeply personal process that catalyzed her to more deeply embody and enact a transnational feminist practice. Professor Mohanty, for instance, shared her experience of becoming: She narrated her struggles, activism, oppression linked to her personal experiences and, later, academic and activist work. In other words, Professor Mohanty scaffolded our own becoming as transnational feminists through mentorship. She helped us think through our own experiences; name these experiences in a new vocabulary that animated their complexity and embeddedness in power relations; respond to and create pathways for our own praxis based on our social locations and political commitments; consider how our own situatedness shapes perspective and praxis; make our work intelligible to those invested in the traditional, hegemonic academy; find ways to resist and bear witness; and support each other in our disparate yet connected fight against colonialism, white supremacy, and heteropatriarchy across borders and difference. In this way, under Professor Mohanty's tutelage, we were able to "see the complexities, singularities, and interconnections between communities of women such that power, privilege, agency, and dissent can be made visible and engaged with" (2003, 523). Knitting together transnational feminist theory and dissident practice, we learned to think differently about academic scholarship—who it is for, what it looks like, how it is created, where it is created. Perhaps more urgently, we learned that we could be activists for social, political, and economic change within the academy as well as outside of it. When collective work, such as our pedagogy project, brings together graduate feminists *across the borders* of the academy's disciplines, then the transformative process of becoming a transnational feminist takes on new epistemic meaning, creating new ways to create solidarities committed to radical feminist work within and outside of the academy. For some of us, this transformative process illuminated these very real possibilities for the first time.

For Nicole, her experience with the course and the pedagogy project felt like a coming of age as a feminist. It sparked critical questions about how this transformative process supports the growth of feminist graduate students. For Meredith, the course and its pedagogy, key components of the transformative process, supported her own growth as a feminist. Having come of age as a feminist in the 1990s, she viewed feminism more in relation to self and her individual experiences; she thought she had a complex view of feminism. Through (re)learning about transnational feminism and participating in Professor Mohanty's pedagogy project assignment, however, she experienced a transformation in her feminism. What was possible within feminist praxis was radically widened and opened her to new possibilities through collaborative and collective knowledge-making processes and activism committed to social justice. She went from practicing feminism in singular ways to understanding how to practice feminism in collective ways that trace our relationality and responsibility to one another.

For Wendy, engagement in the pedagogy project and experiencing the transformative process of becoming a transnational feminist was grounded in *language*: indeed, the language that we use to *name* our worlds is a critical component of transformative experiences. When a person can name something, then there is a shift how she looks at things, and interacts with realities of self and realities of the world. Liberatory pedagogy scholar Paulo Freire (1970) pays significant attention to the powerful, and transformative, experience that naming the world can have on people as individuals or in groups. The power to name worlds/realities through language and to advance critiques of discriminatory practices is decisive because such naming connects with the ability to gain consciousness of experience(s) and be better positioned for liberatory action.

What does it mean, then, to *call* (or name) ourselves transnational feminists in our day-to-day lives as academics and as community members? The transformative process of becoming a transnational feminist implies that in becoming we go beyond a place of understanding, and move into a space of action. But what type of action? In one way, the action may be in the classroom through pedagogy projects that support working collaboratively and in solidarity toward dissidence. The *calling* of oneself also transcends beyond the doors of the classroom. Anya recalls that it was by demanding critical reflections from herself on the implications of her daily life choices that brought her to the point where she could *name herself* a transnational feminist. In what ways? In big ways: academic orientation, a promise to speak out and speak up often, a commitment to creating justice and increasing justice in both her work and personal lives. And, Anya comments, she had to challenge herself to think about such implications at a microlevel: where to shop, what books to read, what language to use with children. For Anya, the process of thinking critically, and responding critically, to such things as white supremacy, class discrimination, and patriarchy began prior to her transformative process. Yet, it was in the transformative process of becoming a transnational feminist (and naming herself as such) that she gained the critical lens to see the interconnections among nation, nation-state, gender, sexuality, race, and class at the global level and in relation to antiracism, heteropatriarchy, and class discrimination. The transformative process developed in her a person mobilized to pursue a lifetime committed to pursuits of justice.

In this way, we envision transnational feminism as a theoretical orientation grounded in radical and dissident thought, a praxis of acting in the world (within and outside the academy), and a commitment to social justice and action weaved into the folds of everyday life. What might such transformative processes, fostered by epistemic friendships, mean for the radical possibilities and feminist work within the academy? How are such investments in radical transnational feminisms negotiated, worked out, and navigated within university space that is at once hegemonic and dissident?

Implications for Transnational Feminist Friendships within the Academy

Given this methodological process of collectively creating a feminist pedagogy project that challenges dominant epistemologies, naming our feminist becoming as graduate students, and mapping the contours of epistemic friendships, this section describes the challenges and promises of building and sustaining such epistemic friendships that rupture particular ways of knowing and interpreting the world. We hope it provides a blueprint and starting point for others willing to build epistemic relationships in the academy without idealizing the process of friendship implied in the concept.

Risk Taking

The many hierarchical and power-laden relations within our own academic disciplines might appear to make it impossible to apply transnational feminist theory and methods in our teaching and research endeavors. For example, when we discover new paradigms that resonate with our own experiences or that of our participants or students, we begin to substantively question our own disciplinary epistemologies, methodologies, theories, and practices. However, this questioning can free us to do research that better answers the questions that could not have been elucidated by past normative knowledge-making practices and methods. These risks permit us a careful reflection or a more critical reengagement with questions we considered unanswerable. Epistemic friendships and the practices such relationships engender, therefore, encourage us to complicate what we may not have been confident, brave, or capable enough to do as individual scholars. These are calculated risks, however. For some of us, our current position in our departments allows us to take academic risks (e.g., we can be creative as long as we cite certain foundational disciplinary fathers). For others, the act of engaging with new forms of knowledge can create roadblocks in our academic path and, thus, keep certain academic activities in the background for some time.

Disciplining Our Disciplines

In some instances, a convergence between our own discipline's paradigms and those constitutive of the transnational feminist canon can be possible. For one of us, in sociology, a transnational feminist lens enriches theoretical choices and allows for new methodological possibilities. Alternatively, for others, a shift in our intellectual practices and disciplinary frameworks can be difficult at best and, at worst, be an isolating struggle in a field where there is no space to practice a scholarship that destabilizes a discipline's status quo. In this frame, our work—unintelligible outside of more traditional, individual forms of scholarship—is reduced to "extracurricular" projects, marked as "unexciting" or "not what we do." We are advised that these scholarly activities will not help us graduate, find a tenure-track job (heralded as *the* successful academic pathway), or earn tenure. The value of epistemic friendships is that they provide a space where transnational feminists do not come just to vent, but where they can accomplish academic and pedagogical goals through the academic labor that takes place in such a collective.

These epistemic friendships, and the political projects that undergird them, can draw us out from our own marginalized spaces at the fringes of our departments. Some of us were already practicing transnational feminism before signing up for the class; others, however, had become distanced from transnational feminist epistemologies for disciplinary (un)reasons. For those who left our cozy disciplinary-made space, the challenge to our old theoretical positions by the resources gained in this collective literally saved us from leaving/giving up academia altogether.

Voice, Text, and Time

Writing an article that makes use of the theoretical resources and methods gained in a transnational feminist seminar will nevertheless need to employ traditional academic practices of writing and editing. Oftentimes, the processes themselves will not make the collaboration process difficult; however, issues arising from the division of labor needed to finish up a product may not be as easily solved in collaborative scholarly writing. Issues of authorship and authorship order, compositional styles, and theoretical density are some issues that might strain the collaborative nature of epistemic friendships. In an epistemic collective, we are already venturing to challenge our own research procedures knowing that the products that will emerge may be different from what we have previously created or even what our disciplines value. Yet, we failed to realize that products created from collaborative dialogue and reflection may take more time to materialize. For some of us where academic timetables dominate how much time is spent doing scholarship, entering an epistemic friendship requires the same commitment one makes when entering and sustaining a friendship in the social sense of the word. Time spent with friends, understandably, is nurtured and is not calculated by setting a timer; epistemic friendships are no different.

(Non)privilege(d) Affection

How do we decenter different forms of privilege during our interactions without alienating members of an epistemic collective? How do we work through the embedded systems of academic privilege (still) operating in our disciplines without undoing the collaborative spirit that animates the friendship in the first place? Dismantling existing power performances can be a tense endeavor. In our collective, "calling out," which was often silently encouraged by other members, interfaced well with some of the group members' personalities. However, not all collectives will find this accountability arrangement workable. We suggest that epistemic friendship collectives need to operate under the essence of "friendship first, academy later." Let us explain. A friend can honestly point out another friend's mistake. *Con cariño* (with affection) and respect, the mistake can be explored and talked about and the friend (oftentimes) will be thankful for the advice. We believe that the same operates with epistemic friendships. A subtle performance of privilege by one friend can be discussed as a group without alienating others. Someone is able to disagree about someone else's editing decisions openly and with *cariño*.

(Un)silencing via Technology

Our biographical differences and the unique experiences with race, class, ability, gender, sexuality, and nation constellated around our identities can also complicate collective knowledge sharing and building. Inspired by transnational feminist theory and practice, an epistemic friendship gives nondominant people the space to make claims with and to feel a sense of ownership in said collaborations. At the same time, it can disallow those sharing ties with the dominant academic culture from truly verbalizing or raising questions in this space. White women, for example, may fail to bring up why we are applying a concept in certain ways, thus defeating the ethos of friendship implied in this collective. In our case, the reiterative processes (revising and meeting to talk about changes and revising again with plans to meet after that round of revisions) and the use of technology provide different mediums to bring out these issues effectively. In the group, someone can make edits to a paper via Google documents and write out their specific justification for certain changes without having to wait to meet as a group and discuss. Such technologies create the necessary space for these discussions across time and place. They also enable conversations that might otherwise not happen in person because of how nondominant people are usually silenced in person. In this way, technology provides multiple mediums for communication, differently utilized by members of the collective to talk and communicate with one another.

Connecting

Epistemic friendships are not exclusionary, and we may belong well among multiple different groups. For this project, our friendship was informed by our intersecting interest in pedagogy and ways to improve how we reach the students we serve. In creating epistemic collectives, we must be attentive that core concepts involved in transnational feminist scholarship will not be for everyone. This may not mean that there is a set criterion of who "can come in and play," and we do not support practices of academic elitism and exclusion. In our case, the organic serendipity of how this group came into existence was bolstered by our relationship to each other as classmates in a specific seminar with specific theoretical aims and pedagogical practices. If we had been searching to create an epistemic collective, however, we would have initially connected through our work as critical and/or activist scholars.

Epistemic friendships will always need to be negotiated, contested, and complicated in academic spaces, making them simultaneously challenging and rewarding endeavors that promise academic and pedagogical transformations. Given these struggles and possibilities within the academy, the next section outlines what such epistemic friendships might mean outside of the academy, engaging in radical dissident politics with communities and invested in social justice efforts that extend beyond the bounds of the university.

Implications for Transnational Feminist Friendships outside of the Academy

Importantly, the course in which we were enrolled was titled Transnational Feminist Theory and *Practice*. This course integrally intended to challenge us to think beyond the academy. Surely, we were meant to learn and think about realms and implications of feminist theory, but always with the aim of understanding and transforming praxis. Our pedagogy project was absolutely a part of this: its product was an academic design, but a design located in a politically contentious space (teaching the Israeli occupation of Palestine within the neoliberal U.S. academy). Quite simply, we should not teach such a course without a clear understanding of our own political and personal commitments or a cogent analysis of the stakes at play. On this level, Professor Mohanty's course assignment forced us to reconcile theory and practice. It also compelled us to think about *how* to integrate our conceptions of feminist theory with our activism in the gritty "real" world. For us, the course also foregrounded the idea of friendship as discussed here, giving us an experience of what epistemic friendship can make possible in radical political work.

As academics thinking "beyond" the university, it is essential to first locate the academy: in the United States, postsecondary institutions of education are part of the neoliberal landscape, whether public or private. Undoubtedly, universities and colleges serve the purpose of further education, but they also act as a nexus between neoliberal governance and control, as sites where public and private money shape research agendas, where what constitutes legitimate knowledge production are political and fraught, and where militarized U.S. supremacy globally are reinforced and maintained (Sudbury and Okazawa-Rey 2009, Giroux 2007). Hence, to think about ourselves—as graduate students in a private northeastern university doing work we consider "feminist" outside of the academy—we must simultaneously be mindful about how our training and allegiance *within* this institutional structure inevitably inform us. That is, as this new epistemological order contests the traditional guard, the corporatization of universities complexly situates the academy as a "contradictory place where knowledges are colonized but also contested—a place that engenders student mobilizations and progressive movements of various kinds" (Mohanty 2003, 170). Despite the colonizing, capitalist forces of these inherited academic structures, universities still act as powerful sites of struggle, particularly through collaborative and dialogic practices across the university-community borders. As critical pedagogues, we must continue to take seriously the liberatory potential of education and the possibility of dissent and disruption of "business as usual" in the space of the academy, both in our scholarship as well as in our classrooms.

In our understanding, whether within or outside of the academy, at its core, transnational feminist praxis is about working toward justice in a complex way. This praxis must account for differences in power on micro- and macrolevels simultaneously, be attentive to intersecting matrices of oppression, and be responsible around areas of representation (Kaplan 1994; McCall 2005; Alcoff 1995). It is "transnational" in the sense that it does this work across borders—and hence, at some level, is always also a critique of neoliberal capitalism (Naples 2002). These components are our "transnational feminist lens" through which we engage in our work—and toward which our "friendship" is aimed. The "implications" of transnational feminist friendships beyond the academy are hypothetically immense—it is a sensibility, an orientation, and a set of commitments, as much as it is a praxis. In thinking through these implications beyond the university, we return to this notion of epistemic friendships through our work within and outside of the university. These examples from our individual work animate the politics of epistemic friendships on multiple terrains of knowledge production.

Immigrant Mothers and Food Justice

One coauthor's work with Latina mothers on issues of food access in marginalized communities of Portland, Oregon, illustrates the challenges of sustaining epistemic friendships outside the academy (Mejia et al. 2013). As we have argued, to build epistemic friendships outside the academy, one must first dismantle myths that knowledge production can only occur inside the academy, the epistemological hallmark of these friendships. In this case, the challenge was building a space where Latina mothers are equally positioned to claim and make knowledge arising from their own lived-experiences without needing an academician to be their interlocutor. The author was initially hired to facilitate a community-based research project using a technique called Photovoice. She coordinated the Photovoice activities of these mothers and delivered a product (pictures taken by the participants) to present to stakeholders. While there are many levels of participation in Photovoice work (ranging from participant-led projects to researcher-controlled activities where participants have limited input), there was much "prep" work that needed to be done before this project could make mothers' knowledge central. One of the earlier forms of prep work was to make mothers aware that their own knowledge was the only one that mattered for the project since they were the community experts. Eventually, the mothers felt confident enough to state that the standard Photovoice methodology would not allow them to truly verbalize their community concerns. Thus, in order to maximize their own knowledge-making possibilities, the mothers (alongside the coauthor) reworked the entire methodology to fit their own notions of knowledge making, friendship, and collaboration. Alternatively, understanding that the academy/community divide could not truly be breached, the coauthor actively focused on "calling out" the processes of privilege and power that were embedded in the institutional assemblage that had initially funded the project. In this case, epistemic friendships outside the academy need to challenge and adapt to the communities with whom they collaborate, taking bold steps to create spaces where not only epistemological, but also political, work is possible.

Urban School Reform

For one coauthor, epistemic friendship includes working with urban youth whose knowledges must be integrated into the discussions school adults have about teaching in and reforming their schools. This work positions urban youth as collaborators in urban school reform, not just as objects of it. Working toward epistemic justice, these collectives seek to center urban children's experiences in and knowledge of their schools and how they work (or do not work). Such collaborations, however, are rife with adult-youth power relations to which adults must carefully attend. As adults working with youth, we must continually push each other to do the epistemic work needed to counterlisten to students, to listen *against* dominant ways of interpreting student voice that so often pathologize urban children and position them as unbelievable or incomplete adults only able to respond in incomplete ways as witnesses of their own lives. To collaborate with young people, in other words, requires we examine our own adult assumptions about what urban children can know and the many ways we exclude young people's knowledges about the schools where they spend their days. Epistemic friendships among coresearchers can push our methodologies in ways that recognize these power differences, hold us accountable for our assumptions, and compel us to self-interrogate and be reflexive about our behavior within these collaborations.

Peace Activism

Another coauthor studies peace activists in the United States. She was struck by how our collective ideas about "friendship" resonate with the work of some of this country's most committed antinuclear and peace activists. As social movement theorist Sharon Nepstad (2004) has clearly demonstrated, to sustain themselves over the "long haul," activists must have a community of support. This community may provide logistical help (childcare, meals, finances) but also offers the spiritual, intellectual, emotional space of "discernment" through which high-risk activism is imagined and subsequently carried through (Nepstad 2008; Koopman 2008). Thus, for Plowshares activists (antinuclear folks who resist U.S. militarism through nonviolent civil resistance), living in community, "house church," and quarterly "retreats" are essential to sustaining the movement. In creating this space, these seemingly social functions fundamentally shape the strategies, focus, and goals of antinuclear activism.

Israel/Occupied Palestine

This chapter cannot close responsibly without some discussion of our pedagogy project's content area, for it was not thoughtlessly chosen. The teaching of the Israeli occupation of Palestine (our very choice of words may foreclose some of our readers' attention, we know) was also not chosen simply because it is a classic "difficult case." In our view, it was chosen because it is a real-time and *harrowing* example of the perpetuation of colonialism, of U.S. military might, of purposeful ignorances, silencing, and political trickery that rely upon notions of sympathy, entitlement, fear, and apology to sustain. It is difficult to teach for very complex reasons that have everything to do with geopolitics, institutional funding, racist calls for "civility," and our students' personal lives. Teaching about this area of the world brings tremendous risks to anyone, including the university-level teacher (see electronicintifada.org): from student outbursts in the classroom to personal censure from our institutions to the denial of tenure. The risks are quite real. And yet ongoing violence at every level is the status quo for the Palestinians, who are daily harassed and worse through the use of U.S. tax dollars, and of whom the average American knows very, very little.

As "transnational feminists" committed to justice work, we cannot ignore this reality. It is part of the difficult and challenging work that we must take on, that we have agreed to take on—and for which we fundamentally *need* the support of friends—if we are to assume the name "feminist" as described here.

Our Final Note: Red Light, Green Light

Informed by the breadth of these research projects and our experiences with them, we acknowledge that, most basically, it is hard to do political work aimed at justice. Sustaining such work requires a community of support. In our shared cradle of rampant injustice, to be courageous enough to be clear and bold in our thinking and action requires a reflexive community that listens, alters, calms, fires up, corrects, humbles, educates, and nurtures. A close example of this, for us, is our teacher Chandra Mohanty's long-standing working friendship with M. Jacqui Alexander. Their partnership provides inspiration and a roadmap—we clearly see how their commitment to each other and their work has generated radical, transformative, foundational theorizing that *could not exist* in the same ways as single-authored texts. We are sure that along with their intellectual insights, the two friends share a camaraderie that enables and sustains courage: the courage to see clearly, to work for justice, to believe that what they do matters, to speak their truths to power, to get out of bed in the morning . . . at some level, epistemic friendship is also just friendship. We have enjoyed and learned much from taking both seriously.

For those who feel a call to pursue issues of justice, one of the most difficult challenges is knowing how to go forward, especially since the university rewards structure incentivizes moderate teaching and the solo production of knowledges while treating activism as something "on the side." What constitutes "good" work is rarely straightforward. Its dangers, however, are striking. Silencing, essentializing, distancing, dehumanizing, (re)marginalizing... and from what we have learned in school, well-intentioned feminists have historically struggled against these challenges. For us, one important way to protect ourselves from reinforcing such dangers is through collective praxis. Working together, across differences, provides a way to "check" ourselves more thoroughly while recognizing that power and privilege persist, sometimes reproduced in our own collectives (see Cole and Luna 2010; Johnson-Reagon 1983). In our activist work beyond the academy, then, the types of epistemic friendships discussed here are essential. We offer that such epistemic friendships, however rife with difference(s), challenge how we think of knowledge-production processes, provide us with the support necessary to sustain our dissident feminist work as graduate students, scaffold our intellectual and activist work, and provide us with clear ways forward in practice. As particularly located graduate students with political and intellectual commitments aimed at social justice and radical pedagogy, the process of applying theory to practice; of establishing epistemic friendships that nurture and challenge our feminist engagements; of working together on a radical, collective pedagogy project; of struggling through and across difference within our epistemic friendship in the collaborative knowledge-making process; of reflexivity considering this collaborative work in relation to our own development and "coming of age" as feminist graduate students; and of learning from the struggles, contributions, and work of the radical feminists of earlier generations has helped us to map out various pathways to engage, sustain, and nurture our dissident feminist politics available to us.

Appendix

Unit Plan Goal

Our goal is to facilitate our students' development of a complex understanding of incarceration as an imperial project. Through an exploration of racist and patriarchal imprisonment systems in the United States, students will first learn theories that articulate incarceration and detention as oppressive strategies of territorial control, imperialism, and colonization. After developing theoretical understandings and methods of critique, students will examine the contemporaneous Israeli occupation through an engagement with Israel's carceral and detention policies of Palestinians, and Palestinian resistance to these procedures that work to maintain Israeli control over Palestinian territory and bodies.

Unit Plan Context

Situated within an undergraduate (200–300) level social science (sociology, political science, anthropology) or humanities (philosophy, history, cultural studies) course of between twenty and thirty students, this unit plan will include a four-class session (one for preparation, two dedicated hour-and-a-half sessions, one for follow-up).

Unit Plan Pedagogical Rationale

Appadurai contends that we do not use the word native "uniformly to refer to people who are born in certain places and, thus, belong to them" (1992, 34). Instead, he argues, "natives are not only persons who are from certain places, and belong to those places, but they are also those who are somehow incarcerated, or confined in those places" (35).

We want our students to think critically about their connection to the occupation of Palestine through U.S. financial and political contributions to the colonization of Palestine through occupation and its attendant structures and strategies. These strategies include penal institutions implemented by Israeli occupying forces, specifically in the form of administrative detention. Centering on the experiences of detainees, our students will utilize gender and class as analytics and participate in critiques of the trivialization of women's resistance. We also want students to consider the methods and modes of resistance strategies exercised by Palestinians as well as U.S. residents.

In designing this unit, we thought about what students know about Palestine and Israel (both in terms of the discourses and narratives readily available to those living in the United States); how to structure their (un/re)learning; how to address the structural, embodied, and resistance levels of Palestinian occupation; and how our students can begin considering their own resistance and activism from their social locations. We imagined our students as undergraduates enrolled in different programs across the university, with our class as an introductory social science or humanities class.

With this in mind, we framed our first eighty-minute session of the unit around an introduction to the Israeli occupation of Palestine, which could serve as a refresher, a disruption of what students have previously learned or known about the occupation, or as a first encounter with it. Specifically, this session would build students' content knowledge of fundamental physical aspects of the occupation. Starting with an orientation to the politics of maps and borders, and a chronological exploration of Israeli incursions into Palestine (focusing specifically on 1946–2012), students will first gain an awareness of what occupation looks like through the geospatial representations of mapping political ideology onto temporal landmass and through bordering space physically.

In preparation for class, students will have watched *Life in Occupied Palestine* for homework in addition to reading the assigned texts. In class, students will collectively build working understandings of the discursive concepts essential to engagement with both the Israeli Occupation and its concomitant penal structures. These concepts include incursion, occupation, colonization, settlement, border patrol, checkpoints, sovereignty, neoliberalism, and mobility.

The second day will build on this foundational and structural understanding of the Israeli occupation by first exploring its political economy, how neoliberalism fuels the maintenance of borders, and the role and implications of U.S. funding to the state of Israel. We are interested in exploring with students how this political economy sustains the occupation circuit that limits the resources and mobility of Palestinians in order to maintain Israeli hegemony.

Next, while working in groups to read assigned texts (as listed on syllabus), we want our students to engage in an embodied, corporeal analysis of detention policies and politics. We draw from specific examples of detention (Khader Adnan) to animate the material effects of this kind of violence, occupation, and intimidation to maintain power and restrict mobility in strategic ways. The UN Women report also illustrates how gender plays a role in occupation, even though much talk focuses on the incarceration of young Palestinian men. Women's voices disrupt this framing and show the differentiated experiences of women not only as they are incarcerated but how their incarceration affects families.

Lastly, we draw from specific cases of Khader Adnan and Hanaa Shalabi to underscore how Palestinians resist the occupation of their land and their bodies by Israeli and U.S. forces through hunger strikes. This focus will segue in a call for students to consider their own social locations within a U.S. institution, to think concretely about different forms of resistance available to them, and to develop an actionable resistance plan (e.g., divestment campaign, pressure on Congress, educating others, reading outside of popular mainstream U.S. media outlets).

In planning this unit, we recognize that students may resist the material depending on their own political stakes in the occupation. As educators who recognize that this unit will disrupt hegemonic U.S. constructions of the occupation, we must strategize how we will speak back to these forms of resistance in a formative way, remembering, as Moya reminds us, that we are "teaching the practice of critical thinking rather than a particular ideological stance" (2006, 113). Our call to students' action and critical thinking, then, is not about aligning their politics with ours, but having students critically engage in an epistemological analysis of what they know, how they have come to know it, and how alternative ways of knowing from other social locations offer other necessary epistemological frames.

Unit Plan Lesson Day 1

DAY 1: INTRODUCTION TO OCCUPATION, OVERVIEW OF PENAL STRUCTURES

Students will come to class having:
Viewed:
Life in Occupied Palestine (http://vimeo.com/6977999)

Read:

- Introduction to Administrative Detention by ADDAMEER: http://www.addameer.org/israeli_military_judicial_system/administrative_detention
- A Reexamination of Administrative Detention in a Jewish and Democratic State by The Israel Democracy Institute (IDI) (Chapter 1: Definition and Post-Chapter: Administrative Detention: An Opportunity for Reevaluation): http://en.idi.org.il/media/1343308/Reexamination_Full_PPE7.pdf
- Israel's use of administrative detention involving Palestinian children (27–30): http://www.unicef.org/protection/files/Administrative_detention_discussion_paper_April2011.pdf

Introduction
Students will walk into class and the following words will be written on poster paper hanging on the walls throughout the room:

- Occupation
- Colonialism
- Neoliberalism
- Border patrol
- Checkpoint
- Freedom
- Democracy
- Shared responsibility

Students will be asked to define these words based on the viewing/reading they did for homework. After each student has commented on each of the poster sheets, the whole class will participate in a silent gallery walk, reading each student-generated definition and reflecting on the multiple articulations as they walk through the room. Once participants have returned to their seats, the class will participate in the generation of collective definition making. Taking each word in turn, students will offer definitions/parts of definitions they would like included for each word and the instructor will facilitate the process of coming to consensus for each word. Through this dialogue, students will flesh out the meaning making they engaged in while viewing and reading the assigned resources.

Administrative Detention as a Structure of Occupational Policy
This section of the lesson serves to strengthen students' understanding of administrative detention, as well as to increase students' awareness of the connection between administrative detention and Israeli occupation of Palestine. Through a dialogue surrounding the following questions, and drawing from the content of the listed readings, which students must have read in preparation for today, the class will discuss: What is

administrative detention? How does international law protect from arbitrary detention? What are administrative law conditions? How does Israel use administrative detention (as collective punishment against Palestinians) in the West Bank? What are the conditions surrounding Israeli detention of Palestinian children? What are the connections to Israeli occupation of Palestine that we can make from what we now understand of administrative detention?

Unit Plan Lesson Day 2

DAY 2: POLITICAL ECONOMY AND EMBODIED RESISTANCE

Students will come to class having read for the first half of the lesson:

- Palestinian workers: http://stopthewall.org/impact-palestinian-workers-under-israeli-occupation
- Globalization and the occupation: http://stopthewall.org/motorola-securing-israeli-occupation
- Women and economic survival: https://occupiedpalestine.wordpress.com/2011/10/17/gaza-women-struggle-to-survive-economically-says-un-study/
- U.S. monetary aid and Palestine: https://occupiedpalestine.wordpress.com/2011/10/01/economic-terrorism-report-us-blocks-200-million-in-aid-to-pa/
- Deaths (names and ages) arising from denied access to medical treatment, 2000–2011: http://www.btselem.org/statistics/fatalities/after-cast-lead/by-date-of-event/gaza/palestinians-who-died-following-an-infringement-of-the-right-to-medical-treatment
- Day-to-day effects (emergency services, fuel, etc.) of the occupation: https://occupiedpalestine.wordpress.com/2010/12/19/gaza-no-water-sewage/ and https://occupiedpalestine.wordpress.com/2012/02/19/crisis-in-gaza-photography/

Students will come to class having read for the second half of the lesson:

- Comprehensive Report on Palestinian Prisoners (from process to larger issues): https://occupiedpalestine.wordpress.com/special-topics/prisoners/
- Khader Adnan and the role of administrative detention in the Israeli occupation: http://www.jadaliyya.com/pages/index/4547/the-hunger-strike-defeated-the-secret-evidence_the
- UN Women report: Suspended lives: Palestinian female prisoners in Israeli Prisons: http://www.pourlapalestine.be/docs/Suspended-Lives-en-Booklet-UN-Women-.pdf
- Hanaa Shalabi on gender, sexual violence, and women's activism in Palestine: http://www.alarabiya.net/articles/2012/03/08/199371.html

The first half of day two's lesson plan focuses on political economy. Students will enter the classroom and be instructed to discuss the following prompt in groups of three to four.

Our current political economy can be thought of as neoliberal. Neoliberalism is a set of economic, political, and cultural practices that are centered on the market, wealth, productivity, and economic gain.

What is the social and corporeal damage of neoliberalist economic practices on the everyday worlds of Palestinians? How are these different groups affected by neoliberalism? Are some groups (i.e., elderly, children) more affected than others? If so, how? How is this political ideology of free market complicit with the occupation? How would this social damage look if our current moment was not neoliberal? Compare the neoliberal landscape (i.e., the social damage) created by market forces and ideologies of free market in Palestine with what is happening at home (i.e., United States). How is this social damage different? How is it the same? How are the things that you buy (e.g., Motorola Android phones) connected to the occupation?

After a half hour of discussion, small groups will be asked to share out to the whole class.

The second half of day two's lesson plan will focus on embodied incarceration and resistance.

After the conversation on the political economy of incarceration, we will segue into the embodied effects of incarceration and forms of resistance exercised by detainees. This part of the class will first begin by asking students to provide responses and reactions to the readings for day two. Afterward, students will break up in small groups (three to four students) to respond to the following questions: Who is detained? Who is targeted? What work does administrative detention do? How does administrative detention support and further occupation? How does violence against women in prisons (and outside) serve as a strategy of occupation? What kind of resistance strategies do detainees exercise? What does the UN Women report tell us about the experience of detention of Palestinian women? How is Hanaa Shalabi's resistance talked about in comparison to Khader Adnan? How are these news reports reproducing normative gender roles? Groups will share out to the rest of the class their responses to these prompts. We will work together to connect these issues to broader course themes of mobility, hegemony, and control.

Action Project

Students will be arranged in small groups of three to four and instructed to engage both research and activism as part of their unit project. The directions for this assignment follow.

> As we learned, the occupation of Palestine by Israel is partially enabled by the global economic and military policies that are structured by the ideology of neoliberalism. Because of neoliberal ideology, there is little to no critical and analytical

discussion of the Israeli divestment campaign in U.S. media. Working in groups of three to four, you will conduct an action research project that meets the following criteria.

- Research representations of the Israeli occupation in U.S. media. You must cite at least three or four articles.
- Building from the topics you found in U.S. media, find three or four more articles covering the same topics in global media, including media from Israel and Palestine.
- Write a one- to two-page (single-spaced) brief explicating the discrepancies in reports and offering an analytical critique of what it means for the reports to be similar/different in the ways you identified.
- From your report, determine what you would like to educate U.S. citizens about (e.g., checkpoints, incarceration, youth and administrative detentions) and the U.S. population that you are most interested in reaching.
- Design and implement a media campaign to teach your chosen population about your topic. You can reach out through editorials, open letters, blogs, Facebook/Twitter blasts, public lectures, art instillations, public performances, etc. Your means of putting your research into action can be as creative as your group chooses, but it must reach an audience and provide content knowledge based on your research. Your presentation (whatever form it takes) must also provide your audience with information on how they can take action and/or share this knowledge.
- You will have two weeks to collect data and write your report. You will have until the last week of the semester to complete your action project. Each group member must write a five-page (single-spaced) paper reflecting on your process as a group, offering an analysis of media representations of the occupation of Palestine, and providing an account of how your action project contributed to re-presenting the occupation in a way that speaks back to the U.S. contribution to and maintenance of neoliberal colonization in Palestine.

Postscript

Every so often in a teacher's life she is gifted with a remarkable testimony of the effects of her labors. This essay is one such gift. It constitutes the generational continuity of political epistemic friendships that have marked my own intellectual genealogy. The pedagogy assignment that Nicole, Wendy, Angie, Anya, and Meredith write about flows directly from my own commitment and accountability to an indigenous and feminist of color solidarity delegation to the occupied Palestinian territories in June 2011.[2] For me the epistemic friendships that resulted from this shared journey, witnessing and reflecting on the everyday life, struggles, and (in)justice in the occupied territories led to a commitment to connect justice for Palestine to the political/intellectual work I undertake within and outside the U.S. academy. The collective pedagogy project that this essay reflects on is thus anchored in my own epistemic friendships forged in the journey to Palestine, and it is one of a series of collaborative practices I have engaged in with my sisters/comrades since June 2011. How amazing that my own feminist solidarities have enabled these young scholars to engage in a collective practice that leads them to craft a notion of "epistemic friendship" that constitutes "a learning with, by, and for social justice with others . . ."

Genealogically, the most important sources of inspiration for my own scholarship, activism, and pedagogy over the last three decades have always been the radical community of activist-scholars and grassroots organizers in feminist, antiracist, anticapitalist, and anti-imperialist movements in the Global South and North. I have always understood that I need to build and nurture the intellectual neighborhoods (the term is Toni Morrison's) I want to occupy. Building these neighborhoods anchored in crossing racial, national, class, and sexual lines over years has been a source of great joy and pleasure. I learned early on that certain ways of thinking and analyzing were dangerous—they posed not just intellectual or theoretical threats but they translated into everyday interactions and relationships at my place of work. After all, the colonial, racialized discourses I was writing about were often inscribed on my own body. It is this deep and inevitable connection between the knowledges I produce, the collectives they are inspired by and anchored in, and the embodiment on my own everyday life and identity that has been most instructive for me in the U.S. academy—what the authors of this essay name "epistemic friendships."

The collective pedagogy project is an example of an attempt to craft such intellectual neighborhoods that sustain pedagogies of dissent and engender transnational, antiracist feminist liberatory projects. Very briefly, the project was designed to:

a. Provide a space for critical, collaborative, action-based, scholarly feminist practice that resists institutional pressures to produce graduates with standard academic literacies in the context of a neoliberal academy.
b. Reinforce systemic political analysis connected to political struggles and movements on the ground (based on the multiple sources of research) and to envision a pedagogy that ethically translates such struggles into the U.S. classroom.
c. Work against the flattening of difference by focusing on place-based knowledge about gender justice connected to alternative colonial histories and social movements anchored in multiple sites of knowledge.

d. Resist individualized, commodified notions of academic performance and success by insisting on a collaborative, collective knowledge-making process that is evaluated at multiple levels in an ongoing process of discussion/reflection.
e. Provide a context for risk taking in the undergraduate classroom that actively connects questions of location, history, and knowledge production with pedagogies of dissent.

Reading Nicole, Wendy, Angie, Anya, and Meredith's analysis, I am deeply gratified to see how generative the project was for them. This nuanced analysis about collaborative process, transnational epistemic friendships, and innovative, cross-disciplinary pedagogical practice is an invaluable testament to pedagogies of possibility and social justice research and activism in the neoliberal, imperial U.S. academy. And it is a testament to the deeply joyful collaborative feminist praxis that keeps many of us keep on keeping on!

Notes

1. This project explores the narratives of forty-two feminists shaped by different historical and cultural contexts.
2. See http://codepink.org/blog/2011/07/justice-for-palestine-a-call-to-action-from-indigenous-and-women-of-color-feminists/.

References

Adams, Maurianne, Lee A. Bell, and Pat Griffin, eds. 2010. *Teaching for Diversity and Social Justice*. 2nd ed. New York: Routledge.

Alcoff, Linda M. 1995. "The Problem of Speaking for Others." In *Who Can Speak: Authority and Critical Identity,* edited by Judith Roof and Robyn Wiegman, 97–120. Chicago: University of Illinois Press.

Alexander, M. Jacqui. 2005. *Pedagogies of Crossing: Mediations on Feminism, Sexual Politics, Memoir, and the Sacred*. Durham, N.C.: Duke University Press.

Alexander, M. Jacqui, and Mohanty, Chandra T. 2010. "Cartographies of Knowledge and Power: Transnational Feminism as Radical Praxis." In *Critical Transnational Feminist Praxis,* edited by Amanda L. Swarr and Richa Nagar, 23–45. Albany: State University of New York Press.

Appadurai, Arjun. 1992. "Putting Hierarchy in Its Place." In *Rereading Cultural Anthropology,* edited by George E. Marcus, 34–47. Durham, N.C.: Duke University Press.

Blackmore, Jill. 2005. "Feminist Strategic Rethinking of Human Rights Discourses in Education." In *Just Advocacy? Women's Human Rights, Transnational Feminisms, and the Politics of Representation,* edited by Wendy S. Hesford and Wendy Kozol, 243–265. New Brunswick, N.J.: Rutgers University Press.

Butler, Judith. 2004. *Precarious Life: The Powers of Mourning and Violence*. New York: Verso.
Case, Kim A. 2010. *Intersections Project*. Accessed April 12, 2012. https://sites.google.com/site/drkimcase/intersections-project.
Cole, Elizabeth R., and Zakiya T. Luna. 2010. "Making Coalitions Work: Solidarity across Difference within US Feminism." *Feminist Studies* 36(1): 71–98.
Freire, Paulo. 1970. *Pedagogy of the Oppressed*. New York: Seabury Press.
Gandhi, Leela. 2006. *Affective Communities: Anticolonial Thought, Fin-de-Siècle Radicalism, and the Politics of Friendship*. Durham, N.C.: Duke University Press.
Giroux, Henry A. 2007. *The University in Chains: Confronting the Military-Industrial-Academic Complex*. Boulder: Paradigm Publishers.
hooks, bell. 1995. "Sisterhood: Political Solidarity between Women." In *Feminism and Community*, edited by Penny A. Weiss and Marilyn Friedman, 293–316. Philadelphia: Temple University Press.
Johnson-Reagon, Bernice. 1983. "Coalition Politics: Turning the Century." In *Home Girls: A Black Feminist Anthology*, edited by Barbara Smith, 356–368. New York: Kitchen Table/Women of Color Press.
Kaplan, Caren. 1994. "The Politics of Location as Transnational Feminist Practice." In *Scattered Hegemonies: Postmodernity and Transnational Feminist Practices*, edited by Inderpal Grewal and Caren Kaplan, 137–152. Minneapolis: University of Minnesota Press.
———. 1996. *Questions of Travel: Postmodern Discourses of Displacement*. Durham, N.C.: Duke University Press.
Koopman, Sara. 2008. "Imperialism Within: Can the Master's Tools Bring down Empire?" *ACME: An International E-Journal for Critical Geographies* 7(2): 283–307.
Lugones, Maria C. 1995. "Sisterhood and Friendship as Feminist Models." In *Feminism and Community*, edited by Penny A. Weiss and Marilyn Friedman, 135–146. Philadelphia: Temple University Press.
McCall, Leslie. 2005. "The Complexity of Intersectionality," *Signs* 30(3): 1771–1800.
McGuire, Kristin, Abigail J. Stewart, and Nicola Curtin. 2010. "Becoming Feminist Activists: Comparing Narratives," *Feminist Studies* 36(1): 99.
Mejia, Angie, Olivia Quiroz, Yoland Morales, and Las Madres del Norte de Portland. 2013. "From Madres to Mujeristas: Latinas Making Change with Photovoice," *Action Research Journal* 11(4): 301–321.
Mernissi, Fatima. 1995. *Dreams of Trespass: Tales of a Harem Girlhood*. New York: Perseus Books.
Mohanty, Chandra Talpade. 2003. *Feminism without Borders: Decolonizing Theory, Practice, and Solidarity*. Durham, N.C.: Duke University Press.
———. 2006. "Foreword." In *Playing with Fire: Feminist Thought and Activism through Seven Lives in India*, by Sangtin Writers and Richa Nagar, ix–xv. Minneapolis: University of Minnesota Press.
Moya, Paula. 2006. "What's Identity Got to Do With It? Mobilizing Identities in the Multicultural Classroom." In *Identity Politics Reconsidered*, edited by Linda Martín

Alcoff, Michael Hames-García, Satya P. Mohanty, and Paula M. L. Moya. New York: Palgrave MacMillan.

Naples, Nancy. 2002. "Changing the Terms: Community Activism, Globalization, and the Dilemmas of Transnational Feminist Praxis." In *Women's Activism and Globalization: Linking Local Struggles and Transnational Politics,* edited by Nancy Naples and Manisha Desai, 3–14. London: Routledge.

Nepstad, Sharon E. 2004. "Persistent Resistance: Commitment and Community in the Plowshares Movement." *Social Problems* 51(1): 43–60.

———. 2008. *Religion and War Resistance in the Plowshares Movement.* Cambridge: Cambridge University Press.

Soja, Edward. 1996. *Thirdspace: Journeys to Los Angeles and Other Real-and-Imagined Places.* Oxford: Basil Blackwell.

Stone-Mediatore, Shari. 2003. *Reading across Borders: Storytelling and Knowledges of Resistance.* New York: Palgrave MacMillan.

Sudbury, Julia. 2009. "Challenging Penal Dependency: Activist Scholars and the Antiprison Movement." In *Activist Scholarship: Antiracism, Feminism, and Social Change,* edited by Julia Sudbury and Margo Okazawa-Rey, 17–35. Boulder: Paradigm Publishers.

Sudbury, Julia, and Margo Okazawa-Rey, eds. 2009. *Activist Scholarship: Antiracism, Feminism, and Social Change.* Boulder: Paradigm Publishers.

Wilson, Robin. 2011, October 2. "Syracuse's Slide: As Chancellor Focuses on the 'Public Good,' Syracuse's Reputation Slides." *Chronicle of Higher Education.* Accessed April 15, 2012. http://chronicle.com/article/Syracuses-Slide/129238/.

Young, Iris M. 1995. "The Ideal of Community and the Politics of Difference." In *Feminism and Community,* edited by Penny A. Weiss and Marilyn Friedman, 233–258. Philadelphia: Temple University Press.

Zuniga, Ximena, Biren A. Nagda, Mark Chelser, and Adena Cytryon-Walker. 2007. *Intergroup Dialogue in Higher Education: Meaningful Learning about Social Justice.* San Francisco: Jossey-Bass.

CHAPTER 2

Meditations on Friendship
Politics of Feminist Solidarity in Ethnography

AZZA BASARUDIN AND HIMIKA BHATTACHARYA

Claiming Friendship and Forming Alliances

Transnational feminist praxis enables epistemological and methodological frameworks that attend to intersectional relations of power (gender, race, sexuality, class, nation) and prioritizes accountability and transparency in understanding women's struggles on their own terms (Chowdhury 2011; Grewal and Kaplan 1994; Mohanty 2003; Mohanty and Alexander 1997; Nagar and Swarr 2010). Feminist ethnographers have addressed questions of representation, agency, emotions, and relationships; worked with decolonizing methodology while subverting the historically loaded idiom of ethnography; and balanced feminist-academic commitments (Abu-Lughod 1986, 1993; Visweswaran 1994; Madison 2005). Central to critical feminist ethnography are reciprocal relations between researchers and their interlocutors: that is, practicing solidarity with those who allow us into the intimate folds of their world through heightened awareness about the implications of inequalities and differences in the hope that such a practice would serve as "a transformative source" (Rowe 2008, 4).

This chapter is a collaborative effort to think through the significance of friendships in the context of feminist ethnography, knowledge production, and writing. It is about the place and role of friendship between people engaged in the research process and within systems of knowledge production that we pledge allegiance to and embrace. It is about thinking through the messiness of *feeling emotions* and *acknowledging* and *working through* contentious issues of power and privilege that exist between our interlocutors and ourselves. It is about thinking through the *cost of feeling* affection and even love in the context of work. We follow Aimee Carillo Rowe to conceive of "love" as relationships beyond lovers and friends to those whose "lives matter to us" (2008, 3). We ask: Do friendships formed in the context of ethnographic fieldwork demand legitimacy in a way that friendships formed in other spaces, across locations, alliances, and axes of identity, do not? What part of the transnational feminist work/labor are these friendships performing? It is not our aim to dwell in the romanticism of friendship ("Oh, why can't we just be friends"); rather, we raise these questions to distinguish between the friendships we form and how we then conduct them in the context of ethnographic representation written onto the lives of our interlocutors, friends, and ourselves, across difference, in solidarity with one another.

Within transnational feminist praxis, *solidarity*, while not assumed or taken for granted, is more often visible as a code of ethics that feminist researchers strive for and abide by to appreciate lived realities, honor differences, and generate knowledge toward transforming power structures. What takes place in the process of building, living, and sustaining solidarity—the intimacies, heartaches, struggles, anxieties, and joys—are generally tucked away in notebooks and recesses of memories/realities, surfacing occasionally in one's writing. Our intent is to make visible the *process* of grappling with the ethics of relationships and friendships formed in the course of our research and to unpack the intricacies of relationality and alliance building. As Rowe writes, "ideas and experiences, values and interpretations always take place within the context of our relational lives. Whom we love becomes vital to the theory we produce and how it might be received. The text is neither produced nor received in isolation. Others are involved" (2008, 15). At the same time, we are invested in carefully thinking through how we understand and practice solidarity. Our attempt is to get to the heart of what it means to embrace friendship as a politic, as part of how we approach feminist solidarity work within and across our research contexts.

From such a lens then, friendships are also political acts. They do not occur in social and cultural vacuums. Our entry points into the various levels of friendship we have cultivated and sustained during research are embedded in power politics, and to a certain extent, filtered through existing epistemological frameworks. How we come to conceive of our research projects, present ourselves personally and professionally, conduct our research, form friendships and relationships, document/write about our research, publish and present our work, and practice accountability is regulated along "power lines" (Rowe 2008). But some of these things, which constitute even political acts of friendship, may simultaneously lie within and beyond "power lines," seemingly unregulated by differences that certain hierarchies of power seek to regulate and contain.

We base this chapter primarily, although not exclusively, on conversations about our respective fieldwork experiences in Lahaul, India (Bhattacharya) and Kuala Lumpur, Malaysia (Basarudin) over the past several years. We take as a point of departure Nagar and Geiger's epigraph and the conceptions of "situated researcher" and "situated solidarities" in order to move beyond the impasse of self-reflexivity and legitimacy into transformative epistemological and methodological approaches to transnational feminist solidarities and systems of knowledge production: "How can we take positionality, identity and reflexivity out of misplaced struggles over legitimacy and transparent reflexivity, and turn them into more meaningful conceptual tools that can help us advance transformative politics of difference in relation to our own research agendas?" (Nagar & Geiger 2007, 272). We articulate here our own process of turning a struggle we both at different points in our work experienced as stagnancy, into an exercise in negotiating power, difference, and privilege to have a productive conversation about the transformative potential of our feminist praxis through, and often because of, these (complicated) friendships. More importantly, we want to shift from a space of always not-knowing and messiness, to understanding how these moments of crises have been productive. By claiming the affections and friendships we experience and share, we reflect on how our work, our solidarity politics, and our feminist praxis have been sharpened. In other words, we consider friendship as the site where ethnographic fieldwork destabilizes the very framework (of rigor and method) it tries to institutionalize. Discussing the politics of friendship as we revisit our respective ethnographic memories becomes the methodology for locating how these friendships form the ground (albeit shaky) beneath our projects.

Bhattacharya and Basarudin carried out ethnographic research in different geographical, cultural, and political contexts and focused on different topics—meaning-making processes in relation to structural violence (Bhattacharya) and women's activism and reform in Islam (Basarudin). We have both struggled with trying to make sense of feminist-academic relationships that emerged during our fieldwork, and evolved over time and across distance. Given the focus of our research, commitment to feminist praxis, and positionality as "native" ethnographers, we are conscious that our fieldwork will, undoubtedly, be messy.

What we continue to struggle with are the intersecting emotional entanglements that characterize our lives and those of our interlocutors, our protectiveness of the intimate knowledge of others, and ourselves and how the choices we make affect directly or indirectly our research outcome. Thus, central to our inquiry is: How do we as feminist ethnographers from the Global South, located in institutions in the Global North, negotiate friendships that cross the boundaries between our professional commitments and personal lives, while remaining accountable to those whose lives and experiences we become a part of?

We consider our writing spaces an extension of the field that allows us to continue negotiating research dilemmas, particularly in confronting subject-object dualisms and representational politics (Lal 1999). Our claiming of friendships is not an indication that we have found a magical solution to the messiness of ethnography or that feminist researchers should aspire to a comparable level of emotional connectedness. We have not transcended the disparity of power and privilege that involves women studying women (Stacey 1988). Rather, we deploy situated experiences of fieldwork and friendships to suggest that genuine affection and love is possible in spite of it. And we do so in celebration of Lila Abu-Lughod's reminder that personal commitment to ethnography can be viewed as "a form of deep respect for 'others' that is rare in the world" (Deb 2012, 4). Moreover, we do so in the spirit of Richa Nagar's (2014) persuasive suggestions that we deeply reflect on our methodological and epistemological practices, in that we make ourselves "radically vulnerable" while remaining politically engaged.[1]

Feminist scholars have shed light on the contested category of "native" ethnographer, stressing that the rigidity and dichotomy of insider/outsider and self/other does not account for the multifaceted lived realities of researchers (Behar 1993; Narayan 1993). They have argued for grounding of subject positionings in an intersectional framework and shifting categories of identities and subjectivities. Our deployment of the term "native" exposes and reinforces its artificial construction and troubles its meaning. Basarudin's research is based in Kuala Lumpur, the national capital of Malaysia. She uses the term "native" to identify herself as a person who was born and raised in Malaysia, hence her national affinity with members of the organization she researched. This affinity does not automatically lend itself to an "insider" perspective, but it serves to problematize rigid conceptions of identity and subjectivity for those who "return" home to conduct research. While the degree and impact of stranger-ness was mediated through her ability to become accustomed to the larger fabric of Malaysian society, as someone who resides abroad, her class, culture, and religious markers of "Malay," "Muslim," and "Malaysian" have also shifted. This is demonstrated by how others perceived her by choosing to converse in English or "Manglish/ Bahasa Rojak" (a particular form of Malaysian English reflecting a combination of various local dialects) even when she was speaking in the local language, Bahasa Melayu/Malaysia. Many assumed she was a naturalized American citizen and inquired whether she needed a support letter from the organization explaining the reason for her visit/research and an extended visa for the duration of her stay. Many were curious (exhibited through humor) about her relationship to the Malay culture: "She has become a *minah saleh* (white woman), *takut makanan pedas* (fears spicy food) and *tak tahan panas* (cannot tolerate the heat). We should Malaycize her." The Malay and Malaysian parts of her identity, as well as her local family ties were suspended in a migrational and citizenship conundrum and replaced by an "American" distinctiveness—an association unfamiliar to her. She then became neither a "native" who entirely belonged nor the "foreigner" who was visiting. Her anecdote is not about romanticizing representational politics and fragmented existence or indicating that the Malay and Malaysian cultures or her interlocutors' identities and subjectivities are static. Rather, she draws attention to the state of nonbelonging within a community, culture, and nation to illustrate the unstable landscape of identity and how it shapes her relationship to people and place, as well as the various ways power and difference continue to define the research process.

Himika's work is based in the Lahaul valley of Himachal Pradesh, India, and is rooted in the friendships and relationships she formed there even before beginning her graduate education in the United States. Her presence in Lahaul has always been a mixed one. On the one hand, she neatly fit the first category in the distinction the Lahaulis use to separate the world into two groups of people: those categorized as *neeche ke log* (people from the plains) and *upar ke log* (people from the higher mountains). On the other, she was also marked as someone who lives in an in-between space, as someone who belongs in both, the plains and the mountains. In Lahaul, especially among the generational members of the women's groups she initially worked with, Himika was always "from the plains" but also with a range of other descriptors, which she has heard repeated over the years by different people there who know her. She heard this idea of being both (of the plains and the mountains), repeated in different ways, and it was best summed up by Pema Dolma, a Lahauli organizer who introduced her to someone saying, "She's caught in-between two lives—her name has our mountains in it[2]—must be connected to a previous life when she was a Lahauli but then in this life, she's from the plains." Different iterations of this idea—whether across lives or within this life—was something she heard people explain her through. Similarly, this idea of "being both" operated in other spaces and identities she was marked by, even as the contours of these ways of being were/are always shaped by power differentials of caste/class/gender. She feels most at home in her status as an in-betweener (Diversi and Moreira 2008) whether in Lahaul or in the United States. While different identity markers (caste/class/gender/race) and subjectivities have obviously shaped her relationship to both places, here she thinks through the feminist possibilities and limitations that emerge from friendships in the context of research, despite the feminist unease that also undergirds the implications of such relationships.

In our analysis, we echo Virginia Dominguez when she asks "how to incorporate and acknowledge love in one's intellectual life, indeed in one's writing, and how to incorporate and acknowledge love in one's politics" (2000, 368). In following several third world writers and feminists who, in Chela Sandoval's words, "understand 'love' as a hermeneutic . . . a set of practices that can access and guide our theoretical and political 'movidas'—revolutionary maneuvers toward decolonized being," we illustrate here how friendship, affection, and love are at the heart of our ethnographic choices and feminist praxis (2000, 140). We begin by situating our research contexts, then follow with our stories, friendships, and solidarities, which demonstrate the methodological, epistemological, and ontological (Nagar and Geiger 2007) shifts we have experienced and that have, in turn, transformed us through immersion in "emotional spaces of research" (Collins 2012, 50).

Journeys, People, and Place

BASARUDIN, KUALA LUMPUR, MALAYSIA

My research is based on fieldwork in a community of Sunni Muslims in Malaysia, a multiethnic and multiconfessional country in Southeast Asia.[3] The population of Malaysia is made up of the majority ethnic Malays (mainly Muslims) and minorities of ethnic Chinese, Indians, Sikhs, and indigenous people. I studied an elite organization of professional Muslim women—Sisters in Islam (SIS)—whose members are academics, entrepreneurs, and journalists. This organization advocates for justice and equality for Muslim women, a contemporary understanding of sources of Islamic tradition, and respect for Malaysia's ethnic and religious pluralism. SIS was founded by a group of friends who came together to address the divergence between their understandings of "ethical" Islam and "establishment" Islam (Ahmed 1992) promoted by the state, which is manifested in the form of laws and policies. The organization's strategy is based on a combination of research and activism. They spearhead initiatives in collaboration with other nongovernmental organizations (NGOs), raise public consciousness through study sessions and public lectures, provide pro bono legal service, and lobby the state through media campaigns. Over the last twenty years, SIS has honed a distinct strategy of translating feminist hermeneutics into activism and led the struggle to promote the rights of Muslim women. The organization and its outspoken feminist founders have a significant, albeit highly contested, presence on the local and international stage.

My path to, and interest in, this organization dates back to a project on Muslim family law I was involved in as an undergraduate student in Malaysia. This project sparked my interest in women's rights in Islam and ultimately led me to pursue graduate work in Women's/Gender Studies in the United States. My research focuses SIS's production and transmission of Islamic knowledge through social and legal activism to effect change in localized cultural mores and family law. Utilizing primary sources (personal interviews, narrative analysis, participant observation, focus groups) as well as secondary sources (newspaper clippings, reports, and media recording), I foreground a geographically, historically, and culturally situated analysis of women activists as agents of contemporary Islamic reform to demonstrate how gender, law, and religion remain inextricably linked to their struggle for self-determination and societal transformation. As someone in solidarity with Muslim women's movements for justice in general, and with the struggle of the Muslim reformers in Malaysia specifically, my political project and intellectual inquiry lie in understanding how these women activists claim, in any way, shape, or form, their space, position of authority, and leadership roles in Islam.

The structure of this organization has shifted since its inception. Previously, the founding members would gather each week in a rather informal manner at each other's houses or flats. Currently, the organization is managed similar to a corporate structure, with a board of directors and a planning committee overseeing the operations of smaller units (e.g., public education, communications, legal services). The founders are articulate, politically savvy, and are cosmopolitan in their worldview and self-representation; many were educated abroad, are frequently interviewed by journalists, have traveled and read extensively, and often invited abroad to speak at universities/research centers. As such, their social standing, life experiences, and professional commitments have imbued them with a relative measure of social/economic power and visibility.

Aware as I was of how power shapes research, studying an elite organization with the founder's positionalities and strategic connections produced a different set of power relations between my interlocutors and myself. My presence notwithstanding, the organizational structure, diverse class and educational backgrounds, and intergenerational makeup of its members (founders, management, and staff) resulted in a strained working environment and a high turnover rate. The founders are mainly those from the upper class and elite class. The managers and staff are of middle class and working class, and the staff members in particular are mainly younger women in the process of starting their careers, testing their endurance for this type of activism, and developing a more rigorous understanding of women's/gender issues in Islam. Insert the researcher who shared their intimate and professional hopes and frustrations, and who was always present (such as when interviews became personal and I was asked to turn off the tape recorder and become "Azza," instead of the "researcher")—all this and more led to heightened levels of power and privilege among us.

I consider the founders and managers acquaintances. They are women I deeply respect and admire, with whom I have a certain level of connection, and, in some instances, by whom I am intimidated, but with whom I am unable to claim the label of friendship. This label, I sincerely believe, can only be fairly applied to the staff members with whom I became close. The contrasting levels of relationships—acquaintances and friendships—that I developed and continue to think about have profoundly influenced the choices I made in the field, the questions I asked, and the stories I tell. These relationships have been instrumental in encouraging me to refine my stake in ethnographic research and the larger goals of my own project, guiding me toward a more honest meaning of friendship and sharpening my feminist praxis across difference.

BHATTACHARYA, LAHAUL, HIMACHAL PRADESH, INDIA

Over the last several years, I have been engaged in different kinds of work, including research, in Lahaul. The most recent of these is a project documenting life histories of women from the region. The first academic research I was engaged in (as a doctoral student) was a collaborative ethnography focused on marriage by abduction in Lahaul, an issue that several women's groups in the valley were fighting against. Before that, my initial work in the valley was as an antiviolence community organizer, when I was involved in the formation of a women's collective and a participatory action research project in the region. Through these different kinds of engagement over the years (since 1999), I have worked in solidarity with different groups of people, particularly women in the area, in their struggles against different forms of oppression, at the intersection of caste, gender, and tribe. How I practice feminist solidarity, and how I may have imagined it starting out, has evolved hugely and certainly become messier over the years.

For this essay, I shall discuss a friendship that complicated my own feminist praxis as an antiviolence organizer working with a women's collective in Lahaul. It forced me to consider the significance of friendship in collaborative work where separating feminist solidarity work and research from the rest of our lives becomes impossible. But first let me provide some context: I first went to the Lahaul valley in 1999 as part of an assignment with the Ministry of Rural Development, Government of India. Subsequently, I stayed on in the valley to work as a community organizer with local women's groups called mahila mandals, continuing to facilitate antiviolence campaigns led by local women. These campaigns were called *kiski izzat gayi* "whose honor is lost" and consisted of village-level meetings between the women who were mobilizing and organizing their community to address issues of violence. This work included working on cases of violence that arose at a day-to-day level, strategizing for future conversations, and planning actions such as valley-level meetings with the men to address issues of marriage practice, honor, and violence. I became involved in a participatory action research project in the valley, which emerged during this period of organizing with the women's groups. The project was to document livelihoods strategies locally; however, the work began to gradually focus on women's concerns with violence. Our final report was a discussion of issues of violence with illustrative cases that local women had been working on, to provide evidence to the state tribal commissioner's office, regarding the pervasiveness of violence, particularly marriage by abduction, in Lahaul.

As a researcher invested in not only understanding, but also in fighting against the violent nexus of Brahmanical patriarchy, tribe and state in India in general, and Lahaul in particular, the research I undertake needs to necessarily be collaborative, in dialogue with the communities my work and my life are situated in. While "solidarity" as an idea and practice is used very widely—and indeed, I, like many others, have been guilty of overusing it (clearly at such times failing completely to do the very things I believe in)—it is also what I understand to be the heart of my work. Thus the manner in which I have approached my work and my research over the years signals who I was/am—what it is I care about and how I have been attempting to learn and engage in solidarity work. Therefore, how I think about my overall research, the subject at hand and the methodology I have adopted in the work, is also my feminist political praxis. My current research project documents and analyzes the (oral and textual) life histories of women across different caste striations from Lahaul, India,[4] with a focus on violence: as experienced, understood, and defined by the women. While the overarching topic of the project is the women's experiences of violence, the lives they narrate of course include much more. Indeed, they spoke in depth about a range of experiences beyond violence, often located on multiple axes of difference, including caste, tribe, and gender. As narrators of their own lives, my cointerlocutors critique, resist, and at times even reify power relations constructed at the intersection of caste, tribe, gender, and state.

The organic manner in which the research emerged, the political potential of the critiques the women narrated, as well as the possibilities and failures of the work I wanted to continue as a researcher, all led me toward a methodology that had at its heart the women's stories. I chose (oral and textual) life histories within a critical performance ethnography framework as my method for this most recent research (now a book manuscript), because I approach oral history as a method that narrates identity and difference as complex, fluid, relational, and political (Moraga and Anzaldúa 1981; Fregoso 2003; Rege 2006). When we narrate our experiences, we tell stories about our experiences of identity (McAdams 1993). When we commit to telling the stories, irrespective of the truth-telling imperative of the testimony (Felman 1992), we engage in a political act. In this spirit, my research is situated within my broader political work and I am interested in bearing witness to the women's life histories, in affirming and in coperforming their stories believing that this knowledge is produced relationally. In such an approach, researcher and narrators are not only cointerlocutors, performing for one another, but they are also connected to each other emotionally, intellectually, and relationally. It follows, then, that my own feminist praxis has been deeply inspired by these connections with the women who have shared their stories with me.

Remembering Friendships

BASARUDIN, KUALA LUMPUR, MALAYSIA

My own process of untangling competing loyalties and visions of solidarities is one that Himika and a few close friends have been privy and central to. Their attentiveness and companionship have helped me arrive at a more political understanding of friendship. Outside the context of ethnography, we develop friendships based on reciprocal trust, ideas, and activities, and although I knew this foundation formed the basis of my friendships in the field, only now am I *in the know* that claiming friendship—with the emotional threads that uphold it—in all its messiness is what shapes and drives my commitment to alliance building and knowledge making. It is my *feeling emotions*, and the *acknowledgment* of them, as well as *working through* the cost of allegiance in the context of research that I can claim transparency/affection/love in reconstituting the significance of friendship and going beyond the methodological and epistemological impasse that is my feminist praxis.

During the course of fieldwork I became close to several women: Tina, Suzila, Rania, and Melia.[5] These staff members were all in their twenties, with the exception of Melia, who is closer to me in age. While these friendships inform my research and influence the stories I tell, my friendship with Melia takes center stage here because she was closest to me and because it is with her that questions of relationality and difference were, and still are, sorely tested. In our friendship, Melia wears many hats. She is a confidant, advisor, mentor, and a research companion. Melia is an activist with an impressive record working on Muslim family law and human rights issues. She brings an extensive combination of consultancy and advocacy at the local and national levels, which allows her to translate abstract theories/concepts in meaningful ways to her audience. She is, I quickly came to realize, extremely well connected in the circuits of civil society. She suggested people I should talk to, integrated me into her circle of friends, navigated the bureaucracy for appointments, accompanied me to interviews (when needed), and cared for me when I was unwell.

When I started research, Melia had been with the organization for many years. Almost six months after I started fieldwork, she tendered her resignation, which required me to negotiate two competing levels of friendship. The first level was with the Melia whom I bonded with through work and beyond; our friendship was strengthened because we saw each other every day and passionately discussed/debated gender issues in Islam and Malaysian cultural politics. The second level was with the Melia who left the organization and with whom I was sometimes at odds because of her expectation (of my loyalty to her) that I disclose organizational activities (e.g., who is carrying on her projects and how) and the office climate (e.g., stories/gossips about her, of how and why she resigned).

These competing levels were made more complex when Melia asked me to bring up issues of class, power, and hierarchy with the organization's founders. In other words, she wanted me to disclose my awareness and knowledge of the ways that the organizational culture and discriminatory practices run counter to the carefully cultivated public image of the organization. Here, my position as an "outsider" is considered advantageous to mediate the tense office environment (between staff and director/managers). While respecting Melia's care of the friends still working at the organization and her commitment to justice, I had to consider my relationship with the founders, managers, and staff, and the implications of such an intervention on my research. More importantly, I was worried about my friend, who was deeply committed to women's rights in

Islam, but who was discouraged that she could no longer be a part of the local struggle in an institutional manner. I was torn between what I knew I should do and what I ended up doing. While negotiating two competing levels of friendship with Melia, I was also balancing the different levels of relationships I had with the founders and managers, as well as other staff members. These different levels crisscrossed too many times, resulting in awkward management, unhealthy silences, and political maneuvering on my (and my friends') part. While Melia understood my discomfort in relation to her requests, my desultory intervention, when it took place, was insignificant and did little to alleviate existing problems. The rest of this section chronicles my friendship with Melia, which is reflected through the notes from a journal I kept in the field.

* * *

Excerpt from field notes, November 2006
Melia was the first person I met. We had breakfast to go over my research process and goals. I felt immensely comfortable in her presence, which I attribute to her bubbly and outgoing personality. That first breakfast turned out to be the first of many of our work meetings and sembang (chat) sessions. We were, over the course of my fieldwork, inseparable. We took advantage of the vibrant social scene and nightlife Kuala Lumpur had to offer, socialized extensively on a daily basis outside the office, and had numerous sleepovers at my flat.

Educated and assertive, Melia was intensely committed to the organization until her (forced) resignation. She was responsible for handling key projects and integral in facilitating a close working relationship with state officials and various NGOs. Her fluency and comfort in switching among English, Bahasa Malaysia, and Manglish, and her ability to negotiate among opposing personalities, agendas, and political pressures made her a valuable asset to the organization. She was also close to the staff members who looked to her for advice and considered her their mentor. Melia reciprocated by watching out for them by way of advising them on issues relevant to the rights of Muslim women and standing up for them in the office during conflicts with founders/managers. Her professional skills and compassion for the staff, I believe, was one of the reasons that made her the target of colleagues who were increasingly uneasy with her competency and influence. Yet, could there also have been other factors contributing to the friction between Melia and the founders/managers that I was unaware of, given our friendship? Did our closeness blind me to other possibilities?

Our friendship did not go unnoticed in the office. From time to time, I overheard conversations on how Melia was sharing too much "delicate" information about the organization and its members with me. I was also asked, when interviewing a manager, if Melia and I were still in touch (after her resignation); the manager then warned me about trusting information that came from Melia because it is "tainted by her frustrations." Our friendship, I realized, was one of the reasons the founders/managers worried I might know too much about power politics, hierarchies, and internal conflicts, and, as a result, that I might not write about the organization in an impartial manner.

* * *

Melia's resignation was the result of a "she said, she said" situation. The official story was that she resigned to seek greater opportunities. The unofficial story, one that was whispered in the halls of the office, circulated on emails, and passed through word of mouth, was that Melia was unprofessional and insubordinate, in that she did not perform what was expected of her. Knowing that I worried about her, but also needing her own time to regroup soon after the resignation, Melia had this to say to me:

> by now I know that you were told that the reason I left was because of poor job performance. Although you know better, I need to say this. I have been keeping quiet because I needed time to figure out my next move and to heal. The decision was difficult for me and those last few weeks were very draining. I felt very hurt and made the decision to be silent because it seems that my words have been wrongly interpreted. I was treated and judged very unfairly . . . and this you know. I choose to disengage, to be "away" from friends and enemies for now, especially when "truths" about me kept finding their way back to me. I am raw and bleeding and I need to heal.

Your acknowledgment pains me, Melia.
Our friendship is important to me.
And I miss our conversations and your wicked sense of humor. Just today Rania was remarking that the workshop we conducted would have been very different—more "grounded" and "lively"—with you anchoring it. Tina said that the unflattering write up about the religious freedom debates raging in the news and the blogosphere and the backlash from the forum they attended might have been less overwhelming with your care and guidance. Our workspace bears your imprint—you are still very much a part of the organization/us even if the physical you is no longer in that space.

When she was ready, Melia and I resumed our contact. I was elated to be in her company, to share her wisdom and humor. As a part of her "healing," Melia wanted to continue analyzing the office dynamics and the debacle surrounding her resignation (she almost always approached it with humor) and to attend various social and political gatherings. We were always worried about running into the founders/managers she was in conflict with, but that never deterred us from taking advantage of the exciting civil society and social events around town. From time to time, the residue of my (lack of/failed) intervention came up and Melia would state how her *trust in me was shaken but that she has come to accept that I did what I needed to do for my research and, perhaps, for myself. But she never engaged in the blame game. Not once. And I did not venture an explanation. I did not want to shake the fragile bonds of intimacy that we tried very hard to reestablish.*

* * *

Melia's resignation and our friendship, my need to remain focused on my research, my desire to balance both my commitment to her and respect for other members, and our shared struggle for greater rights for women in Islam were constant features of my fieldwork. While appreciating Melia's willingness to share details of her work, the organization's institutional memory and its problems, her insightful input became a source of contention between us once she resigned. While employed, her perspectives about my research, the organization, and criticisms of the organization from other NGOs and civil society actors contributed immensely to my understanding of the larger picture of women's struggle for their rights and for their community to be transformed. Her postemployment perspective was meant to guide my research into the direction she thought it should take.

The unguarded moments of her frustrations (about her resignation) were channeled into sharing intimate details of the organization's members' lives, some of which I felt were intrusive and in violation of their privacy. Melia used to tell me stories when she was still with the organization, but the level of details became intensified with her resignation. She called herself "Azza's informer," which was humorous at first but gradually became unsettling to me. It is not that I was never privy to copious amounts of intimate knowledge, as some were made known by their respective owners and others stumbled upon through social gatherings and friendships with many NGO activists. I kept asking myself: If others (nonorganizational members) know of these intimate stories, how private are they? Is Melia really disclosing private information?

If Melia was "guilty" of a level of "inappropriate" disclosure, then I was a guilty of being a curious voyeur, willing listener, and secret keeper. If Melia was guilty of trying to "get back" at the founders/managers for making her resign, I was guilty of not asking her to put a halt to the sharing of intimate information, personal or organizational, for what I now know, I cannot unknow. These intimate and personal details often spilled over into the management context and created a tangled web in differentiating between personal and professional disagreements. In retrospect, however, even without Melia's information I had detected the hierarchical and managerial problems, which were, I told myself, not necessarily distinct to the organization I researched. The problem in managing conflicting personalities, differing perspectives, and competing visions in feminist organizing reflects the normative life cycle of many women's organizations working for social justice. But because it is a women's organization, it is still a disappointment to be confronted with such stark reality, particularly when I believe these issues and conflicts are manageable if open dialogue and respect are practiced. Unfortunately, gossip, dissatisfaction, and heartache prevailed.

* * *

Excerpt from field notes, March 2007
"Are you going to forget us, forget me, when you leave?" Melia ventures.
How can I forget what has transpired here?
Why do you think I might so easily forget?
The personal conflicts—perspectives, class, educational, and generational—within the external struggles against the state, religious bureaucracy, Islamist groups, and ultranationalists—are constantly within my consciousness. As I am willingly/unwillingly dragged deeper and deeper into the web of personal and professional entanglements, I am not certain of what to cling to, and more importantly, how to process it all and decode what it means for my friendships and research. I feel comradeship with you, Melia, as well as others, and at the same time feel alienated, confused, and hopeless. As your friend, I stood by you, but am I guilty for not living up to your expectations? Am I guilty for privileging my research interests? Did I really put my research before you? I was not alone in sensing the injustice that surrounds your resignation. Others were there for you too. We realize the influence the founders have in civil society and what the conflict with them can mean for your ability to secure employment and continue to contribute to the cause you so deeply believe in.
And you so easily think I can forget you, Melia, and all that we have been through. It is simply unthinkable for me. I don't want to forget. I can't.

* * *

"What are you going to write about them [the organization, the founders/managers] and what you have learned, and not learned here?" asked Melia. She goes on to add, "Are you going to share us with the world, share me? How will you write about your role in all of this?"
I have no simple answer to your questions, Melia.
Than again, I know you don't expect that.
Our friendship itself was never simple.

* * *

This fieldwork was, in many ways, trying and painful. But it was also intensely joyful and memorable. While aware that the research process involves negotiation, discomfort, and competing truths, the rising suspicion about me in the office in relation to my friendship with Melia and the way the founders/managers relate to me makes me question my sanity, choice of allegiance, feminist praxis, and my research. Navigating conflicting loyalties without doing damage to any parties, a challenge I thought I was able to handle, may have unraveled, as my intent was not as clear to the founders/managers as I would have hoped. As Suad Joseph suggests, "specification of the ownership of action, however, is often difficult, if not impossible, in connective relationships" (1996, 119).

Should I fault myself for developing a closer relationship with the staff members, and Melia in particular? Should I have been friendlier with the founders/managers? How does one collaborate in spaces with competing visions of friendships—"productive" and "negative" friendships—while staying true to feminist commitments? Should I have made clear that while Melia is my friend, I also value the connections I have with others in the organization? Should I have taken a more decisive stance with regard to the class, power, and hierarchical conflicts? Should I have spoken up about Melia's resignation? Should I have spoken to the founders/managers on behalf of Melia and others and explained how these conflicts affect morale and solidarity? But what would that have done to their (my friends and acquaintances) sense of agency, if I had made such an intervention? Should I have made it known that I have sensitive intimate and organizational information but that I will never use it?

I do not even know anything anymore. I only know that what I am allowed to know and what I do know is tied to what I am not supposed to know.

Melia's predicaments, uneasiness, and questions continue to haunt me. Over the years since leaving the field, we have maintained our friendship and continue to make sense of our shared experiences. She is doing remarkably well in her position with a new organization and has, in the eyes of many, transcended the "stories" that floated about her competency. Her high-level position and influence at this organization is, to her, a vindication of her work ethics. I, for one, am simply in awe of her fighting spirit. In the last conversation I had with her not too long ago, she asked whether I will ever finish the book manuscript I am working on and whether she can read it when it is done. She wants to know of the story that lands on the white pages. I wonder whether she is looking for specifics, of (our) silences surrounding my "intervention yet nonintervention moment" and more. Or not at all. Or does it even matter? Should we let the silences remain as they are? When I mentioned I was still meditating on many of the issues and that at times I am still deeply conflicted about how to write about it all, her advice was seemingly simple: "Finish it [the book manuscript] and you will have done what you sought out to do—to tell the story of how a group of women are seeking their Islamic rights, in all its complexity."

I do not conceive of Melia's utterance as permission or encouragement to retell the (fragmented) story of our friendship within the folds of ethnographic research. Rather, given her deep investment in and profound dedication to the contemporary struggles of women in communities of Muslims for gender justice, I view her utterance as an exercise *in hope* in that moments of uncertainty, conflict, and fragility in friendship are productive in thinking about meanings of solidarity. I take to heart Nagar's (2014) insistence to practice "radical vulnerability"—that alliance making consists of finding the courage to lay bare the ways that love and wounds figure into friendships negotiated in the field and sustained there and beyond. This reflection is undertaken in the spirit of affection and accountability—to continue thinking about how political acts of friendship within the overarching framework of transnational feminism thread through the messiness of lived realities and human emotions.

BHATTACHARYA, LAHAUL, INDIA

This story is about my friendship with Yashodha, which is now mostly a memory reshaped by the ravages of time. Yet, it is one which has shaped my own understanding of how to practice solidarity; how varied its meanings can be; and how painful, messy, and complicated a space it is. In retelling her story of violence (and what followed thereon), I show how my own complicated trajectory as a friend and a feminist is thrown into relief.

Yashodha:

We met in 1999, during a Council for Advancement of People's Action and Rural Technology (CAPART)-funded handicrafts fair in Keylong, Lahaul. It was my first trip to Lahaul, to write a "monitoring and evaluation" report about the fair. Yashodha was the first person I spoke to about how the handicrafts fair was working, and right at the outset she exposed the role of the middle men in the fair, which on paper was to exclusively support local women's handicrafts and entrepreneurship efforts. Eventually she supported me in locating the women whose names were on the files, but who were not the ones running the stalls nor benefitting from the fair, which had been hijacked by middle men from nearby towns and districts. Over the course of the next few months, as I quit my job at CAPART, moved to Lahaul on a fellowship, and eventually began working with a local women's collective (referred to as *mahila mandal* or *mandal* from hereon) there, Yashodha and I began spending time together. She helped me find a room and got me acquainted with my new surroundings, and we would often hang out in the evenings talking about all kinds of things—her growing up in Lahaul, me growing up in Jamshedpur; the state of the world we lived in, the possibilities that the worlds we imagined could bring; love and romance; the trials and tribulations of negotiating with family as we took decisions about our lives as adults; the list is endless.

Repeatedly Yashodha spoke of her dream of eventually moving to Shimla someday with a government job, living close enough to Lahaul, but away from the agricultural labor and life on Lahauli terms she feared she was destined to live. We talked often about escaping our respective "homes" to realize our dreams, about getting away to find our own paths, to do things we believed we could, but just had not yet done. Because I had left the home and town I was raised in several years before I met Yashodha, in these conversations she would often ask me what it felt like—the taste of "getting away" and whether I was lonely without the daily presence of the very familial relationships that I/she were trying to renegotiate through acts/dreams of leaving. I hoped to make a "bigger" escape, to leave the hardships of class and mixed-caste backgrounds behind, also aware that my nontribal and caste-privileged status made such a thing much more possible. Escaping the burdens of what I later understood as my social location was a theme I grew up with from my teenage years and shared in common with a close group of friends in the town where I was raised. Yashodha, too, did the same, but the nexus of tribe-caste-gender-state were mapped very differently onto her context than mine. She talked to me about her escape-dreams, but these were not only dreams, they were plans, which were central to her life until that moment when the same plans could not be part of her landscape anymore.

We also grew closer because during this period she became more and more active in the mahila mandal/women's collective that I was actively working with. Older and younger women who were from the interiors of Lahaul trusted her. She had completed a college degree, could read and write English, which is considered a major asset in many parts of rural India, was fluent in Hindi, and was often seen as worldly wiser than a lot of other local women. She began working on cases of violence—and with her passionate labor, the collective's impact on these issues only grew stronger.

An issue she (and the collective) was working on was the locally specific form of violence prevalent in Lahaul—marriage by abduction. She had begun working on a few cases—supporting women who wanted to take action against their abductors, or even those who did not necessarily seek legal action but needed community support in order to not "consent" to these forced marriages after the abductions. The collective began a campaign called *kiski izzat gayi,* and

Yashodha was among those spearheading it. This was followed by a valley-level meeting on questions of violence, in particular, marriage by abduction. The women's collective stayed active in organizing and seeing these events through to completion, despite a lot of resistance and even direct confrontation with younger men from the community. The group began discussing the possibility of consequences (mainly in the form of backlash), especially for women active in the collective, and advised all its members to take extra precautions as they went about their daily activities.

Journal entry, Lahaul, August 2000

I took the bus from Keylong to Manali early Wednesday morning. After I got in, I called Yashodha's home, to check in with her about next week's plans for the mandal. Her mother, Phuntsok Angmo, picked up the phone, crying. At first I couldn't understand what she was saying, between the bad connection and her crying. Then I figured out that Yashodha hadn't come home all night. Phuntsok Angmo suspected she had been abducted, exactly the night I left to come down to Manali. She was abducted with a group of her other women friends by a man who had been pursuing her (and whose advances she had been rejecting) for over a year now. They abducted her and the other girls as they were walking on the road right behind her house, at 7 or 8 P.M.

HIMIKA: *Do you know where they took her?*
PHUNTSOK ANGMO: *No. I am losing my mind with worry, Himika. I do not know where to start looking. I know it is that man, he was hell bent on marrying her. I don't know what will happen. Her brothers have gone to find out what might have happened and where she (and the other girls) might be.*

"I'm on my way back, I'll take a cab back, Ane, should be there by later today," I said, trying to sound reassuring.

* * *

It took me seven hours to drive back, and I could not stop worrying about the fact that another night would be over before we could reach her, *if* we did so at all. I picked up Ane (Yashodha's mother) and drove to the house of the man we suspected—Tenzin, who had been pursuing her for a while. She had refused his advances and did not want to marry him. When we did arrive at his village, we found his friend's house by asking around. One of the kids who was hanging around us said he had seen Tenzin (Yashodha's abductor, and then husband) drag a woman across the field into a house.

We arrived at the house and knocked. It was nearly 7 P.M. Tenzin opened the door and let us in. He showed us which room she was in and left, saying that he was going to get his family and friends over to complete the wedding rituals. Yashodha sat on the floor, her knees at her chest, unable to speak, unable to move. The three of us sat around her as she cried, holding her hand. Ane kept moving between angry banter and uncontrollable sobs. Yashodha just sat there, quiet. Her mother insisted that she come back home and that she should really decide not to stay with this man, that she did not have to marry him.

Somewhere at this point, Yashodha agreed to go home and take a few days to decide. We bundled her into the car, amid protests from Tenzin and some others from his family, who kept insisting that Yashodha had "consented."

Over the next few days at her mother's house, Yashodha finally decided to go back to Tenzin, marry him, and live with him. She felt that facing the community and villagers as a dishonored woman was something she could not bear. And despite her mother's promises of support, her elder brother (a local journalist) insisted that staying back would be a big mistake, and she would regret her decision when the shame and dishonor would leave her nowhere in her future.

* * *

In subsequent conversations, Yashodha shared details of what had happened the night she was abducted. She also spoke of Tenzin's remorse, that he apologized the same night, begged her to marry him, blaming the abduction and her violation on love. He knew he had robbed her of her dreams and plans and repeatedly asked for her forgiveness and promised to make it up to her.

Over the next few days, she decided that it was her karma that her life had taken such a turn. She accepted his love and decided to forgive and marry him, rather than face the shame she feared would come her way once the incident was known publicly. She decided to step away from the work of the collective and moved to a different location to live with him. She continues to live with Tenzin and their son. They moved to Keylong eventually from his village, and Tenzin has been a "decent husband" (her words) over the last twelve odd years.

Within those messy and traumatic circumstances, this was the decision Yashodha took, and I stood by her. Among the mandal members there were a lot of conflicting ideas about what Yashodha should have done, ranging from how dangerous her decision to stay with Tenzin might be and what was the point of all the activism prior to this if she was unable to take a stand, to what choice did she really have, she did what she had to do, and such. My own position regarding this issue was something that came up for some of the mandal members as "soft." That I did not push her hard enough to make the right choice, of not going back to him, and that I even attended the wedding (none of the other women from the mandal did) despite the position of several others in the group was raised in a meeting.

This raised a lot of difficult questions—for me, as a feminist activist, for those mandal members who were dismissing her decision as a big mistake and for those of us who were close to her, feeling her anguish, but not at liberty to discuss it publicly. I admitted that since she was my friend, even if a fear of consequences had prompted Yashodha's decision to marry him, no matter how messy that decision was, I could not abandon our friendship. The group was split unevenly on this. Some (including me) felt that unless we could really provide an alternative, take responsibility beyond the workings of monthly activities of the mandal, no longer part of her daily life the second she moved away from Lahaul (staying on in the valley after an abduction without a husband was not an option for most women), did we really have the right to judge her decision? In fact, now that she had decided to be with him, did we not also need to share the responsibility of what happened to her, why she was specifically targeted at a particular time in the community, and most importantly, if she was walking into possibly dangerous terrain, should not we stand by her, no matter?

There were several members of the mandal who did raise these questions, but were worried about voicing all of their concerns too openly, especially to the older members. Furthermore, the group included both dalit and caste-privileged women, and in this conflictual moment, too, members of the collective across caste groupings were split. Indeed, I was deeply aware that it was easier for me to articulate these concerns, which some of the younger women may have shared with me in private, because my location as someone from the plains and caste-tribe-privileged always placed me as an in-betweener (Diversi and Moreira 2008).

The conversations within the mandal led to negotiations of various kinds. I was writing a report with/for the group and now we were split in terms of whether or not to include Yashodha's story as part of our "evidence of VAW (Violence Against Women) in Lahaul" section. This led to more discussions on what it would mean to frame these (real) abductions followed by marriage (which were in violation of the customary practice of "marriage by abduction" in the valley) as "violence." What constituted violence, and what kinds of names and categories did we need? These issues became an even bigger part of our discussions following Yashodha's abduction and wedding, and laid the foundation for a number of my subsequent work-related decisions.

During the course of those months, and subsequently too, I found myself asking a range of questions, to which I had no straightforward answers, nor did the others in the mandal, but it did open up possibilities for negotiations and solidarities to be strengthened. Why did Yashodha do what she did—the choices we made, she and the others from the mandal and me—what did any of this mean to feminist interventions in the valley? What types of alliances did we each open or shut ourselves to/from and how did these varying ways of engaging with the same event create a complex space for solidarity, then, and what might that mean now as I reflect upon it here?

Furthermore, as a caste-privileged activist in the context of India, where tribes have been historically disenfranchised, marginalized, and dehumanized, the decisions I made, always, also carried the dirty aftertaste of a violent caste-society, no matter. It also bears mentioning here that the Lahula tribe itself is striated by caste, and like many other nontribal parts of India, the landowning Thakurs, Baniyas, and other privileged castes of the tribe exercise tremendous power over all kinds of goods and things that constitute everyday life in the valley. Yashodha belongs to such a caste- and class-privileged family, and my choice to support her after she made the decision to marry Tenzin despite the fact that several dalit members of the women's collective were against it (there were also other dalit members who supported her) posed a very difficult challenge to my feminist, anticaste, and antiviolence politics. I was aware that Yashodha as a Lahauli woman would not inherit any ancestral property, even though her family occupied a class status that many others who worked in the collective, and indeed myself included, did not. As someone who believes that the onus of marking, thinking, researching, writing, and challenging the violence of caste; of understanding social phenomena in the context of India (or the Indian diaspora) within a framework where the salience of caste is not just acknowledged but also challenged and disrupted in order to bring an end to caste society; to strengthen feminist anticaste alliances and to contribute toward the project of dalit emancipatory movements as allies, lies heavily on those of us who have benefitted from the dirtiness of our privilege, *what did it mean for me to align myself* with Yashodha's decision despite my own concerns on the matter? I desperately wanted to find a way that allowed me to stay accountable to my friend, to the collective, and to my own politics.

I made the decision to support her and continue the work with the mandal even more zealously, and some of the other (mostly younger) mandal members decided the same. It was clear to everyone that this was not really a choice Yashodha wanted to make. Yet, I also understood the mandal's position on the matter as valid. Their critique of this decision arose from the implications for what the mandal members had built so carefully, in order to fight marriage by abduction, to support women who were abducted and to facilitate different decisions than the ones women often felt they *had* to make. And here was one of their own, someone who put so much labor into this movement, doing just the opposite of what the group had been fighting for and facilitating in the valley. Thus, it also made sense to me that several members of the collective felt they could not support Yashodha. Any way I looked at it, this crisis of solidarity was not one that had any clear answers and resolutions.

Over the next year or so while I continued working in the valley, my relationship with Yashodha changed drastically. She (understandably) distanced herself from the collective, and the friendships that she had formed there—something I could not blame her for, but that also worried me. It would not be true if I said I understood completely and did not feel any pain that she withdrew from our friendship, but I revisit it here today to reflect upon what that meant. For me, the process by which the group (and I) negotiated over our friendships, our feminisms, and our work with/in the mandal in order to remain accountable to one another despite differences is the most significant part of this process of embracing the situatedness of solidarities in transnational feminist praxis.

Yashodha's story stands in for the negotiations that occurred then and continued to circulate through various other friendships I formed in the valley, even as we may not have agreed on the specifics of her decisions. We did not include her story in the eventual report (there was no way by which anonymity and confidentiality could be maintained), and so we grappled again, with a different set of questions—this time about who represents whom and why. What would it mean, in fact what did it mean, to the mandal to eventually not include her story? I supported this decision made by the mandal members, even as it displaced Yashodha's labor prior to the violence she experienced.

I stood in the messy space of friendship—in solidarity with Yashodha, and with the other members of the group, while still going against the wishes of the majority of the members of the collective—knowing that I could not choose otherwise. I say I could not because my friend had been violated. She was in pain, in grief, in fear, and most importantly, I (and others in the mandal) knew that while she was afraid to go down a path that would pose everyday barriers of herculean proportions to her emotional and spiritual survival in the valley, the path she had chosen would also be extremely hard and required all the strength she could garner, no matter. For some of us the decision she made was and remains as legitimate a step as what the mandal had hoped for/wanted, wherein she would have fought back, with the group's support. It is not a new idea—that the space of solidarity is not, in fact cannot, be pure. Yet, I tell this story here because this retelling is also part of that unresolvable and messy feminist solidarity work—the labor of friendship.

Toward Transformative Possibilities

We first met when Basarudin was in Syracuse completing her postdoctoral training in Bhattacharya's department. As our friendship evolved, we started sharing more of our research experiences with each other. We talked at length about this impasse. Even though we had arrived at it differently, we found ourselves in the kind of conundrum that Nagar and Geiger (2007) ask feminist ethnographers to work their way out of in order to move themselves into a more productive space of engaging their feminist research dilemmas. For Basarudin, her dilemmas and decisions regarding how to write about aspects of her fieldwork and simultaneously focus on the shared goals with the different women she was engaging with (Melia, founders, managers) as friend and/or acquaintance, researcher, and feminist go straight to the core of the situated solidarities she has chosen as her political site. For Bhattacharya, the friendship and camaraderie with the members of the mandal, past and present, determine the imperative to re-present and consider both the doing and undoing of difference, to continue to strengthen these feminist alliances that form the basis of her work across a range of feminist coalitions. For us the task, then, is to continue to build "differential technologies of oppositional consciousness, as utilized and theorized by a racially diverse U.S. coalition of women of color, demonstrate the procedures for achieving affinity and alliance across difference" (Sandoval 2000, 182) as we build our intersecting paths toward the modes that love and friendship take in our academic-feminist worlds.

Notes

1. Nagar writes,

If the politics of alliance making are about making oneself radically vulnerable through trust and critical reflexivity, if they require us to open ourselves to being interrogated and assessed by those to whom we must be accountable, then such politics are also about acknowledging, recognizing, and sharing our most tender and fragile moment, our memories and mistakes in moments of translation, in moments of love. For, it is in the acknowledgement, recognition, and sharing of these moments, memories, and mistakes that we live our trust and faith, and where we often encounter our deepest courage and insights. It is also in these fragile, aching moments that we come to appreciate alliance work as constituted by fragmented journeys—some fully lived, and others abandoned at different stages . . . interrupted passages through which the co-travellers recognize the power of becoming radically vulnerable together. These fragmented journeys are marked as such by opening ourselves up to the risks of becoming wounded, as they are marked by silences and withdrawals, and by returning to forgive and to love—again and again. (2014, 23)

2. As it happens, my name, Himika, has its roots in "him" or snow and also refers to "of the Himalayas." Funnily enough, ever since I have found myself making active choices about places to work and live, mountains, snow, and, in the instance of Lahaul, the Himalayas have been central to my adult life.

3. I use "community of Muslims" instead of "Muslim community" to indicate agency in organizing society/faith community and determining a collective vision.

4. The Lahaul valley is part of the northern-most district of the State of Himachal Pradesh in India, situated along the Manali-Leh highway (which leads into Kashmir), bordering Tibet on one side and Ladakh on the other. The valley is at an elevation of an average height of eleven thousand feet and is flanked by two high passes—the Baralach La Pass in its border with Ladakh, and the Rohtang Pass, which connects it to the rest of Himachal Pradesh. Its location between the two passes makes the region inaccessible through the winter months (usually between November and May of each year).

5. Their names have been changed and details about their lives altered to protect their privacy.

References

Abu-Lughod, Lila. 1986. *Veiled Sentiments: Honor and Poetry in a Bedouin Society*. Berkeley: University of California Press.

———. 1993. *Writing Women's Worlds: Bedouin Stories*. Los Angeles: University of California Press.

Ahmed, Leila. 1992. *Women and Gender in Islam: Historical Roots of a Modern Debate*. New Haven, Conn.: Yale University Press.

Behar, Ruth. 1993. *Translated Woman: Crossing the Border with Esperanza's Story*. Boston: Beacon Press.

Chowdhury, Elora Halim. 2011. *Transnationalism Reversed: Women Organizing Against Gendered Violence in Bangladesh*. Albany: SUNY Press.

Collins, Dana. 2012. "Performing Location and Dignity in a Transnational Feminist and Queer Study of Manila's Gay Life." *Feminist Formations* 24(1): 49–72.

Deb, Basuli. 2012. "Transnational Politics and Feminist Inquiries in the Middle East: An Interview with Lila Abu-Lughod." *Postcolonial Text* 7(1): 1–12.

Diversi, Marcelo, and Moreira, Claudio. 2008. *BETWEENER TALK: Decolonizing Knowledge Production, Pedagogy, and Praxis (Qualitative Inquiry and Social Justice)*. Walnut Creek, Calif.: Left Coast Press.

Dominguez, Virginia. R. 2000. "For a Politics of Love and Rescue." *Cultural Anthropology* 15: 361–393.

Felman, Shoshana. 1992. "'Camus' The Plague, or a Monument to Witnessing." In *Testimony: Crises of Witnessing in Literature, Psychoanalysis, and History*, edited by Shoshana Felman and Dori Laub, 93–119. New York: Routledge.

Fregoso, Rosa Linda. 2003. *MeXicana Encounters: The Making of Social Identities on the Borderlands*. Vol. 12. Berkeley: University of California Press.

Grewal, Inderpal, and Caren Kaplan. 1994. *Scattered Hegemonies: Postmodernity and Transnational Feminist Practices*. Minneapolis: University of Minnesota Press.

Joseph, Suad. 1996. "Relationality and Ethnographic Subjectivity: Key Informants and the Construction of Personhood in Fieldwork." In *Feminist Dilemmas in Fieldwork*, edited by Diane Wolf, 107–121. Boulder: Westview Press.

Lal, Jayati. 1999. "Situating Locations: The Politics of Self, Identity and 'Other.'" In *Feminist Approaches to Theory and Methodology: An Interdisciplinary Reader*, edited by Hesse-Biber, Sharlene, Christina Gilmartin, and Robin Lyndenberg, 100–138. New York: Oxford University Press.

Madison, Soyini D. 2005. *Critical Ethnography: Method, Ethics, and Performance*. Thousand Oaks, Calif.: Sage Publications.

McAdams, Dan P. 1993. *The Stories We Live By: Personal Myths and the Making of the Self*. New York: Guilford Press.

Mohanty, Chandra Talpade. 2003. *Feminism without Borders: Decolonizing Theory, Practicing Solidarity*. Durham, N.C.: Duke University Press.

Mohanty, Chandra Talpade, and M. Jacqui Alexander, eds. 1997. *Feminist Genealogies, Colonial Legacies, Democratic Futures*. New York: Routledge.

Moraga, Cherríe, and Gloria Anzaldúa, eds. 1981. *This Bridge Called My Back: Writings by Radical Women of Color*. New York: Kitchen Table/Women of Color Press.

Nagar, Richa. 2014. *Muddying the Waters: Coauthoring Feminisms across Scholarship and Activism*. Urbana: University of Illinois Press.

Nagar, Richa, and Amanda Lock Swarr. 2010. "Theorizing Transnational Feminist Praxis." In *Critical Transnational Feminist Praxis*, edited by Amanda Lock Swarr and Richa Nagar, 1–20. Albany: SUNY Press.

Nagar, Richa, and Susan Geiger. 2007. "Reflexivity, Positionality and Identity in Feminist Fieldwork Revisited." In *Politics and Practice in Economic Geography*, edited by Eric Sheppard Tickell, Jamie Peck, and Trevor Barnes, 267–278. London: Sage.

Narayan, Kirin. 1993. "How Native Is a 'Native' Anthropologist?" *American Anthropologist* 95(3): 19–32.

Rege, S. 2006. *Writing Caste, Writing Gender: Reading Dalit Women's Testimonios*. Delhi: Zubaan.

Rowe, Aimee Carillo. 2008. *Power Lines: On the Subject of Feminist Alliances*. Durham, N.C.: Duke University Press.

Sandoval, Chela. 2000. *Methodology of the Oppressed*. Minneapolis: University of Minnesota Press.

Stacey, Judith. 1988. "Can There Be a Feminist Ethnography?" *Women's Studies International Forum* 11(1): 21–27.

Visweswaran, Kamala. 1994. *Fictions of Feminist Ethnography*. Minneapolis: University of Minnesota Press.

… PART TWO

Gender, Nation, Solidarity

I begin with the concept of solidarity itself and why it is important to feminism, and I argue that a discussion of feminist solidarity needs to emphasize women's group identity because women are oppressed *as women*. After addressing the relevance of cultural differences by presenting different feminist approaches to women's solidarity, such as "global sisterhood" and global feminism, I draw on Elora Chowdhury's critique of global feminism. Chowdhury criticizes the problematic construction of global feminism in the U.S. academy, arguing that the politics of global feminism is based on a justification of Western liberal notion of democracy. Chowdhury proposes braiding U.S. antiracist/women of color feminism and third world/transnational feminism to resist both hegemonic White feminism and Western feminism. This approach resembles María Lugones's theory of "world"-traveling, which I utilize to demonstrate that the transcultural approach is present in feminist philosophy and that it is promising for forging women's solidarity because of the ways it helps feminists to challenge gender oppression and to transform the oppressive social structures. I argue that feminist theorists such as Chowdhury and Lugones foreshow an idea of transcultural feminist solidarity although they do not articulate their concepts in this way. To demonstrate how a new solidarity can emerge from the transcultural approach, I show that the transcultural approach is needed to conceptualize collaboration among women in different cultures; for instance, it will help us to understand the relationship between U.S. feminism and Chinese feminism.

What Is Solidarity and Why Is It an Important Concept for Feminism?

Solidarity is individuals acting together with one another with a bond or goal that differs from the pursuit of self-interest in relation to shared or similar life conditions, in other words, certain patterns of oppression. Identity and a feeling of interdependence constitute the basis for solidarity with others. The goal of solidarity is to realize certain personal or collective interests that are not possible without establishing a relationship to others. Solidarity increases strength and influences confrontation with an adversary. It can be expressed in various terms, such as cooperation, shared identification, and shared interests. I define solidarity as collective resistance and empowerment, and I define feminist solidarity as creating a self-consciously constructed space where the resistance to gender oppression is established by forming a coalition around women's group identity and around resistance itself while recognizing the different forms that gender oppression takes. In this sense, the issue of women's group identity and the resistance to gender oppression are connected.

Not all feminists regard solidarity as a necessary component of the feminist movement. For instance, postmodernist feminists do not advocate solidarity or solidarity of all women (though some of them advocate solidarity among certain groups of women). However, the issue of women's solidarity is important for feminism for two reasons. The first reason is that solidarity helps women be aware that women endure oppression as women, and the issue of women's solidarity is in fact an issue of women's collective consciousness raising and empowerment. Feminist solidarity is not a goal or end, but rather a way through which women can act collectively to achieve the goal of ending gender oppression. Women's oppression cannot be eliminated by women individually; rather, the elimination of women's oppression requires collective and political action. For instance, postmodernist feminists criticize feminist multiculturalism, but they do so primarily in a way that stresses limitations of identity politics. They assume that identity politics is built upon a fixed identity and propose a form of political practice that is built upon overlapping alliances, which are formed over common interests instead of identity politics (for instance, see Amy Allen 1999a, 1999b). In other words, they propose coalition politics in which individuals work together upon shared agreements to reach a common goal. As Cressida Heyes observes, these feminists reach "the conclusion that 'coalitional politics' is a more appropriate form of organizing than conventional 'identity politics'" (2000, 60).

The second reason that solidarity is important is that women's solidarity suggests that there should be strong connections among women, but this idea is not illuminated in the positions that address differences among women. Women's solidarity suggests a point where social changes regarding gender inequality can lead. The "difference critique" points feminist scholarship in the direction of multiculturalism. In the context of the "difference critique" and multiculturalism, feminism seems to be drifting away from its initial goal as a collective activity for the elimination of gender oppression by focusing on the discussion of differences (although the discussion of differences might be for the purpose of eliminating gender oppression). Women's solidarity is particularly important for the issues in question of this essay—the increasing divide and fissures of feminism in the past three decades partly due to debates over differences among women—but the divide has less to do with differences than the way some feminists theorize differences among women. Acknowledging differences is a necessary step for eliminating women's oppression, but feminists should gain collective power to achieve the goal of the feminist movement while acknowledging differences among women. As Marilyn Frye rightly points out, "the idea that articulating and elaborating differences among women was a route to viable female identity and solidarity was not an easy idea to grasp; indeed, it has had to be invented" (1996, 1006). Gaining collective power is the key to overcoming women's oppression because resisting women's oppression is impossible to achieve through individual efforts and struggles. Feminists have not reached the consensus that differences among women can lead to feminist solidarity in part because of the pervasive misconception that solidarity must be built upon commonality and sameness.

Different Approaches to Women's Solidarity

Some feminists have attempted to discuss women's collaboration despite their differences, but not many of them have translated their discussions into a useful account of solidarity; thus, solidarity remains a problematic concept in feminism. A number of feminists, such as Robin Morgan (1984), Jodi Dean (1996), Amy Allen (1999a, 1999b), Charlotte Bunch (2001), Sandra Bartky (2002), María Lugones (2003), Chandra Mohanty (2003), and Elora Chowdhury (2009) developed a variety of approaches to women's solidarity. These attempts are related to, but are not the same as, actual political solidarity. For instance, Robin Morgan's concept of "global sisterhood" is frequently seen as a founding element of global feminism (though later global feminism diverges from Morgan's notion of global sisterhood).

Assuming a universal patriarchy and a common experience of oppression of women around the globe, as a representative of early second wave feminism, Morgan believed that women could build a unified front against patriarchy by disregarding divisions of class, race, sexuality, and national origin among women. In the introduction to *Sisterhood Is Global*, an anthology she edits, Morgan argues that what characterizes women across cultures and histories is a common condition and worldview, which is what women share and thus is referred to as the suffering inflicted by a universal "patriarchal mentality" (1984, 1). In Morgan's opinion, women are not different from each other and have an essential bond because they are victims of male supremacy, which is a common condition that is "experienced by all human beings who are born female" (4). Morgan's intent is to further dialogues between women from different social locations. To her, solidarity "as a real political force requires that women transcend the patriarchal barriers of class and race, and furthermore transcend even the *solutions* the Big Brothers propose to problems they themselves created" (18, emphasis in original).

Morgan's idea of global sisterhood presents a widely recognized but heavily criticized notion of solidarity, although her idea is revisited by feminists from time to time. For instance, Charlotte Bunch's scholarship concerns the relationship between diversity and commonality and tries to find a common basis for women to be organized. Bunch proposes a global perspective on feminist diversity through which women can learn from each other. She argues that a global perspective on feminist ethics requires a global vision of feminism—a feminism that is inclusive and seeks to reflect a wide diversity of women's experiences and views. She suggests feminists not only acknowledge and respect differences, but also struggle against social power that divides women along differences. "When diversity is understood as richness of possibility, it is possible to move beyond tolerance toward genuine engagement around difference. . . . Feminist appreciation of diversity must move beyond tolerance to valuing diversity not by condescendingly allowing others to live but by learning from them" (1992, 181). That is, a global perspective is one that regards the domestic life and the international sphere as interconnected. Accordingly, feminists need to go beyond nation-state boundaries to strengthen solidarity. Although Bunch acknowledges the importance of solidarity, she nevertheless argues that the global networking should go beyond solidarity to "a more integrated understanding of the connection between what's happening in one country or another" (2001, 134). Bunch thus advocates women's global networking, by which she means that women need to understand the connections among local issues as well as the connections between local issues and international issues. She argues that although there are differences among women's oppression, feminists need to find a common basis for women's global networking. What she finds compelling is "a commonality in the stories that they told about the discrimination and violence that they faced as women that brought them together in spite of their differences," which justifies her belief that one of the universalities of the feminist struggle is the commonality of women's oppression (2001, 130). Bunch explains that the commonality of women's oppression can be shown in various forms of gender-based violence, such as battery, rape, female genital mutilation, female infanticide, and trafficking, which are human rights violations.

Bunch is actively involved in network-building effects such as the Global Campaign for Women's Human Rights, a loose worldwide coalition of groups and individuals formed in 1993. The driving force of this campaign is a commitment to building linkages among women across multiple boundaries locally and globally. Bunch asserts that women's networking develops a model that affirms the universality of human rights, which includes specifically women's rights, while respecting the diversity of particular experiences. She claims that feminist struggles are based on the commonality of women's oppression and that human rights are universal.

Some feminists not only dispute the commonality of women's oppression, but also criticize the political agenda of global feminism. For instance, Elora Chowdhury launches a critique of global feminism, which she believes to be critical of the notion of global sisterhood but nevertheless attaches itself to earlier Western liberal feminist notions of democracy. She questions the role that global feminism plays when it addresses "women's issues elsewhere" in the U.S. academy and in global feminist politics and argues that global feminism (unintentionally) aids hegemonic maneuvers of the U.S. administration. There are two focuses in Chowdhury's criticism of global feminism: One is her critique of U.S. White feminists assumptions, such as "women elsewhere" are victimized by their cultures or countries, which flattens the oppression of women in other cultures; the other is her critique of the unreflected consequences of global feminist actions such as the advocacy of (a Western notion of) human rights in other countries. Both critiques point to the necessity of bridging U.S. women of color antiracist feminism and third world transnational feminism to resist the hegemony of Western White feminism.

First of all, Chowdhury argues that the utilization of discrete categories such as "women of color" and "third world women" hinder feminist alliances because the former is normally used to refer to women of national minorities within the United States while the latter refers to "women elsewhere." Accordingly, global feminism focuses on addressing "women's issues elsewhere." Chowdhury argues that although the theory of intersectionality is applied to analyze women's experiences in the United States, the intersectional analysis has not yet been utilized to analyze women beyond borders, which leads to the result that "women in the USA become a singular individual with freedom to choose in opposition to her victimized singular third world counterpart" (2009, 60). Although she recognizes the importance of alliances between U.S. women of color and third world women, Chowdhury does not intend to integrate these two categories into one category because doing so "smudges over the necessity of analyses around nation as well as race" (57). She claims that struggles experienced by women of color and third world women are ignored (by White women) because they are divisive. She thus suggests connecting "the struggles of US anti-racist and third world feminists—at times viewed as divisive—in order to envision a collective response to the hegemony of white feminism" (58). In this sense, she acknowledges both the intersections and the divergences of U.S. women of color antiracist feminism and third world transnational feminism.

Second, Chowdhury asserts that global feminism posits itself as a benevolent savior of women in other cultures, which relies on an assumption that the United States is a free country where human rights are respected while women in other countries are abused by their cultures. This opposition between "free us" and "oppressed them" has the consequence of justifying a Western liberal notion of democracy and leaving its role unexamined in the hegemonic reconstruction of a U.S. empire through governmental military intrusion of other countries. "Global feminism aids the US government's political strategy of positioning America as the site of authoritative enunciations of freedom and rights whose representatives can judge the immoral practice of other nation states. Using the logic of global feminism, female US government representatives support US foreign policy strategies and interventions in the name of women's rights activism" (2009, 61).

By doing so, Chowdhury claims, global feminism reproduces "the West as its predetermined default frame of reference" (51). For instance, global feminism uses a universal human rights paradigm to posit itself as the savior of women in non-Western societies. She argues that the advocacy of women's human rights by global feminism perpetuates a framework of commonality of women's oppression because it flattens experiences of third world women into "wounded experiences" by ignoring historical contexts of these experiences; meanwhile, the agenda of global feminism and its political implications remain unexamined.

Chowdhury's alternative to the problematic notion of global feminism is braiding U.S. women of color and transnational feminisms. She claims that braiding U.S. women of color antiracist feminism and third world transnational feminism helps to deepen our understanding of globalization and global feminism.

According to her, this alternative is similar to Chandra Mohanty's mission. Mohanty claims that the common context of struggles against exploitation can potentially create "transnational feminist solidarity" among third world women or women of color (2003, 144). That is, Mohanty promotes an anticapitalist transnational feminist solidarity to struggle against capitalism and globalization. She argues that globalization is a site for recolonization of peoples in the Two-Thirds World, but their exploitation in globalization in turn gives them potential to form a particular form of solidarity that is anticapitalist and antiglobalist. Mohanty uses both Third World/South and Two-Thirds World to refer to women who are the social minority of the globe. One-Third World and Two-Thirds World are categories that incorporate social power relations and are based on a quality of life gradation. Because these women are marginalized and exploited by capitalism's effects, they have the potential ability to analyze and act against capitalism. As Chowdhury comments on Mohanty's account of feminist solidarity, "Drawing connections between the critique of white feminism by women of color and of 'western feminism' by third world feminists working within paradigms of decolonization, Mohanty called for the building of a noncolonizing feminist solidarity across borders" (2009, 73n1). That is, it seems that both Chowdhury and Mohanty argue that the purpose of formulation of transnational feminism is to resist (hegemonic) White and Western feminism.

Chowdhury's and Mohanty's approaches to women's solidarity are similar to what I would call "feminist transcultural solidarity," which utilizes the transcultural approach. In the next section, I will draw on Lugones's theory of "world"-traveling to explain what the transcultural approach is.

The Theory of "World"-Traveling and the Feminist Transcultural Approach

Lugones claims that what is missing in the feminist work that deals with the "problem of difference" is the interactive step. Normally it is not women of color who tell White women that "we" are all alike, rather, it is White women who tell women of color so. Lugones states that when women of color challenge White women on what they mean by "we," they actually call out "an interactive demand, a demand for an answer" (2003, 70). Unfortunately, White women hear that demand as an attack on the activity of their theorizing rather than on White racism. It is this misinterpretation that generates the "problem of difference." That is, the challenge for interaction from women of color to White women is one that White women unintentionally dismiss by labeling the challenge as "difference."

Why is there a lack of deeper interaction between White feminists and women of color, and why do some White feminists merely emphasize their theorization rather than interacting with actual women of color? Lugones explains that it is because racism plays two tricks on White women theorists. The first trick is that White women do not notice women of color, so they do not think that the difference between them is important, which leads to their generalization that all women are the same. The second trick is that White women conceive this lack of noticing women of color as a theoretical problem—the "problem of difference." Lugones argues that what lies at the root of ethnocentrism is racism. According to her, racism is partly due to one's lack of recognition of "the structure and mechanism of the racial state" (44). She asserts that by noticing the race issue, we see "the possibility and complexity of a pluralistic feminism" (77). Lugones argues that theorizing is not the solution to the "problem of difference"; rather, the solution lies with White women interacting with women of color, because by doing so, women of color act as mirrors in which White women see themselves in a way that no other mirrors can reveal.

Lugones presents a consciousness called "world"-traveling as a way of identifying with others and resisting oppression. "World"-traveling is an active subjectivity, which presupposes collective intentionality. "World," for Lugones, does not identify with the physical world in the sense that "world" is not as solidified as the physical world. Through traveling to the "world" of the other, one can identify with her and discover the need of interdependence of each other. By traveling to others' "worlds," we gain knowledge of their "worlds," thus getting to know the people that inhabit other "worlds." Lugones recommends that traveling across "worlds" be partly constitutive of cross-cultural and cross-racial loving as a new meaning of coalition. As mentioned earlier, she proposes a "playful" thought experiment called "world"-traveling as a way of identifying with others. "World"-traveling generates deep understanding and makes one feel at ease. Playfulness is the loving attitude toward others and an openness to uncertainty while traveling, because when we are playful, we are not self-important, nor stabilized in any particular "world," but rather being creative and open to further self-construction and new possibilities. According to Lugones, by traveling to others' "worlds," we can understand what it is to be like others and see ourselves through the eyes of others. The flexibility of "world"-traveling is necessary for outsiders because it is partly constitutive of cross-cultural and cross-racial loving. As Lugones states, "I recommend to women of color in the United States that we learn to love each other by learning to travel to each other's 'worlds'" (78). This identification means that we are disloyal to being arrogant perceivers. If we perceive someone arrogantly, we fail to identify with them, and thus fail to love them. This identification also means that we should quit being servants because love is not the same as unconditional servitude. Lugones thus proposes an I→ we model, which indicates that women inhabit multiple liberatory trajectories. Women engage in interactive multiple sense-making by encountering "at the intersections of local and translocal histories of meaning fashioned in the resisting ←→ oppressing relation" (228). That is to say, the emancipatory sense-making occurs in a complex intersubjective context with a transitional intentionality.

Lugones's account of the need for interaction and "world"-traveling offers feminists a way to explain the intermeshedness of oppressions, which can direct feminism back to solidarity. According to her, knowing other women is a way of loving them, which is intelligible in the sense that women should stop perceiving other women with arrogant eyes because arrogance is a destructive attitude. Lugones rightly believes that the change we need to make to improve women's situations cannot be made without there being solidarity among women of different cultures or ethnicities or class. She implies that women can learn how to generalize the consciousness of playful "world"-traveling into a more political solidarity once they figure out personal friendship, but it remains unclear how women can transit from this personal friendship to a political solidarity. In this sense, it appears that Lugones is rather individualist in orientation, but it is important to note that we cannot lose sight of the impact of women's friendship on women's solidarity and women's personal friendship as a useful component of women's solidarity.[1] Lugones's theory of "world"-traveling demonstrates how to approach women's solidarity by going along with a feminist transcultural approach. In what follows, I will specify what the feminist transcultural approach implies and why it is necessary for feminist theories and practices.

The feminist transcultural approach suggests that feminism must reconcile the competing interests of having a multiplicity of identities and construct a unity based on certain principles of collaboration. That is, each identity might imply distinctive and competing interests. For example, Chinese women who have transcultural experiences would be more likely to understand, sympathize, and incorporate the interests of American women, and vice versa. Over time, those interests would become part of their identities and as a result, their decisions and actions might be an expression of these competing interests. On a similar note, the transformation of systematic structures of social power should be in a collective form as well. Feminism is a collective movement rather than the emancipation of individuals, so an account of collaboration should include various resistant practices, a conception of power, and connectedness. The tension and conflict that results from differences among women can be resolved through transcultural processes and practices, which can in turn inform a new politics of difference in feminism. That is, recognition of and reflection on the shortcoming of each version of feminism or each culture highlights differences among women and encourages the interaction between them. A transcultural approach offers an ethical perspective within which one might work with different identities but also sustain collaboration across these identities. What needs to be noted is that although the feminist struggle is considered a collective one, the idea of collaboration among all women does not necessarily mean that a movement should always consist of every woman. Instead, there may be different kinds and aspects of collaboration, in which subsets of women can be brought together by a universal category.

The transcultural approach is necessary for the feminist political movement for practical reasons: Transculture, by providing a model of engagement and interaction that builds on differences, holds great promise for feminism to find a way to deal more productively with differences among women other than treating feminism as the sum of various kinds of feminism, such as African American feminism, Asian feminism, or Lesbian feminism. Differences among women are concrete and contextual rather than an abstract summary of being simply different in reference to the dominant group, so feminism should treat oppression as multiplicative and concrete rather than abstract because oppressions are intermeshed. The transcultural approach does not simply emphasize that cultures are different, but rather it stresses the significance of interaction and interdependency of cultures. For example, the transcultural practice in which women engage in the interference of different cultures can cure the myopia of viewing women's experiences only through the lens of the Western culture. The transcultural approach would encourage women, especially those in the dominant cultures or those who have privileges, to stop taking undue pride of their cultures or social positions. At the same time, it encourages women in the less dominant cultures to be humble with other cultures and reflect on their own cultures. The category of women, which embraces similarities and differences among women, reminds women in various cultures that they share a collective mission. Employing the transcultural approach thus makes it possible for women to understand each other and share a political solidarity in order to eliminate gender oppression.

Imagining Transcultural Feminist Solidarity

From the previous discussions about the various feminist approaches to solidarity, it seems that one of the issues centered around women's solidarity is: How should a concept of feminist solidarity confront the cultural differences in an increasingly transnational condition? This issue is connected to a concept of solidarity that is similar to transcultural feminist solidarity. In what follows, I will offer a description of the normative ideal of solidarity in order to argue that a transcultural feminist solidarity is related to an adequate idea of women's collaboration in the context of cultural differences. I speculate that as the normative ideal of feminist solidarity, transcultural feminist solidarity would at least include the following two aspects.

From the aspect of identity politics, transcultural feminist solidarity emphasizes women's group identity, which includes identification as women because women are subject to oppression *as women*, so it helps ease the tension between the commonality of conditions and differences among the members from a gender standpoint. It seems that the relationship between commonality and difference plays an important role in the discussion of women's solidarity, which is a practical as well as a theoretical idea. The normative ideal of feminist solidarity recognizes the diversity of individual women but also focuses on building the common cause for solidarity. A category of women can accommodate differences among women rather than reduce differences to attributes or an essence that women share. Transcultural feminism understands these differences as necessary transcultural conditions for women's solidarity, which is different from the universalist understanding that views differences as the primary threat to solidarity. The "difference critique" has launched debates about how relations between White women and women of color have often been constructed to reinforce differences in social and institutional status that are founded on race, class, and culture. In this context, transcultural feminist solidarity should also address class and structural inequality because there is a tension between the commonality of conditions and differences among members from the standpoint of class. Feminist solidarity in the feminist movement does not isolate itself from other social movements because woman is a category concerning racial, sexual orientation, religious, and class differences. That is, feminist solidarity is aligned with other kinds of solidarity.

From the aspect of cultural differences, transcultural feminist solidarity is an account for creating a self-consciously constructed space of transcultural interference where women's resistance to male domination is established by consciously forming a coalition in the name of women. Solidarity connects U.S. women of color feminism with third world transnational feminism. In fact, the divide between these two feminisms is one of motives for transcultural feminist solidarity. The normative ideal of feminist solidarity should provide the flexibility that enables individuals to loosen themselves from certain cultural backgrounds and sample other cultures without pretending to be deeply enmeshed with any particular cultural background. Transculturalism could provide such flexibility because a preliminary summary of transcultural feminism is that it represents a serious attempt to overcome shortcomings of various feminist approaches to solidarity such as global sisterhood, political coalition, and global feminism. Transculture, as it is defined, seeks to move beyond the hegemony of any single dominant culture by recognizing the existence of a multiplicity of distinct cultures, which presupposes an existing interaction between cultures. That is, transcultural thinking aims to broaden one's framework of identification so that one may imaginatively inhabit a range of cultural identities that are themselves shifting and mutable. Transculture means the freedom of every person to live on the border of one's "inborn" culture or beyond it. The transcultural approach has the potential to transform the social structure of power relations into a less oppressive form if we understand the relationship between interference and power and use that understanding as a motivation to challenge the oppressive power relations. For instance, second wave feminists and third wave feminists, Western feminists and third world feminists should all go beyond their racial, class, cultural, sexual orientation differences and engage with each other in order to grow and be liberated collectively. Transcultural feminist theorizations center on differences between women of different cultures and largely appropriate contemporary analysis of transnational capitalism to formulate theories and practices and to understand themselves as generated by a novel transnational condition.

We can see that the concept of transcultural feminist solidarity is already present in the feminist discussion of solidarity when we look at Chowdhury's, Mohanty's, and Lugones's accounts of feminist solidarity. Chowdhury points out the stark distinction between a discussion of the complexity of "our issues" such as the intersection of race and gender and a simplified "their issues" such as the lack of human rights. This shows that some approaches of "difference critique" in feminist theories are unable to capture the complexity of transnational issues. Feminist theorists such as Chowdhury, Mohanty, and Lugones demonstrate that feminists can develop a women's collaboration that is grounded in differences, rather than working toward solidarity that is founded on sameness. The plausibility of Chowdhury's, Mohanty's, and Lugones's accounts of women's solidarity is partly due to, I argue, their employment of something like what I am calling the transcultural approach.

Applying the Notion of Transcultural Feminist Solidarity in the Formulation of Friendship and Solidarity between Chinese and U.S. Women

Previously, I argued that Chowdhury's proposal of braiding U.S. women of color feminism with third world transnational feminism, Mohanty's account of transnational feminist solidarity, and Lugones's theory of "world"-traveling foreshadow a form of transcultural consciousness. To further elaborate on this issue, I will explore the relationship between Chinese women and U.S. women as a way to determine whether transcultural feminist solidarity is helpful for forging mutual understanding and to examine implications of the previous discussions of feminist solidarity in Chinese women's situations. I look at the relationship between Chinese and U.S. women in particular because the two countries are increasingly involved with each other. I will argue that the transcultural approach can help feminists (1) recognize the need to enhance communication between women in China and in the United States; (2) understand the complexity of Chinese women's situations in unique social historical contexts; and (3) examine implications of Chinese women's exploitation in the background of globalization.

First of all, the transcultural approach illuminates that sincere communication on a deeper level between Chinese women and U.S. women is much needed. In U.S. academia, some feminists are challenged by third world women, which has resulted in segregated feminisms such as third world women feminism and various area studies of women. The feminist "difference critique" in the United States occurred concurrently with the Chinese policy of opening its door to the world, but examining how Western feminist theories of oppression, identity, and solidarity apply to Chinese women is an underexplored area of feminist scholarship. For this reason, it is worth exploring why Chinese women are rarely discussed in the multicultural feminist rhetoric and why they are usually placed in stereotypical positions on occasions when they do appear in feminist discourses. For instance, Chinese women are often depicted in the Western feminist scholarship as victims of human rights violations, sexual exploitations, and reproduction control. Uma Narayan makes the case that the image of third world women's victimization is the result of "multiple mediations" that "'shape' issues in different national contexts, and 'filter' the information that crosses national borders" (1997, 104). An example of this is that some Western feminist literature uses foot binding—a phenomenon that is temporally distant to contemporary Chinese women—as a symbol of Chinese women's oppression. Jinhua Emma Teng brings it to our attention that the foot binding practice holds "a particular fascination" for feminist writers in the Western academy when she explores their focus on Chinese women as victims (1996, 124). Following Chandra Mohanty and others, Teng categorizes this phenomenon of Chinese women's victimization into "the marginalization of 'Third World women' in Western feminist discourse" and sharply points out that "this discourse constructs Chinese women as part of a special class of universally subordinated third world women who are even more oppressed than their Western 'sisters.' This phenomenon represented a means not only of understanding cultural differences but also of asserting the superiority of women's status in the West" (125).

Similar to Teng, I argue that the marginalization of Chinese women in (Western) feminist literature (1) presents a distinctive challenge to a Western paradigm case ("free us" versus "oppressed them"); (2) shows us that the complexity and changes of Chinese cultures (and women) remain to be examined more thoroughly by (Western) feminist theories; and (3) demonstrates the promise of the transcultural approach, which not only addresses why there is a lack of

Chinese women's voice in the feminist scholarship, but also offers an approach to forge women's solidarity globally. For instance, there are feminist scholars who manage to forgo the image of Chinese women as victims and instead focus on describing Chinese women as courageous, sophisticated, and freedom seeking. One example is Tani E. Barlow's highlight of "the new woman" in her reading of Chinese literature. "The new woman" characters created in the fiction lived during the 1920s in China, who vacillated between the fear of not being able to "escape the constraints of sexed subjectivity" and the desire to "establish a personal standing in society" (2004, 134) and between "progressive feminism and political anarchism'" (150). Another example is Tze-Ian D. Sang's study on female same-sex desire in modern China. Sang's study investigates "the conditions that enable the emergence of a distinctive lesbian identity in modern literature in Chinese" in the twenty-first century (2003, 34). Barlow's and Sang's accounts of Chinese women make a significant contribution to revealing the sophistication of "Other women" and are good examples of utilizing transcultural experiences acquired from thorough research of Chinese literature and social reality.

Second, the transcultural approach can help us explore the uniqueness and complexity of Chinese women's situations. Chinese women have their own understandings of issues that are of concern to both them and Western feminists; for example, in the context of poverty elimination, Chinese women view reproductive rights differently from U.S. feminists (note that I fall prey to the same feminist discourse by discussing reproductive rights thanks to the great visibility of this particular topic). It is broadly accepted in the United States that women's reproductive rights are women's rights and thus human rights, so the Chinese state regulation on women's reproductive rights is viewed as oppressive and inhuman. However, the assumption that there is a positive correlation between economic growth, population control, and the advance of women is generally accepted without critical examination in China. An immediate but complicated case is the Chinese government's one-child policy, which Western feminists criticize as detrimental to women, but the policy has broad support in China, especially among urban Chinese women. To understand Chinese women's "insensibility" to, acceptance of, and support of policies that are claimed to be anti—human rights, we need to locate these issues within the historical and contemporary context of China rather than speculating and scrutinizing them from a universalist (and Western) point of view. While some scholars such as Susan Greenhalgh are concerned with state control over women's bodies and subjectivities and at the same time being cautiously hopeful about creating "a feminist sphere of public discussion and debate on population" (2001, 874), other scholars are more positive about the impact of the one-child policy on women's lives. For instance, through a study of China's rural daughters, Zhang Hong arrives at the conclusion that "response to and strategies around the state population policy and new employment opportunities may vary from area to area. In some areas the pressure to comply with the birth-planning policy may have intensified son preference and increased daughter discrimination, but in other areas the decline in fertility, coupled with new economic opportunities, may lead to readjustments in parent-child relations and improvement of daughters' lives" (2007, 694).

China is a vast country with great social economic differences among women, so it is not surprising that women hold different or even contradictory views about the state policy. Nevertheless, the issue of reproductive rights does not seem to be the most pressing issue from the perspective of ordinary Chinese people, or at least it does not appear as pressing as it is showed in the Western feminist scholarship. There is a huge contrast in life quality in terms of materials and education within the three decades since the one-child policy took effect, though one may argue that this concurred with the rapid growth of Chinese economy and came with a very high price. Yet to the Chinese, the achievements are visible and immediate, so the price is often overlooked. It can be conjectured that having a better quality of life is one of the reasons that Chinese women support the one-child policy. One may argue that educated Chinese women are "brainwashed" by the government reproduction propaganda while less educated Chinese women remain intact (since the one-child policy encounters more obstacles in rural areas than in urban areas), but it is questionable whether choosing between endorsing an unrestricted reproductive choice and promoting a higher life quality is a hard choice for most Chinese women.

Lastly, the transcultural approach can help feminists understand and address the exploitation of Chinese women in the global market, the purpose of which is to pinpoint the necessity of the collaboration of women globally to eliminate women's exploitation. Similar to women in other developing third world countries, Chinese women face the dilemma of economic development versus capitalist exploitation. China has been going through new class stratification under the influence of capitalization and globalization. More urban professional Chinese women hire women who migrate from rural areas as caregivers, and more Chinese women work in industries that are part of the global economy, either within or outside China. On the one hand, scholars such as Huang Ping worry that young Chinese factory girls in labor-intensive manufacturing industries "enjoy very little in terms of welfare and social security that urban residents take for granted" (2001, 1280). On the other hand, Li Xiaojiang argues that China's development is different from any recognized development model so "a universalist standard of value" (2001, 1276) should be displaced with standards that result from the social reality of China. According to Li, these exploited women's life conditions are much improved compared to what was possible in the traditional social life. After all, "these are all the self-conscious and self-selected choices of Chinese women themselves, and it is possible that they are brief and fleeting" (1278). That is, being exploited is an autonomous choice of Chinese women out of necessity of surviving in current social conditions for the time being. We can see that this survival mode is also present globally; for instance, more third world immigrant women are employed as domestic laborers in the Global North, freeing their female employers to work outside of their home. If we look at this issue by adopting a concept of "coalition politics," then this redistribution of domestic labor would be considered as emerging from a shared agreement since women in the Global North do not force women in the Global South into the international domestic work market. We can even regard this arrangement as some sort of solidarity in the sense of shared agreement because women in the Global South would be empowered at least financially through seeking employment in the Global North. Women in the Global South and North have some common interests and common goals, such as focusing on bettering themselves, but these interests and goals are rather immediate, which mask the hidden conflicts of self-interest. This kind of coalition should be scrutinized because there is also exploitation along with the economic empowerment in the above scenario. Similarly, the elimination of Chinese women's exploitation requires collective consciousness raising and collaboration among women both domestically and globally.

The means to prevent future generations from being exploited in assembly lines and service sectors and to gain opportunities to a better life, for the majority of Chinese, is through education and hard work, which they believe is the most effective way to cast off poverty and improve social status. There is a strong belief in China that education is the most effective means for a country and its people to resist exploitation. With limited education resources and a large population, population control together with the dramatic expansion of higher education is an effective strategy, though remaining controversial to some Western scholars, to guarantee that more Chinese in particular Chinese young women receive higher education. It is not surprising to see that an increasing number of Chinese students and young professionals study and work in the United States. A recent article in the *Chronicle of Higher Education* reports that 47 percent of all foreign applications for fall 2012 graduate spots are from

China.[2] The younger generation has been building a bridge of cultural communication, like generations of Chinese before them, between China and the United States. Their transcultural experiences can greatly change the demography and understanding of cultures, and the resulting interaction between the U.S. and Chinese cultures would demonstrate that cultural boundaries are porous and that individual cultures are dynamic.

The interchange and friendship between Chinese and Americans is not only demonstrated by the increasing numbers of Chinese students and scholars present in the United States, but is also visible in academic collaborations among feminist scholars and activists in both countries. For instance, the Fourth World Conference on Women held in Beijing in 1995 and the associated Non-Governmental Organization forum marks "a historic turning point for the women's movement in China" (Wang 1996). Esther Ngan-ling Chow reports that Chinese women's reactions to the conference were overwhelmingly positive and "many of them showed strong interest in learning about global women's issues and how these issues might relate to their current situations as China transforms socially and economically" (1996, 191). Further interchange between Chinese and American feminist scholars was made beyond Beijing '95. For example, Sasha Su-Ling Welland reviews an international conference titled Feminism in China since *The Women's Bell*, which was held in 2004 in Shanghai and jointly hosted by the Department of History at Fudan University and the Institute for Research on Women and Gender at the University of Michigan. According to Welland, the organizers of the conference Wang Zheng and Chen Yan achieve their goal "to facilitate increased dialogue between China scholars in and outside of China toward the project of engendering the historiography of modern China" (2006, 943). Needless to say, events such as these have a long lasting impact on Chinese and American women both academically and in life, and friendship demonstrated in these events shows Chinese and American women's efforts to forge women's solidarity transculturally.

Conclusion

In this essay, I have argued that solidarity is particularly necessary when the feminist discourse focuses on differences among women to such an extent that there is a divide in feminism. Only by acting collectively and by forging transcultural solidarity will women solve these structural and systemic problems. The divide of feminism is partly due to the pervasiveness of the rigid belief that there are differences between "our culture" and "their cultures" and we (Western feminists) should "help them." This salvation attitude lacks meaningful engagement and does not foster solidarity because of its superficial acknowledgment of differences without addressing the interaction of differences.

It seems that feminists agree that feminists should bridge the divide in feminism, no matter what their opinions about identity politics and cultural differences are. So we need a specific account of women's political solidarity across cultures to address concerns that feminists have about differences among women. A useful approach, which I name transcultural feminist solidarity, endorses women's group identity and addresses structural inequality, global injustice, and cultural differences. Practices or initiatives that draw from the transcultural approach (or at least act in a way that is consistent with such an approach) can foster solidarity. By showing the advantages of transcultural feminist solidarity, I argue that the transcultural approach intends to promote the interaction of feminism, even of those women who are from different cultural backgrounds and class locations. These interactions, such as genuine dialogues between Chinese and American feminists, would benefit from following the transcultural approach and as a result would contribute to women's friendship and solidarity in general.

Notes

1. For instance, Sandra Bartky (2002) emphasizes the function of sympathy in forging women's solidarity from the perspective of phenomenology. According to her, genuine collective fellow-feeling is crucial for the development of feminist political solidarity because fellow-feeling experience can promote the kind of solidarity that encourages attentiveness to difference. However, an endorsement of political fellow-feeling to form a common goal is different from deconstructing gender in the feminist discourse. In other words, solidarity is a political practice rather than a strategic practice of fellow-feeling.

2. Karin Fischer, "Chinese Students Account for about Half of All International Applicants to U.S. Graduate Programs," *Chronicle of Higher Education*, April 3, 2012. Accessed April 4, 2012. http://chronicle.com/article/Chinese-Students-Account-for/131416/.

References

Allen, Amy. 1999a. "Solidarity after Identity Politics: Hannah Arendt and the Power of Feminist Theory." *Philosophy and Social Criticism* 25(1): 97–118.
——. 1999b. *The Power of Feminist Theory: Domination, Resistance, Solidarity*. Boulder: Westview Press.
Barlow, Tani R. 2004. *The Question of Women in Chinese Feminism*. Durham, N.C.: Duke University Press.
Bartky, Sandra L. 2002. *"Sympathy and Solidarity" and Other Essays*. Lanham, Md.: Rowman and Littlefield Publishers.

Bunch, Charlotte. 1992. "A Global Perspective on Feminist Ethics and Diversity." In *Explorations in Feminist Ethics: Theory and Practice*, edited by Susan Coultrap-McQuin and Eve Browning Cole, 176–185. Bloomington: Indiana University Press.

———. 2001. "Women's Human Rights: The Challenges of Global Feminism and Diversity." In *Feminist Locations: Global and Local, Theory and Practice*, edited by Marianne DeKoven, 129–146. New Brunswick, N.J.: Rutgers University Press.

Chow, Esther Ngan-ling. 1996. "Making Waves, Moving Mountains: Reflections on Beijing '95 and Beyond." *Signs* 22(1): 185–192.

Chowdhury, Elora. 2009. "Locating Global Feminisms Elsewhere: Braiding US Women of Color and Transnational Feminisms." *Cultural Dynamics* 21(51): 51–78.

Dean, Jodi. 1996. *Solidarity of Strangers: Feminism after Identity Politics*. Berkeley: University of California Press.

———. 1997. "Feminist Solidarity, Reflective Solidarity." *Women and Politics* 18(4): 1–26.

Frye, Marilyn. 1996. "The Necessity of Differences: Constructing a Positive Category of Women." *Signs* 21(4): 991–1010.

Greenhalgh, Susan. 2001. "Fresh Winds in Beijing: Chinese Feminists Speak Out on the Policy and Women's Lives." *Signs* 26(3): 847–886.

Heyes, Cressida J. 2000. *Line Drawing: Defining Women through Feminist Practice.* Ithaca: Cornell University Press.

Huang, Ping. 2001. "Talking about Gender, Globalization, and Labor in a Chinese Context." *Signs* 26(4): 1278–1281.

Li, Xiaojiang. 2001. "From 'modernization' to 'globalization': Where Are Chinese Women?," translated by Tani E. Barlow. *Signs* 26(4): 1274–1278.

Lugones, María. 2003. *Pilgrimages/Peregrinajes: Theorizing Coalition against Multiple Oppressions*. Lanham, Md.: Rowman and Littlefield Publishers.

Mohanty, Chandra T. 2003. *Feminism without Borders: Decolonizing Theory, Practicing Solidarity.* Durham, N.C.: Duke University Press.

Morgan, Robin, ed. 1984. *Sisterhood Is Global: The International Women's Movement Anthology.* New York: The Feminist Press at CUNY.

Narayan, Uma. 1997. *Dislocating Cultures: Identities, Traditions, and Third-world Feminism*. New York: Routledge.

Sang, Tze-Ian D. 2003. *The Emerging Lesbian: Female Same-sex Desire in Modern China.* Chicago: The University of Chicago Press.

Teng, Jinhua Emma. 1996. "The Construction of the 'Traditional Chinese Woman' in the Western Academy: A Critical Review." *Signs* 22(1): 115–151.

Wang, Zheng. 1996. "A Historic Turning Point for the Women's Movement in China." *Signs* 22(1): 192–199.

Welland, Sasha Su-Ling. 2006. "What Women Will Have Been: Reassessing Feminist Cultural Production in China: A Review Essay." *Signs* 31(4): 941–966.

Zhang, Hong. 2007. "China's New Rural Daughters Coming of Age: Downsizing the Family and Firing Up Cash Earning Power in the New Economy." *Signs* 32(3): 671–698.

CHAPTER 4

For Sister or State?

Nationalism and the Indigenous and Bengali
Women's Movements in Bangladesh

KABITA CHAKMA AND GLEN HILL

This is the story of two women's movements. One is the outwardly successful story of the mainstream Bengali women's movement. The other is the lesser-known and previously untold story of the indigenous women's movement in the remote Chittagong Hill Tracts of Bangladesh. Over the last forty years, the stories of these two women's movements have often intersected. While the two movements are still partitioned, occasions of mutual support and friendship have briefly conquered partisan politics and ethnic difference.

Both women's movements arose from forms of nationalism. The Bengali movement emerged in support of independence from West Pakistan and the creation of the new state of Bangladesh. The indigenous women's movement in the CHT emerged to support the defense of its indigenous population from colonization by the newly formed nation of Bangladesh.

Nationalism is at the root of the state-sponsored and military-backed relocation of hundreds of thousands of Bengali transmigrants onto the land of indigenous peoples, and the violence, particularly the rampant violence against women, that has been the focus of the indigenous women's movement in the CHT. In many instances, nationalism has also been the root of the inability of indigenous and mainstream Bengali *women to build lasting trusting relations and to mobilize against issues that affect all women in Bangladesh.*

Only on occasions where individual activists have moved beyond nationalist perspectives have the genuine friendships between women brought the two women's movements together. Friendship among women offers the hope of a new politics which transcends the intolerance and violence fueled by nationalism.

Political History of the Chittagong Hill Tracts

The Chittagong Hill Tracts (CHT), the traditional homeland of Jumma people, occupies the southeastern protuberance off the main landmass of Bangladesh. The CHT is bordered by the Indian states of Tripura and Mizoram in the north and east, the Burmese states of Chin and Rakhine (or Arakan) in the east and south, and two districts of Bangladesh—Chittagong and Cox's Bazar—in the west. The CHT itself is composed of three districts: Khagrachari in the north, Rangamati at the center, and Bandarban in the south.

Until a few decades ago, the CHT was a sparsely populated, heavily forested, hilly region, cultivated using traditional swidden agroforestry practices referred to locally as *Jum* cultivation. It is significantly different to the adjacent densely populated, mostly low lying, flat, fertile delta of Bangladesh that is better suited to plough cultivation.

The traditional inhabitants of the CHT, who refer to themselves as *Jummas*, are constituted by eleven indigenous groups. Listed alphabetically, the groups are the Bawm, Chak, Chakma, Khumi, Khyang, Lushai, Marma, Mro, Pangkhua, Tanchangya, and Tripura. Numerically, Chakmas are the largest group, Marmas the second largest, followed by the Tripura, Mro, Tanchangya, Bawm, Pangkhua, Chak, Khyang, Khumi, and Lushai.

The Jummas differ from the majority of Bengalis in many aspects, including their physical features, languages, farming, architecture, food habits, dress, and weaving methods. The eleven Jumma groups are ethnolinguistically and religiously diverse. While Chakma and Tanchangya languages are classified as Indo-Aryan languages, the other nine languages are classified as Tibeto-Burman (Chakma 2004, 15). Chakmas, Marmas, Tanchangyas, Chaks, and Khyangs primarily follow Buddhism; Tripuras follow Hinduism; Lushais, Pangkhuas, and Bawms follow Christianity. Mros and Khumis have diverse religious practices, following Buddhism, Christianity, and a new religion, Krama.[1]

At the time of its colonization by the British in 1760, Bengal included both the current area of Bangladesh and the Indian state of West Bengal, but it did not include the hilly hinterland behind the port city of Chittagong now referred to as the CHT. Because colonization of the CHT occurred a century later in 1860, it had a different political and administrative history from Bengal and retained some level of autonomy up until, and even briefly after, the end of British colonial rule in 1947.

As part of the negotiations during the partition of India in 1947, the CHT was "given" to Pakistan, despite its population being 97 percent non-Muslim. In 1971, when East Pakistan won its battle for independence from West Pakistan and the new state of Bangladesh was created, the CHT became part of Bangladesh.

Immediately after the creation of the new state of Bangladesh, the demands by CHT leaders for incorporating CHT's autonomous status into the 1972 constitution of Bangladesh were rejected. The Bangladesh government then began to suppress the early stages of a CHT autonomy struggle that eventually saw the emergence of a political organization, the Parbattya Chattagram Jana Sanghati Samity (JSS), and their associated armed resistance guerilla group known as the Shanti Bahini (peace force). In 1975, when Bangladesh was brought under military rule as a result of a coup in which President Sheikh Mujibur Rahman was assassinated, the CHT became fully militarized. Since 1975, Bangladesh has had both military and democratic governments, but the CHT has remained under military occupation.

The signing of the CHT Accord in December 1997 ended more than two decades of armed struggle for autonomy by the JSS. Although the Shanti Bahini demobilized, the Bangladesh government, in contravention of the accord, maintained its heavy military presence in the CHT. The International Work Group for Indigenous Affairs states that there is now 1 soldier per 40 civilians in the CHT compared to 1 soldier per 1,750 civilians in the rest of the country (IWGIA 2012a, 14). A 2011 report to the Permanent Forum on Indigenous Issues (UNPFII) by U.N. Special Rapporteur Lars-Anders Baer noted that one-third of the Bangladesh military was stationed in the CHT (Baer 2011), which constitutes only a tenth of the land area of the country and about 1 percent of its population.

The UNPFII report documents the occurrence of "arbitrary arrests, torture, extrajudicial killings, harassment of rights activists and sexual harassment," and the continued implementation of so-called Operation Uttoron (Upliftment), an executive order that allows the military to interfere in civil matters beyond its jurisdiction (Baer 2011, 15–16). It also points out that the most important provisions of the 1997 peace accord—the settlement of land disputes, demilitarization, and the devolution of authority to CHT institutions—remain either unimplemented or only partially implemented (Baer 2011, 5).

The Bangladesh military now has six permanent cantonments (barracks) in the three districts of the CHT, which appears excessive considering that there are only fourteen cantonments in the rest of the sixty-one districts of Bangladesh, and that the CHT is not a war zone, nor is there now any counterinsurgency. The heavy military presence in the CHT has been used to facilitate a dramatic transformation of its demography. Between 1979 and 1985, the Bangladesh government, abetted by the military, undertook a politically motivated "transmigration program" in which at least 350,000 Bengalis from the plains were implanted into the CHT, evicting indigenous peoples from their homes and lands. Shapan Adnan, a Bengali socioeconomic scholar, described the program as an act of "demographic engineering" (2004, 53). In 1951, four years after British decolonization, the Bengali population in the CHT was 9 percent. In 1974, three years after Pakistani decolonization, it was 19 percent. The implementation of the transmigration program increased the nonindigenous Bengali population by 150 percent between 1974 and 1991. By 1991, Bengalis constituted about 50 percent of the total population of the CHT.

Although the transmigration program officially ended in the mid-1980s, research shows that Bengali in-migration and the resultant land alienation of indigenous peoples continues both covertly and overtly under the auspices of government agencies (Adnan and Dastidar 2011). A U.N. Development Program survey recently has confirmed that two-thirds of the current Bengalis in the CHT are transmigrants who had settled in the CHT within the last thirty years (UNDP 2009, 46). The Chittagong Hill Tracts Commission (2011), an international human rights panel, concluded that "the alienation of the land of the indigenous peoples by Bengalis continues unabated and is further facilitated, according to widespread allegations, by the acts and omission of civil and military personnel."

The Situation of Bengali and Indigenous Women

According to grand narratives about women's development in Bangladesh, there has been a substantial improvement in women's situation. Over the last three-and-half decades, there has been greater access to education, health, legal rights, and credit. There has also been increased awareness of, and efforts to combat, violence and discrimination against women.

Women's development in Bangladesh has benefited from transformations in the local and international economic and social landscapes. One catalyst has been the introduction of state policies linked to the global discourse on women, beginning particularly with the U.N.'s Women in Development program in the

1970s. Another impetus has been the nation's economic transformation, linked to the globalized economy and fuelled by the economic liberalization programs of the early 1980s. Global funds, particularly from international financial institutions such as the World Bank and the International Monetary Fund, initiated export-oriented manufacturing. Global funds also fueled an exponential growth in Bangladesh's nongovernmental organization (NGO) sector in which women became heavily involved. In the manufacturing sector, a vast number of poor urban and rural women were used as a cheap and easily subjugated workforce. In the NGO sector, urban and rural women were constructed as subjects of development by the new areas of the monetary-based economy.

Globally, women-oriented events that were influential in Bangladesh included the 1975 U.N. declaration of the International Year of Women which began the Decade of Women and Development, the 1979 adoption of the U.N. Convention on the Elimination of all forms of Discrimination against Women (CEDAW), and U.N. world conferences on women in Mexico (1975), Copenhagen (1980), Nairobi (1985), and Beijing (1995). Bangladesh's links to the global development agenda escalated women's participation in the economic sector and in politics, and women came to dominate Bangladesh's development narratives.

Economic and social transformation in Bangladesh, accelerated by international support, saw the consolidation of power and wealth by a new class of politicians and bureaucrats in the public sector, and a new class of business and NGO entrepreneurs in the private sector. A significant number of the new participants in the private sector were women. They were generally affluent and benefited from family and class-based networks. Poor and rural women had mixed benefits from the changes occurring in Bangladesh. While researchers such as anthropologist Lamia Karim (2008, 20–23) and feminist and academic Elora Halim Chowdhury (2011, 17–20) argued that women's progress in Bangladesh was largely based on middle-class urban Bengali women and a small number of rural elites, the work of Shanti Rozario, a Bengali feminist scholar, showed some benefits for poor rural Bengali women (2003), but also scenarios in which poor women could be made poorer by some microcredit arrangements (Karim 2008, 17–20).

Indigenous women do not appear to have benefited from the development windfall enjoyed by many sectors in Bangladesh. There is however very little work evaluating the implication of the global and national economic and social changes for Bangladesh's indigenous women. They are rarely represented in national statistical data and are either presented tokenistically or remain unmentioned in national reports, policies, and laws relating to women.[2] Based on the limited available evidence, indigenous women's access to development, health, education, and justice appear significantly inferior to that of their Bengali sisters.

In terms of access to health, average outcomes for women in Bangladesh have improved substantially and have been acclaimed internationally. At the 2011 U.N. summit on the Millennium Development Goals, Prime Minister Sheikh Hasina was recognized for Bangladesh being ahead of the scheduled reduction in maternal mortality rates. While Bangladesh's health outcomes look positive, the lack of differentiated statistics conceals the poor health situation of indigenous women. In February 2011, the CEDAW committee's working group requested that Bangladesh include information on the maternal mortality rates of minority and indigenous women (CEDAW/C/BGD/Q/7, 2011, para. 20, 3), but the response report from the Bangladesh government failed to provide any disaggregated statistics (CEDAW/C/BGD/Q/7/Add. 1, 2011, para. 43, 10). The UNDP (2008) estimated that the maternal mortality rate in the CHT was two or three times higher than the national average, making it the highest in South Asia. A 2010 study reporting significant improvement nationally in reducing maternal mortality rates projected a requirement of 25 percent reduction in the maternal mortality ratio by 2015 to achieve Millennium Development Goal 5 for Bangladesh (HSB 2011, 4). A similar rate of reduction, however, appears difficult to achieve in the CHT as the UNDP announcement estimated that two-thirds of households in the CHT had no, or very limited, access to basic primary health services. A July 2011 report reiterated that maternal health in the CHT was lagging behind the national average, and infant and child mortality rates in the CHT were higher than the national average. According to the Multiple Indicator Cluster Survey 2009, the three CHT districts ranked among the five worst-performing districts in the country in terms of the Millennium Development Goals (IRIN 2011).

Lack of access to skilled health workers is a primary reason for poor mother's health outcomes in the CHT. While births attended by a skilled health worker increased nationally from 12 percent in 2001 to 27 percent in 2010 (HSB 2011, 2), in 2009 this figure was only 9 percent in the CHT,[3] well short of even the 2001 national average. Nationally, the lowest percentage of births attended by a skilled health worker was in the Bandarban district of the CHT, standing at 8 percent (compared to 61 percent in the most attended area of the country) (*Progotir Pathey* 2010, 19). In 2000, it was reported that there remained a prevalence of chronic energy deficiency in 43 percent of the mothers in the CHT, indicating serious food insecurity (Akhter 2008). In 2009, a UNDP baseline survey on the CHT reported widespread "food poverty." The UNDP noted that about 62 percent of households in the CHT were living below the absolute poverty line (below 2,122 kcal), while 36% percent were considered hardcore poor (below 1,805 kcal). The survey also highlighted that the prevalence of absolute poor was 65 percent and hardcore poor was 44 percent among indigenous peoples in the CHT (UNDP 2009, vi–vii).

In terms of access to education, the CHT remains behind national literacy rates. A 2001 Bangladesh Rural Advancement Committee survey showed that, among the villages studied, there was one primary school for every five villages in the CHT compared to the national average of two schools for every three villages. The survey reported that in the CHT, the average distance to the nearest primary school was 2.5 miles, the nearest lower secondary school was 5.7 miles, and the nearest higher secondary school was 16.3 miles. The 2009 UNDP survey reported that only 8 percent of children completed primary education, while only 2 percent completed secondary education in the CHT (ii).

Women's education in the CHT lags behind that of CHT men and that of Bengali women in other parts of Bangladesh. The 1999 adult literacy statistics showed that there was only a 20 percent literacy rate for females as opposed to 42 percent for males (AIPP 2008, 32). The Bangladesh Bureau of Statistics reported that in 1995–1996 in the three districts of the CHT there were only 10 schools for girls compared to 116 for boys (Gain 2000, 94–95). A 2008 report noted that there was only 1 percent female as opposed to 5 percent male students studying at the level of the secondary school certificate in the CHT (H. Ahmed 2011). In 2009, the average literacy rate for females aged between fifteen and twenty-four years in the CHT was 49 percent, well below the national average of 72 percent (*Progotir Pathey 2010*, table 16, 106–107). Likewise, the 1991 census showed that the literacy rate in the CHT for females aged seven years and above was 18 percent, which is much lower than the national average of 26 percent (Gain 2000, 94).

In terms of indigenous women's access to justice, Bangladesh has remained indifferent to concerns over violence against women raised by national, regional, and international human rights bodies. In 2000, the government directed the establishment of Women and Children Repression Prevention Tribunals in sixty-one districts of Bangladesh, but, significantly, omitted the three districts of the CHT. The high rate of violence against Jumma women reported by national and international human rights organizations should have made tribunals in the CHT a priority. Only as a result of a High Court Order in 2008, and in response to a nongovernmental legal aid organization's writ petition demanding the government show reason why the tribunals were not established in the CHT, were the tribunals finally established in 2009 (BLAST; bdnews 2006). The very small number of cases that are now with the tribunals have yet to find justice as there have been delays and many complications, including reported noncooperation, in many cases from the police department, court officials, and medical officers. The failure of the justice system in the CHT was highlighted by the 2011 Asia Pacific NGO consultation meeting with the Special Rapporteur on Violence Against Women, which noted that "the biggest concern in rape and other violence against women in the CHT now is the lack of access to justice and absolute impunity that perpetrators enjoy" (H. Ahmed 2011, 7).

In the political sphere, nonindigenous women have held progressively more prominent roles in Bangladesh. For over two decades, women have held the positions of prime minister, leader of the opposition, and a number of powerful ministries. There are now fifty reserved seats for women in the Bangladesh national parliament.[4] However, there are no reserved seats for indigenous women or men. In the forty years since independence, only two CHT women have become members of the Bangladesh parliament.[5]

The Bengali and Jumma Women's Movement prior to the 1997 Peace Accord

The Bangladesh Mahila Parishad (BMP) was the first women's organization in Bangladesh. It was established in Dhaka in 1970 as the East Pakistan Mahila Parishad (Women's Association), a voluntary secular nationalist organization supporting independence from Pakistan. The BMP followed the ideas of Begum Rokeya Sakhawat Hussain (1880–1932), a Bengali Muslim feminist writer born in the small Bangladeshi village of Pairaband, then part of British Bengal, who advocated Muslim women's education, was a critic of Muslim patriarchy, and is often considered the first Muslim feminist in South Asia. The BMP's mission was, and remains, the promotion of women's freedom and development, and solidarity with secular, democratic, and progressive movements in Bangladesh.

Subsequent Bengali women's organizations in the early 1970s, which remained predominantly voluntary, continued to focus on women's education, skills, income generation, welfare, and childcare.

In the 1970s, there was a change in the nature of women's work, from domestic, rural, and agrarian to nondomestic, urban, factory-oriented, and monetary-based. The change, which was stimulated by assistance from international governments and nongovernment organizations (NGOs), not only brought about social and economic transformation in Bangladesh, but also transformed the Bengali women's movement. The monetarization of women's labor made possible the direct comparison between the value of male and female labor and highlighted gender inequities. Hameeda Hossain, an eminent Bangladeshi feminist, confirmed that by the 1980s the changing involvement of women in the monetary economy in both the urban and rural sectors was such that "as women entered the work force in greater numbers, either in rural, self employment driven by micro-credit, or in urban industries, women began to construct issues of equality in terms of social justice" (2011). The rapidly growing numbers of NGOs in the 1980s, in which women were heavily involved, pursued both a development agenda and the equity issues arising as an outcome of development. These NGOs not only involved educated urban women, but also a great number of rural women, many through NGO microcredit programs. While urban women became NGO leaders, rural women were more likely to become NGO workers.

The changing nature of women's work from the mid-1970s through the 1980s, and the gender equity issues it exposed, challenged existing patriarchal structures and social relations. This challenge to the traditional patriarchal model[6] added gender tension, evidenced in an escalation (and escalated reporting) of violence and other forms of repression against women. By the 1980s, a growing number of women's organizations were pursuing gender-based discrimination in social, economic, and political sectors, including violence against women, dowry practices, acid attacks, rape, trafficking of women, wage inequality, workplace exploitation, access to credit, and women's underrepresentation in politics. Working through NGOs, the movement against gender discrimination influenced the development of national policies and practices directed toward gaining gender equality and social justice for women.[7] The achievements of women's rights advocacy includes Bangladesh's accession to CEDAW in 1984,[8] endorsement of the Beijing Platform for Action for gender equality at the 1995 U.N. Conference on Women, and adoption of the Optional Protocol to CEDAW in 2000. To date, among the international treaties it has ratified, CEDAW is the only one for which Bangladesh has allowed an individual communications procedure.

The year 1975 marked both the first U.N. International Women's Year and the beginning of Bangladeshi women's entry into development processes. However for indigenous women in the CHT, 1975 marked a more ominous occurrence. It was in 1975 that the CHT was militarized. The subsequent decades of Bangladesh's colonization of the CHT have been a dark period for indigenous women. The Bangladesh government's implementation of the policy of mass transmigration resulted in thirteen major massacres of indigenous Jummas between 1979 and 1992 and has been described as a "creeping genocide" (Levene 1999). Killing, torture, arson, and sexual violence against indigenous women were used to uproot hundreds of thousands of Jummas from their homes in order to take over their lands (Adnan and Dastidar 2011, 97; Mohsin 1997, 178; B. Chakma 2010).

Because the government prohibited the entrance of secular NGOs into the CHT until after the 1997 CHT Accord, the women's movement in the CHT could not operate through NGOs as it had in the rest of Bangladesh. Even since their entrance, the government has applied discriminatory rules against secular NGOs, intimidated local NGO workers, and imposed restriction of movement of international NGO workers in the CHT (bdnews 2012; ICIP-CHT 2012).

The first indigenous women's political organization in the CHT, the Parbartya Chattagram Mahila Samiti (Chittagong Hill Tracts Women's Association), was established on 21 January 1975 by the JSS to help resist the state's political oppression (Chakraborty 2004). It created many village women's councils (*mahila panchayet*) that aimed to provide political education, inspire women to contribute to the struggle, or provide the opportunity for women to give psycho-moral support to other women (Halim 2010, 186). Because its birth coincided with the full-scale militarization of the CHT, it was quickly forced underground.

Later, in 1977, about thirty-five members of the Chittagong Hill Tracts Women's Association joined a women's regiment formed by the JSS, for "self-defense" training. However, due to increased military atrocities across the CHT, in 1983, the JSS deactivated the women's regiment.[9] The association continued working, mainly trying to increase political awareness among women and improve their social conditions.

The economic changes that transformed the women's movement in the rest of Bangladesh in the 1980s had little or no impact in the CHT. Instead, institutionalized gender violence made Jumma women the most vulnerable group in the militarized CHT. Exacerbating the situation, in 1983, a secret memorandum was circulated to all army officers encouraging them to marry indigenous women from the CHT (Chittagong Hill Tracts Commission 1991, 108–109), thus coding Jumma indigenous women as "other" and differentiating them from their own (Bengali) women. The military's policy encouraged the occupation, the colonization, of women's bodies through forced marriage.

Summarizing horrific incidents of gender violence, the report of the Chittagong Hill Tracts Commission's first investigation published in 1991 states simply that "rape is used systematically as a weapon against women in the CHT" (107). In that report, a Jumma refugee woman, who was subjected to gang rape during a 1985 military attack in her village, records her vulnerability: "About 50 army personnel came in the night and rounded up the whole village and gathered in one place. In the morning all the men were arrested. I was tied up hands and legs, naked. They raped me. There were three women there. They raped me in front of my father-in-law. After that we were tied up together naked facing each other. Then they left. Three other girls were raped in front of me. This happened in the month of Ashar (June/July) of 1985" (106).

The revolutionary, militant indigenous women's movement shifted in the late 1980s to emerge in the form of "student activism." The Chittagong Hill Tracts Hill Women's Federation (known as the Hill Women's Federation or HWF) was formed by female Jumma students of Chittagong University on 8 March 1988. The objectives laid out in its constitution show that it was established predominantly to resist all forms of repression against women, establish women's rights as equal rights, and raise awareness about gender violence.[10] But the violent decades of the 1980s and 1990s soon forced these women students to take a robust stand in resisting state colonization of the CHT. At its first convention on 15 January 1995, the HWF demanded autonomy for the CHT (1995; Keokradong 1995, 8). The HWF identified colonization of the CHT via the joint instruments of militarization and transmigration as the root cause of gender-targeted state repression of Jumma women.[11] Personal accounts of leaders and workers of the HWF, who had been refugees in India or displaced persons within the CHT, indicate this as their reason for pursuing "self-determination" or "autonomy" for the CHT (HWF 1999, 25–28, 38, 40–45, 62–64; S. Chakma 2010, 19–20).

The HWF's continued demand for autonomy also manifested in their collaborative campaign work with the CHT-based political alliance, the Hill Student's Council (HSC)[12] established in 1989, and Hill People's Council (HPC)[13] established at the end of 1990, two organizations which publicly resisted militarization of the CHT and transmigration of Bengali settlers. The HWF, like their male-dominated counterparts the HSC and the HPC, assumed that only "self-determination" or "autonomy" of indigenous peoples within the state of Bangladesh could end the nationalist oppression of the state and in turn free Jumma women from the colonizer's ethnic- and gender-targeted sexual violence. This assumption was reflected in the HWF's campaigns, slogans, and public pronouncements throughout the 1990s and into the twenty-first century.

The demand for autonomy, which came to be the major campaign focus of the HWF, may have appeared to deviate from the women's agenda set out at its founding in 1988. But as a leader of the HWF, Kalpana Chakma, made clear in a speech one year prior to her abduction, autonomy and the women's agenda were intertwined: "the HWF's struggle is not only political, but its struggle is against patriarchal repression in social and familial domains" (2001, 23). Ultimately, however, the issues of patriarchal repression, such as the male-dominated customary leadership structure, women's inheritance rights, and violence committed by Jumma men against Jumma women, were left largely unaddressed.

In the period immediately following the 1997 CHT Accord, the HWF divided into two factions, each siding with opposing indigenous political groups. One group was supported by the JSS, a signatory to the accord. The other was supported by a newer group, the United People's Democratic Front, which held that the accord was inadequate. The close alignment of the CHT women's movement with Jumma political parties has left it open to claims of manipulation by indigenous male political activists. Such manipulation was evident during the HWF's preparation for the 1995 Beijing U.N. World Conference on Women, where a male leader of the HSC attempted to impose his view about the use of a logo. The logo, which showed chained female hands, was considered by many of the women as undermining their sense of agency and empowerment and was even ironically interpreted by some of the women as representing the oppression of indigenous male political activists. While most of the women members felt uncomfortable with the logo, some perhaps feared offending a powerful HSC leader.[14] The HWF eventually used both their own preferred logo and the "imposed" logo at the conference, and later abandoned both.

The Differing Characters of the Early Bengali and Jumma Women's Movement

The early Bengali women's movement and the early indigenous Jumma women's movement can be seen to have arisen from different structural conditions. The Bengali women's movement has been predominantly an NGO-dominated movement, strongly connected with economic development (Chowdhury 2001, 203; Chowdhury 2011). Chowdhury argued that the Bengali women's movement "operates inside the structure of NGO with its link to government, donors and other NGOs, and at the same time push[es] their boundaries" (2011, 76). She described it as a class-based movement, which was largely led by "western educated urban elites who advocate women's rights within a secular modernist framework" (160). Acknowledging Karim's (2004; 2008, 22–23) formulation of an entrenched "patron-client" relationship in a culture of institutionalized NGO structures, Chowdhury further suggested two types of Bengali women's subjectivity were constructed: elite women as patrons and poor women as clients, where "elite women working in NGOs feel validated through their work on behalf of other [poor/client] women," and "poor women are perceived as objects of intervention rather than as agents on their own" (2011, 143). In the NGO-dominated women's movement, Chowdhury exposed a power relation where elite women "seek to empower 'other' women, rather than to work for the mutual liberation of all women" (144). While Karim (2004) and Chowdhury claimed that NGO institutional structures enable feminist alliances and transnational networks, Chowdhury also cautioned that they can impede autonomous feminist practices and movements (2011, 186).

The early indigenous women's movement emerged from the larger CHT autonomy movement without links to government, donors, or NGOs. Because the movement remained outside NGOs' development activities, it made no connection either to the global women's movement or to global donors. While the NGO-dominated Bengali women's movement sought alliances with government, pushed their own boundaries in pursuing their NGO work, and connected with the global women's rights agenda, the Jumma women's movement focused on using national and international fora to challenge the government and its policies of militarization and transmigration in the CHT.[15]

Bengali feminist leaders were mainly Dhaka-based urban elites. They were generally well-educated, mature, middle-aged professionals, with links to government, global donors, and NGOs. Their involvement with NGOs provided them further economic security and social status. In contrast, HWF Jumma activists were rural and semi-urban women, who were often young, inexperienced, economically insecure, nonprofessionals without links to government or global donors and without ready access to information networks. While Bengali women were encouraged to be involved in women's organizations related to NGOs, Jumma women activists were discouraged because of the risk of being targeted by state agencies and because state authorities harassed not only HWF activists but also those who assisted them.[16] One small benefit of their lack of ties to government and nongovernment sectors was their relative freedom in choosing their agenda. But as their agenda was not in alignment with national women's agenda, it failed to gain prominence at national and international levels.

While the early HWF activists failed to influence Bangladesh's mainstream women's movement, they nevertheless played a valuable role in resisting oppression against women in the preaccord CHT. And because the indigenous activists did not match the profile of their Bengali sisters, they also represented a challenge to the ethnic and class hegemony of Bengali feminism.

Shifting Alignments between Indigenous and Bengali Women's Organizations before the 1997 Accord

During the 1970s and early 1980s there was almost no meaningful communication between mainstream Bengali and Jumma women's activist groups. However at an individual level, there were a small number of indigenous women attending university who became involved in left-wing student politics and developed social connections to other women activists. These included Ma Mya Ching, who was politically active at Dhaka University, and was later elected as a member of parliament for the right-wing Bangladesh Nationalist Party, and Bithika Chakma who was a political activist at Chittagong University.

With greater numbers of Jumma and Bengali women attending universities, the opportunity for personal interactions between women activists at colleges and universities increased during the 1980s. However at the organizational level, the links being forged between women's groups and development-focused NGOs during the 1980s did not offer a place for indigenous women activists to raise issues over institutionalized gender violence under colonization and militarization.[17]

Only in the 1990s was the indigenous women's organization, the HWF, able to build connections with Bengali women's organizations. Signs of solidarity were evident when the HWF joined the rally of the national women's gathering in Dhaka to celebrate International Women's Day in March 1994. As an outcome of this cooperation, the HWF joined the National Preparatory Committee Towards Beijing, which worked for eighteen months as part of a coalition of over two hundred individuals and various NGO organizations to prepare a status report on women in Bangladesh for the upcoming U.N. Fourth World Conference on Women—Action for Equality, Development, and Peace in Beijing in September 1995.

The HWF was part of the Sanmilita Nari Samaj (United Women's Society), a coalition formed in Dhaka in August 1995 and led by mainstream Bengali feminist organizations, including human rights organizations, development-oriented organizations, women from the Left, trade unions, and individual women activists such as lawyers, academics, and students. The coalition emerged as a result of an incident of sexual violence against a thirteen-year-old Bengali girl, Yasmin, who was raped and then killed by three policemen in the northern district of Dinajpur in August 1995. The HWF spontaneously joined Bengali women on the streets of Dhaka as part of the Sanmilita Nari Samaj protests against sexual violence.

Being part of the coalition allowed Jumma women activists to understand the spectrum of violence being committed against Bengali women, including dowry violence and acid attacks that were almost unknown in the CHT but prevalent in the plains of Bangladesh.[18] It led the HWF to demand punishment for the perpetrators of acid attacks on women in its first national conference in June 1995 (*Kalpana Chakmar Diary* 2001, 50). Naripokkho (pro-women), a leading feminist advocacy group, later went on to champion the anti–acid violence campaign (Chowdhury 2011, 29–30, 62).

The cooperation between Bengali and Jumma activists was short-lived, however, as the relationship fell out during the preparations for the 1995 Beijing conference on women. One point of disagreement was a key section heading in the report being prepared for the conference. The report was first written in Bangla and then translated into English. Jumma and Bengali activists started working on a section titled "*adibasi nari o paribesh*," meaning "indigenous women and the environment." But when the final draft was prepared by the drafting committee, largely composed of highly educated Bengali women NGO leaders, they unilaterally translated *adibasi nari* as "ethnic women" rather than "indigenous women." The unspoken nationalist subtext was that even admitting the possibility of the existence of indigenous peoples undermined the ambition of Bengali sovereignty over every corner of the country. The term "ethnic women"[19] was considered offensive by the HWF, but their protestations failed.

Another disagreement occurred over the text of the section on indigenous women. Jumma delegate's primary concern of sexual oppression by the military in the CHT was entirely written out of the final set of issues presented at Beijing. It was not that Bengali women activists were unaware or disbelieved the occurrence of gender and ethnically targeted state violence in the CHT. Rather the issue neither fitted with the development-oriented framework of their campaign, nor could they accept the implied critique of the nationalist agenda being played out in the CHT. Unable to present the situation of indigenous women in the CHT through the national women's coalition, the HWF prepared its own leaflets for the Beijing Conference on Women and sought global solidarity with other indigenous women from Asia.

After Beijing, many Bengali feminists and their organizations painstakingly developed the conceptual packaging of campaigns against gender violence experienced by Bengali women to fit them into the twelve critical areas of the Beijing Platform for Action (for instance, acid violence against women was packaged under the area "the girl child" focusing on child acid victims; Chowdhury 2011, 48). But there was no accommodation of Jumma women's issues.

It was only later, in 1996, when Kalpana Chakma, the young organizing secretary of the HWF, was abducted, that Bengali women activists took up the issue of violence against indigenous women. Kalpana was allegedly abducted by a group of security personnel led by Lieutenant Ferdous Kaiser Khan, commander of the Kojochari military camp (Seventeenth East Bengal Regiment) situated near Kalpana's village. They were armed but in plain clothes. She was abducted from her home along with her two brothers, and in front of her mother and sister-in-law, in the early hours of 12 June 1996, the day of the national elections. Kalpana and her two brothers' hands were tied, and they were blindfolded. One brother was taken knee-deep into the nearby lake by one of the abductors, who had been ordered to shoot him, but both brothers managed to jump into the lake and escape. Kalpana was heard crying "*dada, dada*," meaning "brother, brother." She has not been heard from since.

The abduction of Kalpana awakened many Bengali women's rights and human rights activists in Bangladesh to the plight of indigenous women. Some Bengali women activists, risking the rainy season and the perils of the long journey, traveled to Kalpana's remote village to investigate the incident. They were instrumental in publicizing Kalpana's abduction in the national media and breaking a long public silence about violence against women in the CHT. As a result of the visceral trauma of this event, the Bengali activists appeared to have set aside considerations of ethnicity and nationality to become purely women—women who could understand the grief of losing a daughter or a sister.

In the period immediately after Kalpana's abduction, cooperation between a coalition of Bengali women's organizations, particularly the Sanmilita Nari Samaj and the HWF, were further strengthened during their campaign against the lack of action over the abduction. As a result of the campaign, NGOs and civil society organizations (CSOs) from thirty-seven countries asked the Bangladesh government to urgently find Kalpana and conduct an inquiry into the incident. For a short time at least, Kalpana's disappearance brought together indigenous and nonindigenous women in Bangladesh with other women from around the world.

The strong cooperation between the HWF and Sanmilita Nari Samaj in protesting Kalpana's abduction and demanding her rescue broke down again after the signing of the Chittagong Hill Tracts Accord in 1997. The Sanmilita Nari Samaj split along political lines over the accord. One faction supported the then ruling government's commitment to the accord; the other faction supported the opposition party's rejection of the accord (Guhathakurata 1997; 2001, 287). The split was evidence of the presence of nationalist politics operating within the Bengali women's movement.

Jumma and Bengali Women's Activism after the 1997 Peace Accord

While the 1997 accord did not bring any cessation of the military-facilitated colonization of the CHT or the associated violence against indigenous women, it did allow the CHT a limited degree of openness to the external world. One significant effect was the entrance of numerous NGOs to the CHT, and the new associations this allowed between indigenous women activists and women-oriented NGOs.

New Jumma women's organizations and networks that have emerged since the Peace Accord include the Women Resource Network, a women-managed CSO, and the CHT Women Organizations Network (CHTWON), a network of forty-nine local women-oriented NGOs.[20] Mainstream Bengali women's organizations have also opened local branches and begun to work in the CHT. In October 1998, Bangladesh Mahila Parishad, the oldest women's organization in Bangladesh,[21] opened a branch in Rangamati, the largest town in the CHT, involving both Jumma and Bengali women. The large Durbar Network, a national coalition of over 550 women-oriented organizations formed prior to the 1995 Beijing Conference and led by Naripokkho, has now established linkages with women's organizations in the CHT. The activities of the network include advice to victims of gender violence, advocacy of women rights, and moral and practical support to CHT women in legal matters. One early Durbar Network campaign made a significant national impact in a protest over the rape of two indigenous Marma women in the CHT, who were abducted from their homes by Bengali settlers during an attack at Maischari, a Marma village in the north of the CHT. In this protest, women activists from the network simultaneously formed human chains in front of deputy commissioners' offices in all sixty-four districts of Bangladesh (Eskildsen 2012).

A national conference of indigenous women, the first of its kind, was held in Dhaka from 31 March to 1 April 2012 and brought together many of the fifty-four indigenous communities from all over Bangladesh (IWGIA 2012a). As an outcome of the conference, a network of twenty-three indigenous women's organizations from both the CHT and the plains of Bangladesh was formed under the title Bangladesh Indigenous Women Network (BIWN). Its stated aim was "equal dignity and rights for indigenous women to ensure a violence-free life." Because the twenty-three indigenous organizations were dispersed across the country and had limited experience and little access to technology and communication, the BIWN would have had only limited impact on its own. But new friendships and coalitions between activists of the BIWN and some leading mainstream women organizations, including BMP, Bangladesh Nari

Progati Sangha (BNPS),[22] and Karmojibi Nari (KN),[23] enabled the BIWN to achieve outcomes in its first year.

Against the background of a rise in reported violence against indigenous women throughout the country, these organizations held a collaborative press conference to demand an end to recent violence against indigenous women, the arrest and punishment of perpetrators, and compensation for women victims. Journalists were called upon to raise awareness of indigenous peoples' conditions and draw public attention to escalated violence against indigenous women. The press conference pointed out that the rape and murder of indigenous women has been part of a strategy of intimidation ultimately aimed at taking over land owned by indigenous people. It detailed nineteen incidents of violence against indigenous women between January and June 2012. Eleven of the nineteen cases of sexual violence against indigenous women and girls were in the CHT, where the alleged perpetrators were all migrant Bengali settlers (BIWN 2012). Over 50 percent of the victims were girls under fifteen, and included an eleven-year-old primary school student, Sujata Chakma, who was raped and murdered.

A campaign of BNPS, a Bengali women's organization, demonstrates how collaboration between indigenous and Bengali women activists has facilitated a broadening of the gender issues being pursued by indigenous activists. As well as the long-standing demands for an end to sexual violence, the campaign (and a remarkable poster art that supported it)[24] demanded a range of gender issues that included constitutional recognition of indigenous people, a marriage registration system for indigenous women, equal status for indigenous women, equal inheritance rights, equal access to justice, equal opportunity for participation in private and public life, and equitable representation in all levels of government.

While greater collaboration and understanding developed between Jumma and Bengali activists, the points of disjunction were still not erased. The circumstances surrounding the introduction of a major piece of legislation affecting women, the National Women's Development Policy, 2011, demonstrated again the nationalist fear of admitting the existence of indigenous peoples in Bangladesh because it undermined their colonizing ambitions. While the policy is directed toward all women in Bangladesh, it substantively omits indigenous women. Indigenous women are placed in the category *pratibandhi nari, khudranrigosthi nari* (literally meaning "handicapped women, small anthropological group women"). Under this grotesque new category there are vague references to "rights" without any definitions, and without formulating any strategy, work plan, financial source, or nominated implementing institution to achieve these "rights" (Chakma 2011). Although the Samajik Pratirodh Committee (Social Defense Committee), a platform of sixty-seven feminist- and social justice–based NGOs and CSOs, acknowledged the shortcomings of the policy, they nevertheless gave it full support because it contained important measures for reducing women's poverty, enhancing women's economic and political empowerment, food security, health, nutrition, education, training, employment, improving the status of girls, and resisting violence against women.[25] The committee thus made a pragmatic decision to sacrifice indigenous women's issues for the sake of achieving much of their own agenda.

A Future for Bangladesh's Women's Movement beyond Colonialism and Nationalism

Perhaps unusually, both the indigenous and Bengali women's movements could be conceptualized as arising out of nationalistic resistance to colonial domination. In the case of the Bengali women's movement, the early organizations arose to assist in the struggle for independence from West Pakistan and the establishment of the new state of Bangladesh. In the case of the Jumma women's movement, early organizations arose to defend indigenous women from the violence ensuing from the military-supported transmigrant colonization of the CHT by the new state of Bangladesh.

With the overthrow of the Pakistani regime and the emergence of the new nation of Bangladesh, Bengali women were able to move on and address issues beyond the fight for independence. However indigenous women in the CHT were never free of military-facilitated colonization and its associated violence, and therefore they largely restricted their campaigns to these issues.

Both Bengali and indigenous women appeared torn between women's issues and nationalist agendas. For many Bengali women, the autonomy movement in the CHT was a threat to Bangladesh's unity and strength. While for indigenous groups in the CHT, militarization and colonization produced an artificial unity and pride akin to nationalism in their identity as Jummas. And while Jummas have never campaigned to secede, they sought autonomy within Bangladesh.

Prior to the signing of the 1997 Peace Accord, short-lived collaborations between indigenous and Bengali women's organizations arose primarily in response to injustices committed against individual women such as Yasmin, the thirteen-year-old Bengali girl, and Kalpana Chakma, the young indigenous activist. Here nationalist sensibilities were suppressed in favor of the empathy felt by both Bengali and indigenous women activists for these personal tragedies.

Disheartened by the nationalist hegemony of the Bengali women's movement and referring to the legacy of Kalpana Chakma, the Bengali anthropologist Zobaida Nasreen argued that "if the women's movement in Bangladesh fails to overcome its nationalistic attitude it will fail not only to stand for Kalpana but will fail to stand for violence against women" (2006, 103).

Although the CHT Peace Accord remains largely unimplemented, only since its signing in 1997 has there been an opportunity for Bengali and indigenous women to rise to Nasreen's challenge and widen their agenda beyond nationalist concerns. Cooperation in shared struggles to overcome injustices that touch all women have become more frequent, evidenced by events such as Durbar Network's campaign of protests in all sixty-four districts of Bangladesh over the abduction and rape of two indigenous Marma women in the CHT; BNPS's campaign to highlight broader gender issues affecting indigenous women; and the 2012 national conference on indigenous women organized through the partnership of the BIWN and prominent Bengali women's organizations. These moments, where nationalism has been suppressed in favor of the shared concerns of all Bangladeshi women, allow a glimpse of the possibility that friendships between indigenous and Bengali women activists may allow the emergence of a new politics that transcends the intolerance and violence fueled by nationalism.

Notes

1. Krama was founded by Manle Mro between 1985 and 1986.

2. Bangladesh census reports have yet to present any data on indigenous women. For instance, the 2011 CEDAW Committee's working group pointed out that Bangladesh's "report does not provide any information on the situation of minority and indigenous women, especially those living in the Chittagong Hills" when it responded to Bangladesh's "Combined sixth and seventh periodic report of state parties: Bangladesh, United Nations Convention on the Elimination of Discrimination Against Women." Concluding Observation of the Committee on the Elimination of Discrimination Against Women, Bangladesh, 4 February 2011, CEDAW/C/BGD/Q/7, 24 March 2010, para 28, 4.

3. Calculating the average for the three CHT districts from IRIN's 2011 report: 11.5 percent in Rangamati, 9.1 percent in Khagrachari, and 7.6 percent in Bandarban district.

4. The number of women's seats in the parliament was raised through the Fifteenth Amendment of the constitution on 30 June 2011, article 65, clause 3A.2.

5. Sudipta Dewan was selected in the 1970s and Ma Mya Ching was elected in two elections during the 1990s. In the current parliament, Ms. A Thin Rakhain, an

indigenous woman from the plains of Bangladesh, represents her own constituency Cox's Bazar and the CHT.

6. It was argued that in rural Bangladesh the work of development NGOs and feminist organizations challenged patriarchy in three areas: economy, law, and politics. Karim (2004), 300–301.

7. The work of feminist NGOs was instrumental in state recognition of women's rights and adoption of the CEDAW. Advocacy work later by Sanmilita Nari Samaj, Nijera Kori, Nari Pokkho, Ain O Salish Kendra, BMP, BNPS, Prabartana, Women for Women, etc., is noteworthy in implementing the CEDAW in national laws and policies.

8. Because of Islamic religious sentiment, Bangladesh maintained reservations to CEDAW articles 2,13.1[a], 16.1[c], and [f], which ensured equal rights for men and women in social, economic, and family life.

9. However, there was no formal deactivation of the regiment by the JSS. Written communication with Mangal Kumar Chakma, Information and Publicity Secretary, JSS, 17 August 2012.

10. The five objectives of the HWF are (1) to bring an end to all forms of repression and deprivation of women by making them aware about those; (2) to establish equal rights and dignity for women; (3) to practice hill nations' age old traditions and cultures and carry out their development; (4) to cultivate fraternity and solidarity among different nations of the CHT, and to integrate women in protection of their national existence and establishment of their own rights; and (5) to help neglected and repressed women in building their own future.

11. On 16 January 1995, the issue was further discussed among the convention participants and many other Jumma rural and urban women in an open field in front of the Khagrachari Town Hall. I (Kabita Chakma) was present at the postconvention meeting.

12. The HSC, known as the Pahari Chattra Parishad or PCP in Bangla, was established in 1989 by Jumma university students from all over the country. It was jointly convened by two students, Bidhan Chakma and Dhiraj Chakma, of Bangladesh University of Engineering and Technology, Dhaka.

13. Pahari Gana Parishad or PGP in Bangla.

14. As a member, Kabita Chakma was present in most of the HWF's meetings in Dhaka from June 1994 to June 1995.

15. Although work at the international level was limited, the HWF made a number of statements at different international fora. For example, two of five demands (1. Immediate demilitarization of the Chittagong Hill Tracts and 4. Resettlement of the plain settlers to places outside the CHT) clearly demonstrated the HWF's campaign in a statement by Bartika Chakma, vice president, CHT Hill Women's Federation on Agenda Item 5: Review of Developments, The Commission on Human Rights, UN Working Group on Indigenous Populations, Thirteen Session, Geneva, 24–28 July 1995.

16. For instance, in the 1990s, a number of Jumma government officials (distant relatives and acquaintances), who sheltered the HWF activists in Bandarban,

were harassed by security and intelligence officers. The house owners later received untimely transfer orders to remote locations. A practical reason to agree to accommodate the HWF activists was that there was no suitable commercial accommodation for women in the town. Kabita's discussion with Nairanjana Chakma, a former activist of the HWF, July 2012, Chiang Mai.

17. Similarly, in the 1980s, there was very little space in the women's rights movement for *beerangana* (war-heroines, mostly Bengali women), who were victims of rape and other sexual abuses during the war of Independence of Bangladesh.

18. The Ministry of Home Affairs' record on violence against women, January 2010 to December 2011, listed only three dowry-related incidents of violence, and no acid violence among a total of fifty-six cases filed with the courts in the three districts of the CHT.

19. The term "ethnic women" was coined by the Bengali women's leadership in 1995 to replace "indigenous women" and is still widely used by many seemingly progressive national NGOs and national independent institutions and publications, including the *New Age*, which is regarded as one of the most progressive dailies of Bangladesh.

20. CHTWON is not only a network of women's organizations, but it also includes other local organizations in the CHT that are sensitized in gender and working for women's rights and welfare. http://www.chtwon.org/

21. One of the largest organizations with fifty-nine braches in the country.

22. The Nari Progati Sangha (Association of Women for Progress) was established in 1986 with the aim of establishing equal rights for women from the family to the state level.

23. Karmojibi Nari (KN), meaning "working women," was established in 1991. Its aim is to establish women's "identity" as "working women" and to provide them a "platform" at the national and the grassroots level. KN states that "it is not a women's organization in the conventional sense; not even a trade union in the traditional sense." It is an organization of woman-workers, who are striving to establish rights, dignity, and the authority of woman-workers. KN's goal is to liberate the women's movement from the domination of upper-class women and to liberate the labor movement from the domination of patriarchy by upholding the agenda of woman-workers. KN envisages itself as a vanguard for social changes in Bangladesh.

24. The image used in the poster is by Kanak Chanpa Chakma, a well-known Bangladeshi artist. She also holds an executive post with the BNPS.

25. However, in response to this committee's positive call to the government, a coalition of left-leaning women's organizations, trade unions, and activists got together to form an open platform named, Shomo Odhikar Amader Nunotomo Daabi (SAND), meaning "Equal rights is our minimum demand." At their rally held in Dhaka, on 24 May 2011, they put forth the demand for a new Women's Policy. SAND's formation is in response to the NWDP, 2011, which they deem unsatisfactory as it does not include women's equal inheritance rights, a long-standing campaign of the women's rights movement in Bangladesh. Rahnuma Ahmed (2011).

References

Adnan, Shapan. 2004. *Migration Land Alienation, Migration Land Alienation and Ethnic Conflict: Causes of Poverty in the Chittagong Hill Tracts of Bangladesh.* Dhaka, Bangladesh: Research and Advisory Services.

Adnan, Shapan, and Ranajit Dastidar. 2011. *Alienation of the Lands of Indigenous Peoples of the Chittagong Hill Tracts of Bangladesh.* Copenhagen: IWGIA and the Chittagong Hill Tracts Commission.

Ahmed, Hana Shams. 2011. "The Multiple Dimensions of Women's Equality." Submission on the CHT at the Asia Pacific Regional Consultation with the UN Special Rapporteur on Violence Against Women, Its Causes and Consequences, Kuala Lumpur, 11–12 January.

Ahmed, Rahnuma. 2011. "A Postscript." *New Age,* 23.

AIPP (Asia Indigenous Peoples Pact) Foundation. 2008. "A Brief Account of the Human Rights Situation of Indigenous Peoples in Bangladesh." In *Indigenous Peoples' Human Rights Report in Asia 2008: Bangladesh Burma Lao, pages.* Chiang Mai, Thailand: AIPP.

Akhter, N., H. Torlesse, Sde Pee, QIU Ibrahim, G. Stallkamp, D. Panagides, and M. W. Bloem. 2003. "Nutritional Status of Young Children and their Mothers in the Chittagong Hill Tracts, Bangladesh." Hellen Keller International Bangladesh. Accessed. https://centre.icddrb.org/pub/publication.jsp?classificationID=1andpubID=4717.

Baer, Lars-Anders. May 2011. "Study on the Status of Implementation of the Chittagong Hill Tracts Accord of 1997," Permanent Forum on Indigenous Issues, Tenth session, New York, 16–27 May, UN Economic and Social Council, E/C.19/2011/6.

bdnews24.com. 2006. "HC Rules over Establishing Judges' Courts, Tribunals in CHT Districts," 1 February. Accessed 2 August 2015. http://ns.bdnews24.com/details.php?id=26508andcid=3.

———. 2012. "Foreign Journalists Barred from CHT," 5 August. Accessed 2 August, 2015. http://ns.bdnews24.com/details.php?id=229703andcid=2.

BIWN. 2012. "*Sampratik samaye adibasi narider upar hatya, dharshan o apaharnsaha byapak sahingsata rodhkalpe doshi byaktider greptarpurbak dristantamulak shasti pradan ebang khatigrasta narider khatipuraner dabi*"—a collective initiative of Bangladesh Indigenous Women's Network (BIWN), Bangladesh Nari Pragoti Sangha, Bagladesh Mahila Parishad, Karmajibi Nari, Press conference, 16 June 2012, Reporters Unity, Dhaka, Bangladesh.

BLAST (Bangladesh Legal Aid Services and Trust). 2009. "BLAST vs. Bangladesh and others ['CHT Courts' Case] Writ Petition No. 606 of 2006," 61 DLR (2009) 109. Accessed. http://www.blast.org.bd/issues/adivasi/198.

CEDAW/C/BGD/Q/7. 2011, Concluding Observation of the Committee on the Elimination of Discrimination Against Women, Bangladesh, United Nations Convention on the Elimination of Discrimination Against Women, 4 February, para. 28, 4. Accessed. http://www2.ohchr.org/english/bodies/cedaw/docs/co/CEDAW-C-BGD-CO-7.pdf.

CEDAW/C/BGD/Q/7/Add. 1. 2011. List of issues and questions with regard to the consideration of periodic reports, Pre-session working group, Committee on the Elimination of Discrimination Against Women, 17 January–4 February. Accessed. http://tbinternet.ohchr.org/_layouts/treatybodyexternal/Download.aspx?symbolno=CEDAW%2FC%2FBGD%2FQ%2F7%2FADD.1andLang=en.

Chakma, Bhumitra. 2010. "The Post-Colonial State and Minorities: Ethnocide in the Chittagong Hill Tracts, Bangladesh." *Commonwealth and Comparative Politics* 48(3): 291.

Chakma, Kabita, ed. 2001. *Diary of Kalpana Chakma*. Dhaka, Bangladesh: Hill Women's Federation.

Chakma, Samari. 2010. "Untitled." Translated by Hana Shams Ahmed. In *Between Ashes and Hope: Chittagong Hill Tracts in the Blind Spot of Bangladesh Nationalism*, edited by Naeem Mohaiemen, 19–20. Dhaka, Bangladesh: Drishtipat Writers' Collective.

Chakma, Sugata. 2004. "*Parbatya chattagramer bibhinna bhasha o upabhashar moulik shabda sangraha ebang bishleshan purbak tader prathamik shrenikarn*" [Collection of basic vocabulary of different languages and dialects of the Chittagong Hill Tracts and their primary classification]. *Upajatiya Gabeshana Patrika* (Research Journal of Tribal Cultural Institute) 3. Rangamati, Bangladesh: Tribal Cultural Institute.

Chakma, Tandra. 2011. *Bangladesh National Women's Development Policy 2011: Subject Indigenous Women* [Bangladesh Nari Unnayan Niti 2011: Prasanga Adibasi Nari]. 21 August. http://w$study.com/?p=2247.

Chakraborty, Eshani. 2004. "Understanding Women's Mobilization in the Chittagong Hill Tracts Struggle: The Case of Mahila Samiti." Paper presented at the 15th Biennial Conference of the Asian Studies Association of Australia, Canberra, Australia, 29 June–2 July.

Chittagong Hill Tracts Commission, The. 1991. *Life Is Not Ours: Land and Human Rights in the Chittagong Hill Tracts Bangladesh*. Copenhagen: IWGIA.

———. 2011. "CHT Commission Concludes Sixth Mission." Press Release, 30 November.

Chowdhury, Elora Halim. 2011. *Transnationalism Reversed: Women Organizing against Gendered Violence in Bangladesh*. Albany: State University of New York Press.

Chowdhury, Najma. 2001. "The Politics of Implementing Women's Rights in Bangladesh." In *Globalization, Gender and Religion: The Politics of Women's Rights in Catholic and Muslim Contexts*, edited by Jane H Bayes and Nayereh Tohidi, 203–230. New York: Palgrave.

Dabinama (demands) of the HWF, May 1995. 2001. In *Kalpana Chakmar Diary* [Diary of Kalpana Chakma], edited by Kabita Chakma et al., 50. Dhaka, Bangladesh: Hill Women's Federation.

Dewan, Ilira. 2011. "Hill Women in Exercising their Rights: Media, Management and Institutions" [*Khamata carchai pahari nari: ganamadhyam, byabastha o pratishthan*]. In *Jum Paharer Adhikar* (Rights of Jum Hills). Dhaka, Bangladesh: Shuddhasbar.

Eskildsen, Tom. 2012. "Doorbar Network in CHT: Women Joining Hands to Break Down Walls and Transform Society." In *The Jumma Voice*, 75–79. Seoul: Jumma Peoples Network—Korea.

Gain, Philip. 2000. "Women in CHT: Some Facts." In *The Chittagong Hill Tract: Life and Nature at Risk*, edited by Philip Gain, 94–95. Dhaka, Bangladesh: Society for Environment and Human Development.

Guhathakurata, Meghna. 1997. "Overcoming Otherness and Building Trust: The Kalpana Chakma Case." In *Living on the Edge: Essays on the Chittagong Hill Tracts*, edited by Subir Bhaumik et al., 109–125. New Delhi: South Asia Forum for Human Rights.

———. 2001. "Women's Narratives from the Chittagong Hill Tracts." In *Women, War and Peace in South Asia: Beyond Victimhood to Agency*, edited by Rita Manchanda, 252–293. New Delhi: Sage Publications/South Asia Forum for Human Rights.

Halim, Sadeka. 2010. "Insecurity of Indigenous Women." In *Between Ashes and Hope: Chittagong Hill Tracts in the Blind Spot of Bangladesh Nationalism*, edited by Naeem Mohaimeen, 183–189. Dhaka, Bangladesh: Drishtipat Writers' Collective.

Hossain, Hameeda. 2011. "Bangladesh: Women Development Policy—Pushing the Boundaries." *Daily Star*, 4 April. Accessed. http://www.thedailystar.net/suppliments/2011/anniversary/part7/pg1.htm.

HSB (Health and Science Bulletin) 9, 2. June 2011. Maternal Mortality and Health Care Survey 2010. Dhaka, Bangladesh: International Centre for Diarrhoeal Disease Research, Bangladesh.

HWF. 1995. *"Hill Women Federationer 1st kendriya sanmelaner dak: nari adhikar pratishthar sangrame egiye asun"* (Call of the First Convention of the Hill Women's Federation: Join the movement of establishment of women's rights)," 15 January, Town Hall, Khagrachari.

———. 1999. *Silenced Voices: Oppression and Resistance of Hill Women* [Paharer rudhhakantha: pahari narider nipiran o pratirodh]. Dhaka, Bangladesh: Hill Women's Federation.

International Council of the Indigenous Peoples of CHT (ICIP-CHT), 7 August 2012, a letter to the Prime Minister of Bangladesh include raising concern on restriction of entry to Bangladesh of an international aid worker who works in the CHT.

IRIN (a service to the UN office for the coordination of humanitarian affairs). 2011. "Bangladesh: Health Indicators Lag in Chittagong Hill Tracts." 14 July. Accessed. http://irinnews.org/report.aspx?reportid=93224.

IWGIA. 2012a. "Bangladesh: Indigenous Women form a Network Aiming at Realizing their Rights through United Movement." *International Work Group for Indigenous Affairs*, April 4. Accessed April 4, 2012. http://www.iwgia.org/news/search-news?news_id=566.

———. 2012b. "Militarization in the Chittagong Hill Tracts, Bangladesh: The Slow Demise of the Regions Indigenous Peoples." *International Work Group for Indigenous Affairs*, May. Accessed. http://www.iwgia.org/news/search-news?news_id=568.

Karim, Lamia. 2004. "Democratizing Bangladesh: State, NGOs, and Militant Islam." *Cultural Dynamics* 16(2/3): 291–318.

———. 2008. "Demystifying Micro-credit: The Grameen Bank, NGOs, and Neoliberalism in Bangladesh." *Cultural Dynamics* 20(1): 5–29.

Keokradong: The Mouthpiece of the Hill Students Council [Pahari chattra parishader mukhapatra], 2 April, 1995.

Levene, Mark. 1999. "The Chittagong Hill Tracts: A Case Study in the Political Economy of 'Creeping Genocide.'" *Third World Quarterly* 20(2): 339–369.

Mohsin, Amena. 1997. *The Politics of Nationalism: The Case of the Chittagong Hill Tracts*. Dhaka, Bangladesh: University Press Limited.

Nasreen, Zobaida. 2006. "Abduction of Kalpana Chakma and Women's Movement in Bangladesh [Kalpana *Chakma apaharan o bangladesher nari andolan*]." In *Solidarity: Indigenous Peoples Have the Right to Territory Land and Natural Resources* [Sanghati: Adibasi anchal, bhumi o prakritik sampader upar adibasider adhikar nishcit karte habe], edited by Sanjeeb Drong. Dhaka: Bangladesh Indigenous Peoples Forum.

Nath, Samir Ranjan. 2001. "Enrollment and Literacy." In *Counting the Hills: Assessing Development in the Chittagong Hill Tracts*, edited by Mohammad Rafi and A. Mustaque R. Chowdhury. Dhaka, Bangladesh: The University Press Limited.

Progotir Pathey. 2010. *Bangladesh: Monitoring the Situation of Children and Women, Multiple Indicator Cluster Survey (MICS) 2009*. Vol. 1: *Technical Report*. Dhaka: Bangladesh Bureau of Statistics (BBS) and UN Children's Fund (UNICEF).

Rozario, Shanti. 2003. "Gender Dimension of Rural Change." In *Hands not Land: How Livelihoods Are Changing in Rural Bangladesh*, edited by K. A Toufique and C. Turton. Dhaka: Department for International Development, UK, and Bangladesh Institute of Development Studies.

UNDP. 2008, National Health Management Specialist, Dhaka, Bangladesh. 7 July. Accessed. http://jobs.undp.org/cj_view_job.cfm?job_id=5326.

———. 2009. "Socio-economic Baseline Survey of Chittagong Hill Tracts." Dhaka, Bangladesh: Chittagong Hill Tracts Development Facility.

CHAPTER 5

Solidarity through Dissidence

Violence and Community in Indian Cinema

ALKA KURIAN

In this chapter I examine cinematic portrayal of dissident friendships, in particular among women, located across differences of class, caste, faith, and ideological positions, expressed particularly during moments of extreme crisis. I aim to investigate the persistence of these antihegemonic solidarities between the privileged and those located in communities decimated as a result of communal and state-led violence. To illuminate my thesis I will investigate cinematic narratives set against two of the most challenging periods in the history of contemporary India: the 2002 anti-Muslim attacks in Gujarat and the 1970s suppression of the Naxalite movement. In the first instance, I will look at Nandita Das's *Firaaq* (2009) that explores the plight of the Muslims during the 2002 Islamophobic communal flare-up in the country. Second, I will explore Govind Nihalani's *Hazaar Chaurasi Ki Ma* (1998) and Sudhir Mishra's *Hazaaron Khawishein Aisi* (2001), both of which take on board the 1970s brutal suppression of the Naxalite resistance movement at the hands of the hegemonic imperialistic Indian state.

In their deliberate distancing from majoritarian, mainstream, and industrial filmmaking style, *Firaaq* and *Hazaar Chaurasi Ki Ma* could be classed as parallel, art, or middle cinema, that is, a genre of cinema that refuses the crutch of sentimentalism to illuminate the systemic regime of oppression perpetrated against the country's minority communities or their antiestablishment resistance forces. Popular among a sizeable section of the urban middle-class India, this style of film has recently acquired other appellations, including *Hatke* Cinema for being located outside Bollywood's "star" hierarchy and the country's mainstream award system, or multiplex cinema for being screened in small-sized, upscale, multiplex theaters located in India's gleaming shopping malls. The "thinking" sections of the educated class of Indians are attracted by the alternative cinematic narratives offered by this genre of films, deemed more "authentic" than the so-called song-and-dance formulaic commercial cinema. Usually shot on location, most of the roles in these films are played by nonactors.

Hazaaron Khwaishein Aisi, on the other hand, falls very much within the category of crossover cinema, which, while exploring the cracks and fissures within neoliberal, postcolonial India, combines filmmaking practices of middle and commercial cinema with the aim of appealing to a wider section of the population. This can be gauged by its reliance on Bollywood's star power and formulaic filmmaking strategies through casting well-known Bollywood actors and including nondiegetic songs, powerful dialogues, exaggerated acting style, expensive sets, etc. This star-studded film, for example, garnered the country's prestigious and glamorous Filmfare "Best Story" award, and one of its central male actors, Shiney Ahuja (now a popular Bollywood actor), won the Filmfare "Best Debut" award.

Despite the films' formal differences, they all foreground the construction of subjectivities of women who rise above their situation of privilege through forging with members of minority communities bonds of sympathy and solidarity. In my discussion, I am informed by Elora Chowdhury's (2011) understanding of the politics of solidarity where it is not just goodwill or a hollow commitment alone to concepts of secularism and pluralism by the privileged that counts: what matters more is their tangible support and assistance to the disadvantaged. Real transformation, asserts Chowdhury, will not transpire until people undertake to critically interrogate the ways in which others have been disadvantaged as a result of their hegemonic cultures and reach out to them in a meaningful gesture of assistance. Solidarity and self-determination go hand in hand and necessarily involve working across difference by renouncing one's class-based privileges. My chapter also draws on Uma Narayan (1988), who argues in favor of the moral and political necessity of working across differences "in the elements of background and identity [as they] can be enriching resources, epistemologically, politically and personally" (32). And finally, I rely on Leela Gandhi's (2006) political articulations on the significance of anti-imperialistic relationships that took shape in Europe to elaborate my arguments on dissident friendships as an expression of "an improvisational politics appropriate to communicative, sociable utopianism, investing it with a vision of radical democracy" (C. F. Andrews 1914, cited in Gandhi 2006, 19).

Anti-Hindutva Dissidence

Indian cinema's fascination with Islam, Islamic ethos, and the Muslim culture—Urdu language, literature, and poetry—dates back to the 1947 Partition of the Indian subcontinent and the creation of Pakistan. There have been various genres of Islamicate films ranging from Muslim historicals that focus on the Islamic high life, its glory and decadence, and Muslim socials that center on Muslim lives, love, marriage, and family. Over the past decade or so, however, there has been a marked shift in Muslim representation in popular mainstream Indian cinema where the narrative is structured in a way to simultaneously center and "other" Indian Muslim subjectivities. This shift in Muslim representation is put in place through strategies of their exoticization (highlighting Islamic decadence), marginalization (relegating the Muslim presence to the margins), or demonization (portraying the Muslims in negative roles) (Chadha and Kavoori 2008, 134).

Firaaq could be seen as an example of a nonmainstream filmmaker's response to popular representations of the othering/demonization of Muslims in the context of the growing tensions in the 1990s between Muslim minorities and Hindu fundamentalists. The film is set against the ramifications of the 2002 accidental burning of a train carriage in which nearly sixty Hindus perished followed by statewide anti-Muslim attacks. The Hindu train passengers were traveling back home in Gujarat after offering their voluntary services in the rebuilding of the Rama Birth temple in Ayodhya.[1] The then chief minister of Gujarat, Narendra Modi, made unsubstantiated remarks about Pakistan's involvement in the torching of the train, a comment that was followed by the unleashing of a violent spate of anti-Muslim attacks throughout the state that left more than 2,500 Muslims dead and nearly a quarter of a million Muslims forever displaced. A tragedy of this scale shocked those who believed in the country's secularism rooted in the tradition of respect and tolerance of India's minorities.

Other films that have dealt with this theme are Rahul Dholakia's crossover feature film *Parzania: Heaven and Hell on Earth* (2005) and Rakesh Sharma's documentary film *Final Solution* (2005). Both films offer a searing critique of the Hindutva-led anti-Muslim violence in Gujarat, the so-called crucible of Hindutva hegemony. Their contribution in unraveling the mask of hypocrisy from the face of a democratic, shining India, is laudatory indeed. What is worrying, however, are representational gaps in these narratives, in particular their inadequate portrayal of expressions of friendship, compassion, and solidarity by nonradical Hindu subjectivities toward the Muslims. Despite the filmmakers' claim to offer a dispassionate exploration of the situation, they end up representing the majority Hindu masculinities as barbaric, jingoistic, and inhuman as a collectivity. Also, their focus on cultural explanations, sweeping under the carpet questions of class and economy, are equally unsatisfactory. They focus, therefore, on the erasure of people's humanity during crises and not on the rise of forces of resistance that have the potential to disrupt people's savagery. Dholakia's *Parzania* portrays a White American scholar rescuing a middle-class Parsi family so that representation of sectarian and ideological moderation is located outside the Muslim minority—Hindu fundamentalism equation. Furthermore, in his unapologetic assessment of the Hindutva savagery, Rakesh Sharma's *Final Solution* alludes to moderate Hindus only in passing.

Nandita Das's *Firaaq*, while sharing its ideological agenda with Sharma's and Dholakia's films, is different in that its narrational focus includes expressions of dissent against heteronormative Hindutva forces through proactive acts of solidarity among a plethora of classed, sectarian, and gendered characters: this underlines the film's subversiveness. It offers a nuanced representation as, despite the nobility of their intentions, lower-/working-class subjectivities struggle to maintain dissident connections across sectarian and class divides, while secularity and class privilege buffer middle-class members from the unfolding communal tension and violence. However, despite its insistence on the precariousness of such cross-communal harmony, *Firaaq* must be recognized for its exploration of the ways in which a complex intersection of class, faith, and hegemonic ideology simultaneously subjugates the other as well as opens up for it possibilities of dissent. The film debunks the idea of essentialized, universalized, and ahistorical antagonisms among people and offers creative ways in which individuals come together in relationships of dissident friendships, as they unplug their rootedness in family, community, faith, or ideology, in spite of their relative class privilege/disadvantage. In this process, they "defiantly" breach strategies of divisions, censure, elimination, and marginalization put into effect by modern oppressive states, thereby expressing their "non-violent resistance through an anarchist politics of immediate conjunction, coalition, and collaboration between the most unlikely of associates" (Gandhi 2006, 20).

Synopsis of the Film

Firaaq is Das's directorial debut film and focuses on the impact of the anti-Muslim violence on the lives of a diverse group of people and their interpersonal relationships. It articulates its narrative from multiple points of view—Hindu, Muslim, male, female, young, and old—as it puts into perspective their search for and construction of their identity. Set in Gujarat, a month after the 2002 carnage, the film's narrative unravels over a period of twenty-four hours the physical and emotional journeys of those who perpetrated violence, those who suffered violence, those who did not quite know what to make of it, and those who watched silently. The film traces five sets of relationships intersected by multiple locations of class, religion, gender, and ideology—some of them intersect each other while others remain independent. The opening scene in the film shows truckloads of corpses (of men, women, and children) being dumped in a Muslim graveyard. Munna the grave-digger looks overwhelmed and panic-stricken, his uncle seeming to be on a breaking point. The narrative quickly shifts to Ahmadabad a month after the carnage. A young working-class Muslim couple, Muneera and Hanif, take stock of their house that has been burnt down during the attacks. The loss takes a toll on Muneera's friendship with and loyalty to her best friend Jyoti, whose family, Hanif suspects, was responsible for torching their house. A lower middle-class Hindu housewife Aarti, living in an abusive patriarchal joint family and victim of domestic violence, is haunted by the memory of a badly wounded Muslim woman whom she had not been able to shelter during the anti-Muslim attacks. Aarti tries to make amends by unsuccessfully taking under her wing a little Muslim boy, Mohsin, orphaned during the attacks. On the eve of their relocation to Delhi, a middle-class man, Sameer Shaikh, discusses with his Hindu wife, Anuradha Desai, whether running away from the site of violence will really free him from the burden of his Muslim identity. An idealistic elderly musician, Khan Saheb, refuses to fault religious tension in the city for the dwindling number of his students, to the exasperation of his caretaker/friend Karim. And finally a group of working-class men, including Hanif, tries to settle scores with the Hindus through violence, an effort that ends in tragedy. While the film illuminates expressions of solidarity among a multiplicity of subjectivities, this chapter restricts itself to the forging of such bonds among women.

Dissidence through Solidarity

Muneera and Hanif's world appears to come to an end as they step foot inside their charred house. They have lost everything in the fire, including a large amount of borrowed money that Muneera had secreted away in an old tin can in the kitchen. The future looks frightful, and Hanif suspects foul play on the part of Mehul, Muneera's Hindu friend Jyoti's brother. The force of his anguish and despair at their loss confuses Muneera so that she ends up internalizing his suspicion, which would later put her friendship with Jyoti under enormous strain. However, unaware of the couple's misgivings, Jyoti brings them food, offers to look after their baby, helps clean the house, and organizes for Muneera a henna application job at a Hindu wedding. Jyoti, in this regard, does all that she can to comfort her friend during this moment of tragedy even though she is troubled by the latter's continuously questioning gaze. It would be useful to examine the dynamics between Muneera and Jyoti by exploring the idea of "friendship between women" emanating from disparate backgrounds, as elaborated by Elora Chowdhury (2011) in her analysis of Triti Umrigar's novel *The Space Between Us* where she makes useful observations on the politics of dissident friendship or solidarity among women across difference. Inspired by transnational feminist analysis, in particular that offered in Kumkum Sanghari's essay "Consent, Agency, and Rhetoric of Incitement" and Leela Gandhi's book *Affective Communities*, Chowdhury complicates the notion of solidarity by defining it in the following two ways: On the one hand, it can be understood as an expression of philosophical commitment by members of the majority community to notions of pluralism and secularism. On the other hand, solidarity can be defined in terms of proactive offers of assistance—rather than "goodwill" alone—by those who disregard their situation of privilege and reach out to the victims of their hegemonic culture, at times even at the cost of their personal safety. For example, while underlining Jyoti's working-class background, which is possibly not too dissimilar to Muneera's, the filmmaker's camera captures Jyoti's awareness of and the resultant discomfort with the privilege that comes to her simply because of her majority Hindu credentials, something that she uses nonetheless to their collective advantage. She makes sure, for example, to swap, when required, her bindi[2] between herself and Muneera as she gives a ride to her friend—without the knowledge of their families—on her two-wheeler scooter, steering her through crowded streets, past various police checkpoints, all the way to the wedding house for the henna application job. While the bindi swapping action on Jyoti's part in itself is seemingly innocuous, given the context of the communal tensions, however, the absence on her forehead of the bindi can potentially jeopardize her own safety. However, the expression of her political agency as an "ethical agent" surfaces her "ethico-existential capacity for the radical expropriation for self-othering" (Gandhi 2006, 20) and her action therefore becomes subversive in that it illustrates a deliberate fracturing and manipulation of iconic religious symbols. On the one hand, the resultant fluidity of identities is used by Jyoti as a measure of precaution in a place where the Muslims are being hounded by the state's coercive arm. On the other, it signals the futility of religious markers that separate and alienate people with a common racial, cultural, and historical heritage.

It is important, however, not to romanticize this dissident friendship and to point out its relative ineffectiveness as there are several challenges that come in their way. The relationship between Jyoti and Muneera is marked and shaped by patriarchal oppression. While the relative anonymity of the city enables Jyoti to navigate through its streets (including at night), her gendered self loses agency, as she has to hide Muneera's presence in her house inhabited by her radical right-wing patriarchal brother. As a result, while *Firaaq* refuses to essentialize the majority-minority communities by articulating "contrapuntal perspectives" (cited in Chowdhury 2011) that center the human connection between people from heterogeneous communities, its location within the context of class-based patriarchal oppression chips away at its efficacy.

In another moment in the film's narrative, Aarti's attempts at sheltering the orphaned Mohsin come under enormous strain. Both Aarti and Mohsin have been traumatized by the recent events. She is troubled by the memory of the wounded Muslim woman she was not able to shelter in her household controlled by her abusive, right-wing Hindu fundamentalist husband. Most of Mohsin's family has been killed during the communal carnage. In him Aarti sees her redemption. In her tenderness, Mohsin recognizes a mother that he has lost. She gives him a Hindu name of Mohan as a measure of precaution, feeds him, and soothes his injured forehead. He shares with her the burden of witnessing his family's murder. This connection between them, nonetheless, has to be evaluated within the politics of religion, class, and gender, and Das unambiguously portrays the unfathomable gulf that separates them: not only is his Muslim identity stripped away but also can he only be recognized within the subordinate position of a servant boy. Despite Aarti's unambiguous compassion for him, her oppression undermines her agency so that, bullied and terrorized by her husband, her son, her brother-in-law, and her father-in-law, she hovers at the margins of her household, watching through barred kitchen windows, as Mohsin runs away from her clutches. And when Aarti does step over the threshold of her home, and leaves her husband, rejecting in the process her unacknowledged subservience to patriarchy, it is too late, as she will never be able to find Mohsin, lost among thousands of refugees scattered across the city. While Das's film complicates simplistic binaries of communitarian identities and offers an insight into complex intersection between classed and sectarian communities that shape possibilities of alliance among disparate people, the narrative falls short of comprehensively evaluating dissident friendships across cultures, dissipating in the process the force of the filmmaker's contention that "in the midst of all this madness, some find it in their hearts to sing hopeful songs of better times" (Das 2011).

Such examples of "dissident friendships" (Leela Gandhi, cited in Chowdhury 2011) nevertheless fissure commonly held perceptions of sectarian communities as bifurcated into simplistic binaries of "oppressed" and "oppressor" or "colonized" and "colonizer." They help us unravel the processes through which members from diverse groups, despite being asymmetrically located within the social hierarchy, resist this politics of hate. It can be argued that "dissident affinities," established among disparate people from diverse conditions and power hierarchies—for example between Jyoti and Muneera and Aarti and Mohsin—help them better understand the other as well as themselves through their response to violence rooted in a "sense of collective desire and hope to understand this complex and violent world we inhabit and a palpable need for peace" (Das 2011). And even though such relationships are not entirely effective, it would be useful to think through them with the view to unpicking the fragility of the colonized/colonizer binary and to understand how, through resistance to neocolonial processes colonizing people's minds and bodies, they articulate possibilities for social and political transformation—either individually or collectively. Chowdhury insists that rather than "pity, condescension, or self-righteousness," these dissident friendships must be understood as "a gesture towards human connection" (2011, 3) so as to realize "a politics based on concrete heartfelt understanding of what it means to be Other" (Adrienne Rich, cited in Chowdhury 2011, 3). It is in its recognition of plurality of subjectivities and situations that friendship sets off a process of self-reflection by means of which one is able to work one's way across difference and enter into a "human connection that nourishes self-growth as well as fosters community" (Cherrie Moraga, cited in Chowdhury 2011, 5). Das's film suggests, therefore, several possibilities of "dissident friendships" that, given their "'overlapping' and 'intertwined' histories and realities" (Chowdhury 2011, 2), signal the weakness of the Hindutva hegemony.

The Naxalite Uprising

The Naxalite or Naxalbari movement, variously referred to as a peasant uprising, an urban middle-class youth rebellion, or the culmination of the Indian communist movement, unambiguously endorsed the belief that social and political transformation—both personal and collective—is possible through collective resistance rooted in dissident solidarity among a cross-section of people. The genesis of this movement lay in the May 1967 police atrocities committed in the Naxalbari area, West Bengal. Ten agricultural workers, claiming their rightful share of the season's harvest from the landowner, were ruthlessly killed by the police. The event lit the fuse of a simmering discontentment in the region and under the guidance of the Communist Party of India (Marxist), took the shape of a widespread, armed uprising of agricultural and tea-garden workers. The state of West Bengal witnessed an unprecedented outpouring of solidarity toward the agriculturalists by urban artists and intellectuals who, outraged at the slaying of the peasants, carried out mass demonstrations and organized meetings to think through strategic ways of supporting the peasants' struggle. Inspired by the 1949 Chinese Revolution, the Naxalites and their supporters challenged the forces of neocolonialism and the continuing hold of feudalism. India's decolonization was meaningless, they claimed, if large sections of the country's poor (agriculturalists, tribals, workers) were evicted from their ancestral land, forced into debt-bondage, treated as criminals, and had their basic human dignity removed. The Naxalites set off an antiestablishment "armed peoples' war" against the Indian state, which they saw as the "primary enemy of the people," so as to bring about "peoples' democracy." Mobilizing landless peasants and casual workers and instilling within them class consciousness, they urged them to take over the state and decimate the class enemy (the police, industrialists, businessmen, landowners, and politicians). In her support of the specific form of tribal dissidence that unraveled in the process, Mahasweta Devi claims, "I think that as far as the tribals or the oppressed are concerned, violence is justified. The system resorts to violence when people rise to redress some grievance, to protest. India is supposed to be a non-violent country. But in this country, how many firings, and how many killings by bigots take place every year? When the system fails an individual has a right to take to violence or any other means to get justice. The individual cannot go on suffering in silence" (cited in Spivak 1995, xi–xvii). The coercive arm of the imperialistic Indian state, however, responded by brutally crushing the movement, whereby a large number of Naxalite leaders were incarcerated, tortured, disappeared, or killed. This, along with political differences among the activists, weakened the movement so that it collapsed by 1975, the year when the state imposed the Emergency rule in the country.

Some of the most significant works on Naxalbari (Banerjee 1980, 1984; Ray 1988) characterize it as an urban middle-class movement. While these works no doubt illuminate the economic, political, and cultural background to the movement, what is glaringly absent in these writings is the expression of solidarity put forth by female Naxalites in this resistance movement, in the process undermining the party's progressive image. This is all the more puzzling given the nineteenth-century women's education that was slowly transforming private and public gender relations in the country (Sinha Roy 2010). Equally surprising is their indifference to women's involvement in transnational revolutions—in China and Russia—that had inspired the Naxalite intelligentsia in the first place. Elaborating on the contribution of rural Naxalites, Edward Duyker's work (1987) too falls short of acknowledging women's participation despite his claim that "whole families of Santals joined the movement . . . [and] kinship organization began to parallel guerilla organization . . . husband/wife, uncle/nephew, and father/son relationships existed in . . . Bolpur and Illambazar action squad" (cited in Sinha Roy 2010, 27). The disregard of gender as a crucial unit of analysis resulted in the erasure of the culture of dissident friendships and solidarity among and by female activists toward the movement, leading to their "double marginalization," dissipating in the process the history of radical feminine activism (Sinha Roy 2010, 27). While Mallarika Sinha Roy's debunking of an essentially masculinist nature of the Naxalite movement is comforting, her reference to feminine participation as "magic moments" is disconcerting. This is because, rather than being sporadic or occasional—as Sinha Roy's notion of magic moments would tend to suggest—women's participation in social and political struggle resulted from their sustained and collaborative resistance against institutional oppression (Sawant 2011).

In 1967, seven Naxalite women died during a police shooting of an armed peasant protest in the Naxalbari area. Dominant historiography, however, has tended to sideline women's contribution despite ample evidence of their dedication to the Naxalite movement where they worked as leaders, in women's armed groups, or in guerilla squads (Sinha Roy, 2010). Feminine presence in the movement mobilized support from school and college girls, most of whom had never been exposed to left-wing politics. Women Naxalites became role models for members of their families, including spouses, which launched political careers for many of them: some went in for full assimilation with marginalized workers and peasants, others filled the ranks of the movement, and still others passed on secret messages, or simply chose to house wounded Naxalites.

Most of the films made on the subject of the Naxalite rebellion have also tended to foreground city-based masculinities either romanticizing, supporting, or directly engaging with this powerful left-inspired antiestablishment movement in the country. Films by Satyajit Ray and Mrinal Sen are counted as significant markers in this area.[3] The cinematic narratives that I would like to explore in this section are different in that they foreground feminine contributions to this revolutionary movement. Govind Nihalani's *Hazaar Chaurasi Ki Ma* (*HCKM*) (1988) and Sudhir Mishra's *Hazaaron Khawishein Aisi* (*HKA*) (2003), for example, offer a sustained critique of this middle-class masculinist history and its cinematic representations. Crucial to my understanding of the construction of the feminine Naxalite subjectivity are women's efforts at alleviating pain and suffering through the fundamental human emotion of empathy and friendship. I argue that such emotions, apart from having been relegated to the margins, have not been adequately explored in the elaboration of dissident grass-roots social movements. This omission is all the more inexcusable because it fails to recognize the "thick" or embedded nature of ethico-political agency of the initiators of these bonds who, conscious of their "ethical obligations to all those who are not part of [their] own nation, family, republic, revolution" perform their dissident deviancy despite being put at "risk precisely from those who are questionably [their] own" (Gandhi 2006, 24–25).

Synopses of the Films

Nihalani's *Hazaar Chaurasi Ki Ma,* set in the 1970s, relates the story of a middle-class woman, Sujata Chatterji, whose Naxalite son, Brati Chatterji, and four of his comrades, including his best friend Somu, have been killed in a savage police-instigated attack. Afraid of losing his family's honor, Sujata's philandering husband, Dibyanath Chatterji, has the event hushed up. Sujata grieves not only the loss of her son but also her blindness to his work with the socioeconomically marginalized sections of the society. As the Chatterjis get on with their lives, Sujata reaches out to Somu's mother and Brati's girlfriend Nandini to learn the truth about Brati's Naxalite past. She begins to openly question her husband's hypocrisy and refuses to perform her duty as a wife and mother. On the day of their daughter Tuli's engagement, while the party is on, Sujata's appendix, the condition of which she had been concealing for years, bursts. Over time, Sujata and Dibyanath make peace with each other and, together, they work in a human rights office to carry forward Brati's work. The film ends on a dramatic note: one of Brati's Naxalite friends is shot dead by a couple of unnamed men in front of Sujata, who in turn lunges toward them, catching hold of one of them, not letting him go until she is assisted by passersby.

Set in the 1970s, too, Mishra's *Hazaaron Khwaishein Aisi* centers on the lives of three Delhi University students. The upper-middle-class Naxalite Siddhartha Tayyabji relocates to Bihar to work with the peasants, leaving his lover Geeta behind in Delhi. Geeta's secret admirer, the lower-middle-class Vikram Malhotra has no faith in the Naxalite ideology and follows his dream to become a successful business man in Delhi. Geeta divorces her husband Arun to join Siddhartha and, once in the village, begins to work along with the peasants, giving them lessons in literacy, both of them doing their work secretively. The police finally catch up with them: Siddhartha is brutally beaten up and Geeta is raped. Rescued by Arun's political connections, Geeta pleads with Vikram to get Siddhartha out of jail. In the meanwhile, however, with the help of his Naxalite comrades, Siddhartha escapes from jail and Vikram pays the price for this by being savagely attacked by the police. Siddhartha relocates to London, and Geeta goes back to work with the village women, taking along a severely brain-damaged Vikram.

Gendered Dissent from Within

HCKM and *HKA* characterize masculine Naxalite politics as essentially rhetorical, rooted in a pedantic understanding of suffering and oppression, and therefore ineffectual. The quintessentially Naxalite Brati (in *HCKM*)—male, middle-class, college-bred, intellectually gifted—is keen on eradicating asymmetrical wealth distribution and injustice through a class-based revolution. Unfortunately, all that he has to offer is his goodwill and intentions. Not only does he lack the "epistemic privilege" of the oppressed but also he has an abstract understanding of the Naxalite ideology. Behind closed doors of the party office, he and his middle-class "comrades" debate the Naxalite strategy, cut off from the real meaning of lived oppression, indulging in abstract intellectualism, and as informed revolutionaries (Bhatia 2005, 1540), they attempt to control from afar. Some talk about annihilating the class enemy through solidarity with the urban poor, while others insist on mobilizing the villagers to bring down the state apparatus in the cities. Eventually they all fall victim to internal differences and are brutally massacred.[4] As a bleeding-heart revolutionary, Brati hovers on the verge of social transformation, desperate to embrace the metaphorical reward that came with solidarity with the downtrodden: martyrdom. In reality, though, it turns out to be an empty and reckless death, turning Naxalite solidarity into a mere fantasy for the young.

The central theme of *HCKM* is not Brati's revolutionary zeal but the "awakening of the apolitical mother," articulated through the character of his mother Sujata. Her deliberate and willful journey into her dead son's past radicalizes her consciousness, which helps her transition from dream space into wakefulness. If getting to the truth of Brati's life is important for Sujata, she can no longer keep away from "working together continuously across [her] differences" (Narayan 1988, 34). To make sense of Brati's disillusionment with life she must cross over the threshold of home and tradition and connect in a relationship of understanding and solidarity with Brati's friends located outside her caste and class privilege. Uma Narayan underlines the moral and political imperative of engaging in a conversation with and reaching across people from heterogeneous groups: "Both in political contexts and in the context of friendship, such differences in elements of background and identity can be enriching resources, epistemologically, politically, and personally. Learning to understand these differences can make more complex our understanding of ourselves and our societies, can broaden the range of our politics, and enrich the variety of connections we have as persons. But such efforts are not without cost" (1988, 32).

However, in order to initiate this process of crossing over and transformation, Sujata must first disengage herself from her present circumstances so that the coalitionary politics of equality, solidarity, self-definition, and hence dissidence, that she wishes to strive for, is founded on the negation of class-related privilege and entitlement that she inhabits. To recall Gandhi here, the mode of friendship with which she strikes out is "predicated upon a [suddenly acquired] principled distaste" for the politics of exclusivity practiced by her class that is convinced that "the promise of the good life for some requires consigning others to the . . . various inhospitable borders of modern civility" (2006, 29).

Having spoken for the first time with Nandini, Brati's girlfriend and political comrade, Sujata is struck by an unusual feminine consciousness in her—bold, self-assured, and more importantly, independent and free—which has an immediate impact on her. On the day of her daughter Tuli's engagement party, she confronts her husband on his philandering and refuses to put the kumkum[5] in the parting of her hair, rejecting in one go Hindu patriarchal notions of femininity and her self-inflicted and internalized sense of secondariness, emerging, consequently, as a politicized consciousness. During the party, appalled by the reveling family and friends, openly berating Brati and his idealistic politics, Sujata has a visceral reaction to the hypocrisy that surrounds her: she lets out a scream, bringing the celebration to an end. The unraveling of her body is precipitated by her despair so that the condition of her appendix, which she had been disregarding for years, resurfaces and bursts. The physical unbearability of her pain is significant in that it underlines a crucial moment of transition in her life. The sinister ways of the interlocking system of oppression—state, institutional, caste, and Bhadralok patriarchy—becomes suddenly clear in her eyes. Using her words as her weapon, Sujata accuses the middle-class complicity with the state apparatus for killing Brati and erasing the dissent of the marginal, the weak, and the subaltern. Unafraid of using her emotions to communicate her despair as "emotions must be taken seriously and not regarded as mere epiphenomenal baggage" (Annette Baier cited in Narayan 1988, 32) and rejecting the cold rationality of reason, Sujata undergoes a radical transformation so that the rupturing of her appendix sets off the process of decolonization of the self and centers her back within her mind, which was previously cluttered by the Bhadralok morality.

While the rest of the family moves on with their lives, in the stillness of the mind that follows Brati's death, Sujata willfully recalls and articulates his memories. This process becomes crucial for the politicization of her consciousness and to complete the "gaps, erasure, and misunderstanding of hegemonic masculinist history" so that she can carve out a "space for struggle and contestation about reality itself." Drawing on Dorothy Smith, Chandra Mohanty argues that "if the everyday world is not transparent and its relations of rule, its organizations and institutional frameworks, work to obscure and make invisible inherent hierarchies of power (Smith 1987 cited in Mohanty), it becomes imperative that we rethink, remember, and utilize our lived relations as a basis of knowledge. Writing (discursive production) is one site for the production of this knowledge and this consciousness." The inherently transformative process of remembering and speaking becomes for Sujata a crucial act of resistance that allows her to "write selfhood, consciousness, and identity back into daily life" (Mohanty 1991, 34–35). With the clarity of mind, she is able to see through the state's invidious attempts to misrepresent the truth and rewrite history as it destroys Brati's written words (poetry, posters, books) and masks its brutality by disposing of young bodies too soon. She also understands her husband's hand in the erasure of Brati's dissident voice by eliminating his name from the newspapers.

In her "Feminist Communities and Moral Revolution" chapter, Ann Ferguson underlines the need to deliberately create "oppositional communities" with "actual or imagined others" who reject dominant heteropatriarchal definitions of women/mothers and come together on a collective project for social transformation (1995, 372). Engaging with this project, argues Ferguson, involves reassessing one's belief system and reconstructing one's identity so as to break out of the negative stereotypes associated with femininity and become a "woman-identified-woman." By questioning and removing herself away from the trappings of the Bhadralok bourgeois heteronormative household, Sujata is able to engage "the very institutional power structures" (Mohanty 1991, 1) that had defined, circumscribed, and buffered her from the sinister world that Brati had been working on transforming. But Sujata's rebellious process of identity-politics must involve "affinities and political affiliations with those in other identity positions who share critiques of the dominant order" (Ferguson 1995, 371). Remorseful for not empathizing with Brati's politics during his lifetime,

Sujata initiates the act of putting together the essence of his world by crossing over to the other side of the borders where she seeks an alternative value system and structure of support to sustain her newly constructed self. But given the "historically constituted relations of power [and] privilege" that she inhabits, engaging in the act of friendship and solidarity with Brati's friends will never be easy; Sujata will be agonized by the sentiment of mistrust and rejection that she stumbles across as she reaches out to connect with the other. In other words, this "ethic of fidelity to strange friends" marked by the Epicurean "philoxenic solidarity" can only be performed at the profoundly existential risk of "self-exile" (Gandhi 2006, 29).

As a city-bred, educated, and already politicized consciousness, Nandini is a fully committed party member of the Naxalite movement who writes revolutionary poetry with Brati without, however, sympathizing with his excessive romanticism. She is not blind to the strength of their opponents and understands why, motivated by the very base human emotions of hunger for money and leadership, some of the party members might eventually betray the movement. Not only does she spot the traitor among them (disregarded by Brati and who would eventually lead to his murder), she also demonstrates her ideological tenacity by not divulging the whereabouts of her Naxalite comrades despite being viciously tortured in police custody. Sujata's act of reaching out to Nandini can be read at several levels: her desperation to vicariously know her dead son from his lover, her anguish at the deception within which her life had been mired and which Brati despaired, or her resolve to recognize the lives of people who are more disadvantaged than her, to empathize with their struggles even though she has nothing in common with them, and to eventually dismantle the oppressive structure of power.

But no sooner than Sujata makes forays into Nandini's world does she understand that as a member of the privileged class, it would take her much more than "good-will" to repair the historically fragmented lines of communication between the two world orders and systems of being: rich and poor, traditional and modern, political and apolitical, just and unfair, oppressor and oppressed. However, and this is the first wave of struggle she faces on crossing the border, as a member of the advantaged group, she is "wrong to expect [her willingness] to be sufficient to cause strong, historically constituted networks of distrust to simply evaporate into thin air. If anything, such good-will must help sustain communication through situations, issues and discussions which inevitably cause resurgence of mistrust" (Narayan 1988, 34). Sujata has now made peace with Brati's death and seals herself way from the hurt so that when she says to

Nandini that the previous uncertainties and danger appeared to have passed, Nandini points out the older woman's blindness to the poison that continues to lurk beneath the surface. Sujata must know why Brati died.

> **NANDINI:** Like always, you never know. You people are oblivious to what happens. Events occur and are forgotten . . . We were betrayed . . . it is still going on. You may feel that the arrests have stopped just because newspapers are silent about them. It doesn't mean that what is not reported is not happening . . . The same injustice and tyranny continues. Behind the shield of silence, a whole generation between the ages of 16–40 has been wiped out. A generation that picked up arms on behalf of the poor, demanded land for the landless, and liberation for the oppressed, a generation that had the courage and dream to change the whole system . . .
> **SUJATA:** But it is more peaceful than before . . .
> **NANDINI:** (*shaking Sujata by the shoulders*) No, no. Never say that! There was no peace ever. And won't be in future. It is like the stillness inside a police morgue, a silk sheet covering a blood-soaked body. It is not peace, no.
> (*HCKM*, my translation)

Nandini's outburst against Sujata needs to be interpreted in the light of her deeply seated suspicion of the repressive state and its sinister allies that continue to haunt her: her body remembers the cost she has paid for what lies at the core of her being and ideological beliefs. She is more wounded by the callousness of the privileged Sujata's insistence about the political calm in the city than if the older woman had deliberately set out to hurt Nandini.

Sujata's middle-classness comes under suspicion by Somu's family too. Brati's loss brings her again and again to Somu's house, reevoking memories of the night the young were savagely killed in front of his family, repeatedly traumatizing Somu's mother who goes into loud fits of wailing. Somu's sister is deeply skeptical of her brother's abstract and inherently deathly—and therefore self-serving—ideology. Buried underneath Sujata's grief, she spots an essential greed of a privileged mother who laments the loss of her son but is oblivious to class oppression: murderous goons continue to lurk the neighborhood, preventing her from going out to work, crushing the family further with hunger. She yells at Sujata and her mother: "Somu, Somu, I am sick of Somu. Look at what he has done to us!"

The presents that Sujata brings for Somu's family—a gift to soothe a "sister's" misery—belie the bourgeoisie's moral commitment toward the poor and not for want of alternatives. She does not see the blind spots in her own philosophy that reinforce the inherent classism; focusing on her persecution as a woman/

mother, she deludes herself by considering the loss of Brati and Somu's lives as a homogenizing experience and, using the "ideology of common oppression" (hooks 2015, 9), she reaches out to the other woman in a relationship of "sisterhood," disregarding their class difference.

Clearly, like Brati, Sujata too does not share the "epistemic privilege" of Somu's family members—the historically oppressed and disadvantaged—who have "a more immediate, subtle and critical knowledge about the nature of their oppression" (Narayan 1988, 35). Uma Narayan complicates the category of "insider" and "outsider" to oppression by claiming that the insider to one kind of oppression can be a source of oppression to another and therefore becomes an outsider. "Explanatory theories and conceptual tools (like 'class structure' and 'patriarchy') that help us understand the specificities of a certain form of oppression and its link with other forms are often developed by people who are not members of the oppressed group and whose relative privilege in that regard has given them greater access to the means of theoretical reflection and production" (36).

Such a position, I argue, contradicts Narayan's previous understanding of the insider/outsider overlap and proceeds from the assumption that the oppressors are always privileged. Being simultaneously an insider (ideological) and outsider (class) to oppression, Nandini has unique insight into how oppression works. (Similarly in *Firaaq*, as a member of the Hindu majority community, despite her sectarian privilege, Jyoti does not have the conceptual tools to understand her own oppression at the hands of her brother. All that she has is an instinctive consciousness and not an elaborate theoretical perspective.)

I am willing to concede the validity of this analogy but what becomes problematic is the author's denial to the oppressed of "a detailed causal/structural analysis" of the basis of their oppression (Narayan 1988, 36). Despite being uneducated, Somu's mother (unlike Sujata) understands why her son, running from place to place just to stay alive, was brutally decimated for his beliefs. She is familiar with the wretchedness of life in the slums of Calcutta; she recognizes the exact processes of dispossession put in place by the privileged that take poor peoples' land away and relocate them along urban margins. The historical expulsion of millions of disenfranchised people (mostly tribals, peasants, and the adivasis) from their homeland by colonialists and neocolonialists is permanently traced within her physical and psychological makeup. Endorsing the resolve of the disposed—like Somu—to cross "over . . . to the side of armed struggle" (Arundhati Roy 2009, 166), she is not the one to be surprised at their anger, as she says: "Whenever [Somu] spoke, he was always rough, incensed! After being kicked around by everyone, a pauper has to turn rough and thick skinned, like a horse ... You've seen the poor's plight. How can one sit by idly and do nothing? Why should our blood not boil? So they agreed to join hands" (*HCKM*, my translation).

Sujata will need to rethink the structure of solidarity: Empowering herself as a woman will necessitate thinking through the "power-over dynamics that continue to exist between [her and Somu's mother] due to institutionalized and internalized ... ethnicism ... and classism" (Ferguson 1995, 375). It will mean recognizing that since her gendered identity is inextricably linked to her other identities (class, caste, and ethnic), she will need to engage with a multiplicity of communities of opposition. By opening her postretirement human rights office as a platform for establishing her political and emotional commitment toward working with and for the oppressed, she uses this as an opportunity to also deal with "the man question." She does not see herself as embedded within the "limited, liberal 'women's rights' individualistic focus" but in an all-encompassing, and "a more productive 'feminism as a philosophy'" tradition (Mohanty 1991, 8). As a result, rather than separating from or rejecting Dibyanath (as an oppressor), she pulls him along in her community work, which gives support to the likes of Nandini, who had initially rejected her. Clearly, this female solidarity stems form the "revolutionary love" among women despite their political, class, caste, and ideological differences from each other. Sujata demonstrates this revolutionary love by internalizing the ethics of social justice, constructing an imagined empathetic community with those who have been denied social justice, and making efforts to give up the class privilege so as to be able to meaningfully address social inequalities (Ferguson 1995, 382).

Geeta is portrayed in *HKA* as an eroticized desiring subject where, untroubled by social morality, and as and when needed, she relies on the various men in her life: for romantic gratification with Siddhartha (whom she loves), for stability with Arun (with whom she has a short-lived marriage), and for rescue with Vikram (who loves her). It is while in the village, where she frequently travels to be with Siddhartha, that she undergoes a radical transformation of the self as she becomes aware of the glaring disparities between her privileged self and the villagers. As a thoroughbred British university-educated cosmopolitan, she begins to make a difference by offering adult literacy classes to the village women and, in the process, reaches out to the other side of the class and caste divide. In the end, abandoning her wealthy, cosmopolitan life with Arun as well as domesticity with Siddhartha, she chooses the alternative space of independence. Like Sujata, the previously apolitical Geeta too witnesses the coming into being of her feminist identity based on a gradual politicization of her consciousness where her allegiance with Siddhartha is substituted with solidarity with the underprivileged. In the process, through this defiant politics of dissident solidarity with "foreigners, outsiders, and alleged inferiors," she ends up representing (and is later penalized for) "the politics of 'betrayal,' 'departure,' 'flight,' 'treason' ... [of] metropolitan anti-imperialists" (Gandhi 2006, 2).

Despite his firebrand demeanor, a Che-Gavaraesque nonchalance toward class privilege, the willingness to forge dissident alliances with his disadvantaged rural cocountrymen by immersing himself totally in the real site of oppression—the village—Siddhartha's revolutionary experiment fails. In spite of his goodwill to fracture the country's inequities through working across difference, he lacks the "epistemic privilege" of the subaltern and leaps blindly into a rather daunting ground reality. The traditional caste and class hierarchy is too powerful for the local people to shake off as they are anxious about violent retribution for collaborating with the Naxalites. As a result, Siddhartha is constantly on the run from the police, which leaves his politics of class solidarity in tatters. While Siddhartha's charm and revolutionary idealism had drawn Geeta toward him, she is disconcerted by being regularly abandoned by him in the city and, after relocating to the village, by the unraveling of his politics. Worse still, she is baffled with him deriding her practical method of bringing about self-sufficiency among rural women through adult literacy classes: these he refers to as a bourgeois feel-good factor.

As compared to Sujata, Geeta's politicization does not result from sharing secondhand, real-life stories of the subaltern but through a direct involvement with the poor where she experiences firsthand the true essence of marginalization, oppression, and sexual brutalization. Her dissident friendship and solidarity stemming from her work with the women and children of the village instills in her the spirit of the subaltern struggle, which helps shape the construction of her oppositional agency. Unlike Siddhartha, instead of getting frustrated by not being able to gain philosophical insights into the perennial hold of the oppressor over the oppressed,[6] Geeta takes a proactive role in demonstrating her commitment to the oppressed. One of the key scenes in the film signals her agency as a site of dissidence. The scene is set in the village Bhojpur where she now lives, and the time frame is 1975, the year the country was put under Emergency rule. Accused of murdering a policeman, the village men have all been put behind bars and their houses burnt by the police. The women, beside themselves, run in vain to the police station for help. Geeta and one of her Naxalite comrades from the city, Shankar, intervene in the situation and talk to the police.

THE POLICE INSPECTOR: (*to Shankar*) We know who you are. You are the one who is instigating the villagers. Trouble maker! Get the hell out! Or else I will shove saw-dust up your ass.

> **GEETA**: (*to the police officer, speaking in the village Hindi dialect*) There is no basis for the arrest of these men. They are simple laborers. Why did you arrest them?
> **POLICE INSPECTOR**: (*to Geeta*) They are not as simple as they look! These vermin killed a police officer near the rail track last night.
> **GEETA**: That's ridiculous. There is no evidence to support that.
> **POLICE INSPECTOR**: (*looking at her sari blouse*) So you are going to teach me about evidence? You know how serious an offense killing a police officer is?

Just then one of the female Naxalite comrades informs Geeta that the police officer who was deemed to have been "murdered" is alive after all. He was found inside a bullock cart, drunk, and singing at the top of his voice.

> **GEETA**: (*screaming in English at the police officer*) And you beat up and tortured an entire village for nothing!
> **POLICE INSPECTOR**: (*embarrassed and defensive*) Don't bloody show off your English! Someone was killed, wasn't he?
> **GEETA**: It could have been anybody! It could have been a guard who fell from a train!

The police inspector begins to walk away.

> **GEETA**: (*screaming even louder*) It could have been anybody, for God's sake! Who do they think you are? You are not Gods. (*HKA*)

Apart from underlying the gendered difference of Siddhartha and Geeta's expression of dissident solidarity toward the subaltern in the same village, this scene crucially highlights a general level of masculine erasure through arrest (of the village men), banishment (Shankar's from the police station), absence (Siddhartha's), or embarrassment (of the police inspector). As a result, what we see here is the "collective consciousness," agency, and solidarity among the women that overrides the masculine imperative of writing history, surfacing in the process, the "leakiness of [heteronormative] boundaries" (Gandhi 2006, 3). In lending her support and voice to the subaltern, Geeta takes on the abusive and corrupt state machinery.

Despite paying the price for her role in publicly humiliating the state (she is arrested and sexually brutalized by the police), unconsciously, Geeta's agentic-self proceeds to collaborate with victims of institutionalized abuse. Her former incentive to visit Bhojpur for Siddhartha is substituted by her dissident friendship toward the villagers. Unbeknownst to Siddhartha, whose misogynistic actions and condescending attitude toward Geeta can be traced back to the Naxalite Party politics,[7] Geeta quietly reaches out for sympathy and offers sympathy to those who, like her, are victimized by a system that marginalizes as it pretends to protect. This manifest omission on the part of a patriarchal Marxist Siddhartha represents his simultaneous rejection and reproduction of a feudal, masculinist, and neocolonial ideology. While he comprehends rural oppression that was rooted in the "landlessness of about 40 percent of rural population, the backbreaking usurious exploitations, the ever-growing evictions of poor peasantry coupled with the brutal social oppression... reminiscent of the medieval ages" (Sumit Kumar Ghosh 1992, 46, cited in Sinha Roy 2006, 213), he is blind to the ramifications of his sexist actions. In the end, a defeated Siddhartha apologizes to Geeta for having failed her in a place that had brought him nothing. By now, Geeta knows Siddhartha well enough to see through the compassionate façade of his patriarchal self. She says: "It's not about you anymore. *I* want to be here" (*HKA*). This gradual loss of self-belief in Siddhartha is a counterpart of Geeta's self-assuredness. She does not accompany him to London (where their son lives with Siddhartha's grandparents) and returns instead to Bhojpur to complete her work with the village women. Clearly, her dissident revolutionary politics is now firmly rooted in an ethical agency "tutored in the habits of invulnerability to the anarchic domain of desire and inclination" (Gandhi 2006, 21).

Conclusion

Firaaq, Hzaar Chaurasi Ki Maa, and *Hazaaron Khwaieshein Aisi* illuminate the surfacing of women's political agency, translated into the politics of dissident solidarity as a tool of resistance against oppression: class, caste, patriarchal, or neocolonial. A multiplicity of femininities in these films—Jyoti, Muneera, Aarti, Sujata, Nandini, Somu's mother, and Geeta—are portrayed as already politicized or endowed with a nascent germ of rebellion. Suppressed underneath various forms of subjugation, the women experience personal and communal transformation of their identities, bringing to the fore Patricia Jeffrey's contention that the "question is not whether women are victims or agents, but rather what sorts of agents can women be despite their subordination" (cited in Sinha Roy 2009a, 161). The films in this manner can be understood as part of the revisionist historical narratives both in theory and practice. Furthermore, the films do not pretend to excavate the feminine history as a "submerged territory" but by a careful interjection of women's narratives with the view to reinscribing and rewriting women's mobilization as a strategy of intervention in exploitative situations where they have, first and foremost, reached out to and worked with people across difference, with all the muddle and chaos that this dissidence might have entailed.

Notes

1. In 1992, under the leadership of the Bharatiya Janata Party, the sixteenth-century Babri mosque in Ayodhya, North India, was demolished by Hindu fundamentalists as the site was deemed to have been the birthplace of the god Rama. The Hindu pilgrims in the train had probably gone to Ayodhya to help construct the Rama temple.

2. A bindi is a spot on the forehead, marker of Hindu identity. Jyoti uses the fashionable stick-on variety that can be easily removed and put back on again.

3. Satyajit Ray's *The Middle Man* (1975), *The Company Limited* (1971), *The Adversary* (1970), and *Days and Nights in the Forest* (1969), while tackling the theme of people's disillusionment with an ineffectual state, offer urban masculine imaginings of a utopian existence, drawing strength from and entering into relationships of solidarity with revolutionary adivasis and tribal people leading peripheral lives in villages and forests. In Mrinal Sen's 1972 film *Calcutta 71*, a middle-class, urban-bred, and college-educated young man dies for the cause of the oppressed laborers and peasants, mythicizing in the process the figure of the middle-class urban masculine Naxalite hero. Bollywood's representation of Naxalism—for example, Prakash Jha's *Chakravyuh* (2012) and Ananth Mahadevan's *Red Alert* (2009)—also reinforces masculine Naxalite renditions.

4. Kshama Sawant (2011) points out the flaw in the Naxalite ideology where initiating its struggle in villages and forests and then spreading out to the cities would not be enough to undermine the force of the capitalist class and state in India. The crucial Naxalite weakness stemmed from them not communicating with the struggling urban masses who could have offered a meaningful postrevolution plan rather than be seen as a "sympathetic spectator in the revolutionary events" (4). The misplaced Naxalite strategy of not collaborating with their urban peers cost them their goal. As a result, the urban oppressed (Somu and his friend Partho) are not part of these discussions.

5. A red powder that Hindu women apply in the parting of their hair to signal their marital status.

6. *HKA* offers an interesting contrast between Siddhartha's and Geeta's reaction to a real-life situation of oppression. When a young girl is raped by the village chief, Siddhartha mobilizes the local people to march toward the village chief's house, asking for justice. Feeling threatened, the chief has a heart attack and the villagers run around, trying to get him a doctor. Baffled by the ease with which the villagers give up their fight, Siddhartha withdraws from the scene and, in a letter to Geeta, expresses his bewilderment about the situation: "I have seen this strange compassion of the villagers towards their oppressors. It taught me something—what, I am still trying to understand" (*HKA*).

7. The silencing of Naxalite femininities clearly needs to be problematized, especially since this radical political movement had resonated with some of the most progressive sections of the society, be they male or female. On the basis of her extensive research on Naxalism, Mallarika Sinha Roy argues that this leftist movement developed at a time when the first wave of the 1960s and 1970s feminism was in the

throes of its formation. And if the urban middle-class Naxalites were keeping pace with other significant political debates taking place globally, how could they have entirely bypassed international-level conversations of women's rights, an idea voiced by the authors as a "strange and unhappy coexistence of a patriarchal structure, and a revolutionary ideology" (2006, 209)?

References

Anzaldúa, Gloria. 1987. *Borderlands/La Frontera*. San Francisco: Spinsters/Aunt Lute.
Banerjee, Sumanta. 1980. *In the Wake of the Naxalbari*. Calcutta: Subernarekha.
———. 1984. *India's Simmering Revolution: The Naxalite Uprising*. London: Zed.
Bhatia, Bela. 2005. "The Naxalite Movement in Central Bihar." *Economic and Political Weekly* 40(15): 1536–1549.
Chadha, Kalyani, and Anandam P. Kavoori. 2008. "Exoticized, Marginalized and Demonized: the Muslim Other in Indian Cinema." In *Global Bollywood*, edited by Anadam P. Kavoori and Aswin Punathambekar, 131–145. New York: New York University Press.
Chowdhury, Elora. 2011. "The Space between Us: Reading Umrigar and Sanghari in the Quest for Female Friendship." Unpublished paper.
Das, Nandita. 2011. "Firaaq—A Mirror of Life Time Experiences?" Frequently Asked Questions provided to the author on May 22, 10:40 A.M.
Duyker, Edward. 1987. *Tribal Guerillas: The Santals of West Bengal and the Naxalite Movement*. Delhi: Oxford University Press.
Ferguson, Ann. 1995. "Feminist Communities and Moral Revolution." In *Feminism and Community*, edited by Penny A. Weiss and Marylin Friedman, 367–398. Philadelphia, Pa.: Temple University Press.
Firaaq. 2009. Directed by Nandita Das. DVD.
Gandhi, Leela. 2006. *Affective Communities: Anticolonial Thought, Fin-de-Siècle Radicalism, and the Politics of Friendship*. Durham, N.C.: Duke University Press.
Guha, Ranajit. 1997. Introduction to *A Subaltern Studies Reader 1986–1995*, edited by Ranajit Guha, ix–xxii. Delhi: Oxford University Press.
Hazaar Chaurasi Ki Ma. 1998. Directed by Govind Nihalani. DVD.
Hazaaron Khawishein Aisi. 2001. Directed by Sudhir Mishra. DVD.
hooks, bell. 2015. *Feminist Theory: From Margin to Center*. New York: Routledge.
Mohanty, Chandra Talpade. 1991. "Cartographies of Struggle: Third World Women and the Politics of Feminism." In *Third World Women and the Politics of Feminism*, edited by Chandra Mohanty, Ann Russo, and Lordes Torres, 1–50. Bloomington: Indiana University Press.
Narayan, Uma. 1988. "Working Together Across Difference: Some Considerations on Emotions and Political Practice." *Hypatia* 3(2):133–140.
Ray, Rabindra. 1988. *The Naxalites and Their Ideology*. Delhi: Oxford University Press.
Roy, Arundhati. 2009. *Field Notes on Democracy*. Chicago: Haymarket Books.

Sawant, Kshama. 2011. "Marxism and the Maoist-Naxalite Movement in India." Unpublished manuscript.

Sinha Roy, Mallarika. 2006. "Speaking Silence: Narrative of Gender in the Historiography of the Naxalbari Movement in West Bengal (1967–75)." *Journal of South Asian Development* 1(2): 207–230.

———. 2009a. "Contesting Calcutta Canons: Issues of Gender and *Mofussil* in the Naxalbari Movement in West Bengal (1967–1975)." *Contemporary South Asia* 17(2): 159–174.

———. 2009b. "Magic Moment of Struggle: Women's Memory of the Naxalbari Movement in West Bengal, India (1967–75)." *Indian Journal of Gender Studies* 16(2): 205–235.

———. 2010. *Gender and Radical Politics in India: Magic Moments of Naxalbari (1967–1975)*. London: Routledge, Taylor and Francis Group.

Spivak, Gayatri Chakravorty et al. 1995. *The Spivak Reader: Selected Works of Gayatri Chakravorty Spivak*. New York: Routledge.

Stone-Mediatore, Shari. 2003. *Reading across Borders: Storytelling and Knowledges of Resistance*. New York: Palgrave Macmillan.

Tagore, Proma. 2009. *The Shapes of Silence: Writing by Women of Colour and the Politics of Testimony*. Montreal: McGill-Queen's University Press.

PART THREE

Neoliberalism, Agency, Friendship

CHAPTER 6

Kinship Drives, Friendly Affect

Difference and Dissidence in the
New Indian Border Cinema

ESHA NIYOGI DE

Some years back, Maria Lugones persuasively argued that friendship is more appropriate as an ideal for feminist bonding than any model of relationship associated with family and kin. A kin metaphor such as sisterhood presumes, on the one hand, that women will bond together "unconditionally" rather than out of particularized "appreciation" for another (1995, 136). It derives, on the other hand, from an institution of relationships based in blood and heterosexual marriage and, by implication, in their gendered constructions of power and purity. Conversely, friendly relations rest on the presupposition that bonds have to be cultivated between different agents and, as such, that these are conditional to "failures" (142) in the commitment to appreciate and understand the other. In the words of Lugones, the friendly bond is a "wholly individuated ... practical love that commits one to perceptual changes in the knowledge of other persons" (142). A similar argument for individuated perceptiveness is made also by Deleuze and Guattari. Friendship, in their view, is a "vital relationship with the Other" (1991, 4)—that is, a way of interacting with the singularity of another's worldly circumstances and affective vitality that enables one to become different from one's identity (Berardi 2008, 138–139). These feminist and postmodern theorists of friendship agree that the critical potential of the ideal lies in its individuation of otherness and the proactive agent, and that this emphasis on singular agency sets this concept of relationship apart from models based in the institution of the family and allied structures of kin-identification or alienation (nation, religion, race, caste, able-ness).

This chapter addresses a conundrum born of this emphasis on individuality shared by theories of friendship as praxis. I examine whether friendship is useful as a metaphor for gendered solidarities across difference in cultures wherein ideas such as individuated and conditional love, challenge to patriarchal family customs, and sensitivity to difference come to be recognized as the norms for socioeconomic progress, or even as marketable tropes of (neo)human connectivity. My chapter delves into this concern through exploring one influential lens of neoliberal imagination. I look at commercially released Indian "border" cinema centering on women who are proactive in forging friendly solidarities in the breach of familial boundaries (heteropatriarchal; ability-centered; national and racial; religion-, clan-, caste-based).

Across the spectrum of independent and popular-industrial productions, Indian films today tell cross-border stories. These filmic narratives cut across "geographic . . . [and] cultural boundaries" (Naficy 1996, 119) through portraying how mutual ties develop between two individuals at odds with institutional structures of relationship and difference. As the builders of unorthodox bonds, women characters appear also to be diverging from their assigned role in postcolonial nationalism. Far from being the keepers of home, national tradition, and a pure and able patriline, they act as self-propelled agents of affective understanding who break down inherited kin structures and sexual beliefs. The complexity of this seemingly radical trope of the friendly woman is that it goes hand in hand with the discourse of neoliberal transnationalism. Specifically, it accompanies the motifs of individual motivation, women's empowerment, and flexible connectivity, which recur on the screens of postliberalization India. As Stuart Hall cannily noted in the early days of the new liberal globalization, deregulated capital works "through difference." It seems to build bridges between national, regional, religious, racial, and sexual borders because it is utilizing and combining a variety of labor forces, economic sectors, and consumer groups (1994, 29). A new wave of Indian cinema appears in this vein to be embracing difference and building bridges between people and geographies. Common to this "deterritorialized" cinema (Naficy 2001, 4) are portrayals of unregulated friendships, born within such practical circumstances of global mobility as urban roads and parks, journeys, vehicles, and border zones. I have discussed elsewhere that the emotional appeal of present-day media images that particularize and interconnect persons in this fashion, however, is that while they respond to the multiple aspirations and fears being generated across various sectors in these mobile times, they direct public emotions such that identities are regrouped and the others demarcated (De 2011a, 18). Mass media's inflections of public emotion, then, contribute to flexible, neoliberal imperialism insofar as empire, in the words of Edward Said, begins with pitting "one race, society, culture against (on top of) another" (1994, 228). In the process, the trope of the woman's love of difference very well can get deployed to eroticize the purity and superiority of certain identity groups in comparison to others. Indeed, biopolitical boundaries between identity and alienness routinely are recharted by Indian border cinema in the very name of women's tender feelings for the different or the outsider.

Does this mean that the feminist notion of friendship—which privileges individual motivation over institutional relationships—loses its critical potential in a neoliberal conceptual climate wherein such ideas as individuated love, the self-propelled woman, and connectivity across difference are utilized as instruments of capital and empire? Far from it. I argue that friendship as a metaphor for solidarity across gendered borders is very useful under present-day neoliberalism precisely *because it helps us to distinguish between the various prevalent ways of relating to, understanding, and desiring the different*. We are able to make distinction between a friendly feeling that drives toward institutionalized patterns of bonding and hostility and another, dissident form of friendliness. The dissident feminist friendship characteristically disorients accepted familial and geopolitical feelings. Instead, it follows a vitally affective course of understanding the other and learning how to care at odds with one's institutional identity and filiative loyalties.

The following sections explain this distinction through a comparative reading of women-motivated friendships, respectively, in a popular-industrial film (the Bollywood blockbuster *Veer Zaara,* 2004) and in critical feminist cinema from India (Aparna Sen's *House of Memories/Paromitar Ek Din,* 2000, and *Mr. and Mrs. Iyer,* 2002). As we will see, narrative Indian film is a potent register of the distinction I explore here not simply because the trope of cross-border friendships recurs. Equally germane to my effort to discern the dissident friendly affect is the aesthetic work done upon the "human sensorium" by neoimperialist narrative cinema, and a consideration of the ways in which friendly sensations could be "reshaped" through alternative storytelling on postcolonial film (Ponzanesi and Waller 2012, 2). While the aesthetic register of film has long been recognized as evoking a "veritable festival of affects" (Heath 1981, 53)—through its techniques of interrelating bodies, objects, lands, and nature—narrative cinema also is well-known to modulate spectators' feelings such that they desire for an order of meaning with an origin and an end, a narrative comprehensible from a coherent subject position. A close look at cinematic friendships across gendered institutions thus enables us to distinguish relationships that narrativize a coherent identity from dissident feminist stories of sensory understanding that reshape identitarian emotions.

Women Friends, Difference, and the Narrative Drive: Neoliberal Empire and Indian Cinema

In a recent book, Eve Kosofsky Sedgwick draws a contrast between affect and the drive of desire that is helpful for distinguishing between friendship stories on film. In her view, affect has "texture," that is, "an array of perceptual data ... whose degree of organization hovers just below the level of shape or structure" (2003, 16). When evoked on the movie screen, this (dis)array of perceptual data—which very well could intensify seeing and hearing by combining with sensations of bodily motion, touch, smell, or taste—refuses to make sense in terms of the storyline of interpersonal relations unfolding thus far and creates a narrative space for interrelating bodies and persons in other ways. Desire, on the other hand, is a libidinal drive constituting a "social force ... that shapes an important relationship" (Sedgwick 2003, 18). Since the drive of desire is both the "glue" and the "vehicle" of the said relationship, it also can manifest as "hostility or hatred" (2003, 18) toward outliers. By invoking the desire to comprehend a storyline, modern narrative film develops a quintessentially Oedipal drive to discover the origin or father figure and to cohere family structures through the narrative form (Barthes 1975, 10). Film narrative techniques typically put "pressure" on images to link up with what happens next (Seymour Chapman 1980 quoted in De Lauretis 1984, 146), thereby gluing together affective evocations and reinstating heteropatriarchal identities and national kinships. Along these lines, Yash Chopra's *Veer Zaara* utilizes a transgressive story of friendship between different women as one emotional vehicle for spectators to arrive at the erotic glorification of the superior man and his liberal nation and religion, and of an originary "father" figure at the pivot of it all.

The Bollywood melodrama *Veer Zaara* (2004) is a narrative about building emotional bridges across the border of two nations torn by a long history of ethno-religious conflict, the border between India and Pakistan. It depicts a romance between an Indian Air Force officer and an elite Pakistani woman that endures through a twenty-two-year separation caused by xenophobic nationalism and sexual rivalry on the part of Pakistani family men. This heterosexual romance is catalyzed, mediated, and sustained by ties between women that flourish within the heterogeneous structure of South Asian family life. The situation for the romance between Indian Veer Pratap Singh (Shah Rukh Khan) and Pakistani Zaara Hyat Khan (Pretty Zinta) in the breach of national and religious kinships arises in the first place because Muslim Zaara crosses the Pakistan-India border to fulfill her filial duty toward her Sikh Indian "grandmother" (Zohra Sehgal) by performing the last rites at a holy site in India. While the Sikh is a serving woman who raised her, Zaara has adopted the serving woman as her grandmother or Bebe. Enabling Zaara's acts of rupture and crossing—of the boundaries imposed, respectively, by the patriarchal family, the nation-state, and religion—is the loving assistance of her declared *dost* (friend), Shabbo (Divya Dutta).

The egalitarian companionship between Shabbo and Zaara itself bridges difference. Shabbo is another serving woman, possibly Zaara's childhood companion, whose social standing is far apart from her mistress's elite bloodline, propertied status, urban background, education, and speech. Without a doubt, breaches such as these of the division of proprietorship and servitude have appeared through the decades in Indian family films (a memorable instance is to be found in the 1972 hit Hindi film *Bawarchi*, starring Rajesh Khanna, and its 1966 antecedent on the Bengali screen, *Galpo Holeo Satti*, starring Robi Ghosh). In these narratives of employer-servant bonds, we encounter residues of the affective habits common to the household practices of South Asia. In the story of Zaara's tie with Shabbo (and for that matter, with the Sikh serving woman she adopts as her grandmother) we meet, in other words, the non-Western cinematic tradition of rooting filmic narrative in the region's "collective memories" (Gabriel 1989, 58) of cohabitation and family-making. Yet the Zaara-Shabbo story of friendship significantly departs from the similar portrayals we encounter in earlier decades of Indian cinema. Whereas earlier narratives typically contained transgressions of hierarchy within the heterogeneous affects of patriarchal family life, *Veer Zaara* emphasizes how the indomitable vitality of a servant-mistress tie ruptures the codes of family and habitation. Shabbo's particularized appreciation of Zaara's self-expression and choices enables a reshaping of the normative sensorium of kinship and property relations wherein Zaara's life at first is contained. Moreover, the story of this vital bond between the friends is situated within the practical conditions of an elite household and, in a realistic vein, made to escape its hierarchy only in stages.

The germination of mutual understanding hand in hand with egalitarian sensations between the two women is portrayed through the course of a song-and-movement montage. We first see the two together in Zaara's bedroom the morning after her betrothal. Shabbo is humorously trying to carry out the orders of Zaara's mother by teaching the girl to get up on time and learn discipline in preparation for life as a housewife. Zaara shows her defiance of the disciplinary measure by unfurling her body into a frisky dance on the bed accompanied by a song of self-assertion that could be taken as an address to her "friend": "Hum To Bhai Jaise Hain Waise Rehenge" is translatable either as "I am as I am and so will I stay," or as "I am, my friend, as I am, and so will I stay." On her part, Shabbo responds to this egalitarian call for friendly understanding with a caressing look of affection and joy. This reverse shot at medium-close range evokes vision as a form of "tactile" contact (Marks 2000, xi), lending texture and intensity to Shabbo's routine activity in this mise-en-scène. As if learning from physical contact with the frisky body of her friend, Shabbo's own body soon comes alive with the same movement language as Zaara's. At one point, we view the two *dosts* performing identical defiant movements on either side of Zaara's disapproving mother. As such, this momentary dance of cooperative defiance conjoining the intentions of the friends throws into perceptual disarray the overarching narrative logic—driven, at this stage, by mother Mariam Hyat Khan's (Kiron Kher) tension over preparing her free-spirited daughter for the marriage to come. Mariam's disapproval of the defiant dancing couple—a frown of reprimand leveled, predictably, at the servant rather than at her own kind—stems from her fruitless effort to calm her daughter down so that tailors are able to measure and clothe the bride-to-be in the colorful raiment of fertility and wedding. Growing increasingly prominent through the course of the montage, these perceptual disruptions of the principle narrative logic depict a bond between Shabbo and Zaara that is sovereign, in other words, independent of social differences and sensory norms.

Zaara's song soon recedes to the soundtrack, following a trend in New Bollywood Cinema of disconnecting the narrative from the sensations of song and dance such that social identities are allowed "access to sovereignty" (Gopal 2011, 57). As we hear the song playing on, we follow on screen the blossoming of sensory cooperation between the two young women, reflected in the framing of space, body, and movement. Underscoring the free and sovereign status of their friendship, the women relate to each other at a distance from the elite patriarchal home and its strictures. Medium-long shots show them riding down a road on bikes side by side or clutching at the same umbrella as their rhythmic movements meet at midpoint in an open courtyard under a pouring sky, while close-ups capture the texture of their unregulated tastes and tactile pleasures. At one moment, we see the two in an open park, on a picnic with grandma Bebe, licking at ice-cream bars with childlike relish. All in all, this montage accompanying Zaara's self-expressive song of freedom captures the growth of perceptiveness between two "sensing bod[ies] in movement" (Manning 2007, xiii)—moving bodies that refuse identification in terms of the dominant narrative of elite patriarchy and property relations. Still, the sovereignty of their feelings is limited at this point, being pressurized to fit into the principle narrative drive of preparing the woman for a lavish wedding. Moreover, this libidinal drive to glue together an elite kinship through the exotic display of a beautiful female body, in an appropriate realistic vein, reinforces also Shabbo's social and physical difference from Zaara. The pressure of the marriage narrative upon the friendship story proves, however, to be short-lived.

The desire to see a wedding spectacle unfold of course is not simply internal to the narrative of *Veer Zaara,* it is also generic to the glittering Indian romantic film of the Bollywood vein. If the New Bollywood film of postliberalization India is at the forefront of merchandizing high-end lifestyle items and fashions (Gopal 2011, 18), the big-budget-wedding film surely leads this trend of consumer erotics. Narrativizing this logic of spectacle, the song-and-movement sequence montage described earlier has the camera revolve around the autoeroticized body of the bridal heroine and make all other bodies-in-movement satellites to this center. This focus on the exotic bride-to-be and the normative emotions enabling her path to marriage predicts that Shabbo's support of Zaara's individuality likewise will be sutured to the narrative drive for patriarchal kin formation. As such, Shabbo's body language comes across as plainly conflicted at this stage—torn between her love and solidarity for friend Zaara's inclinations, on the one hand, and the pressure, on the other, to acquiesce to household discipline by becoming the bearer of the parental look toward the offspring in her care, exactly as a servant should. For one such as Shabbo, different and lower in social status to the family she interacts with, the pressure to belong to a family narrative has to go hand in hand with the logic (internal to the narrative) of belonging securely in a master's home by facilitating the normative desire of domesticity. Even though Shabbo's help and money enable Zaara to go to India to perform Bebe's last rites—in other words, to move across national and religious differences—the assistance is shown to come not as an act of pure solidarity but also due to some degree of coercion. We learn that had Shabbo not yielded, Zaara would have wrested the money from her. Yet precisely this coercive edge of the differential friendship is a passing phase of the women's relationship. For it gives way to their radical responsiveness toward each other, an intensity of feeling that throws into disarray the familial sensorium of difference and hierarchy.

Or so the narrative trajectory would lead us to believe. Thinking from a feminist perspective, we must ask if the disruptive friendship does, in fact, liberate the spectator from an Oedipal drive to know the end of the family narrative and demarcate the outlier. Conversely, is this story of an individuated friendship deployed to satisfy the conflicting desires of an Indian spectatorship under neoliberal capital: the desire, on the one hand, for self-propelled and unregulated interpersonal relationships, and a drive, on the other, to recognize a higher (imperial) narrative order of differences pitting one kind of family relationship, national value system, and manhood on top of another?

Events take a disruptive turn moments before Zaara's engagement, provoked by a deeper understanding between the friends and an ensuing sense of purpose in Shabbo. No longer able to contain her anguish at being forced into an unwanted marital life, Zaara discloses to her mother and Shabbo her desire for another man. They are told of her feelings for Veer Pratap Singh, the dignified Indian officer who had rescued her from an accident, accompanied and nurtured her, and subsequently dedicated his love to her—all without once touching her or objectifying her body. Shabbo at first is inclined to follow in the line of mother Mariam's emotional reaction to this disclosure. She expresses shock, pursues Mariam's orders to bring the disaffected Zaara to her senses, and cooperatively joins Mariam in a ritual dance to usher the groom's party to the engagement. But her attitude undergoes a fundamental change from the moment a weeping Zaara locks her in an embrace of desperate entreaty. Evoking the power of tactile perception, a medium close-up depicts a new sense of resolution creeping into the tearful eyes of Shabbo as she holds on to her friend while their bodies rock together in a synergy of understanding. Through the depth of this affective contact, Shabbo acquires a new level of commitment to the "perceptual change" (Lugones 1995, 142) that has occurred in her childhood *dost,* a commitment that finally permits her to risk her own security out of love for her friend. From hereon, Shabbo is intrepid about breaching authority structures—patriarchal, national, or religious. She puts a call through to Veer Pratap Singh and arranges such that he is able to come to Pakistan, intercept the prenuptial rites at a mosque, and reunite with Zaara. And even though the Pakistani family narrative seems once again to take over the plot—the intruder steps away in deference to her parental wishes and Zaara's marriage takes place as scheduled—the interruption of narrative and breach of borders brought about by the strength of Shabbo's friendship proves to have longevity. The film closes with the revelation that Shabbo and Zaara have moved to India and are living in the model village established by Veer's parents in order to fulfill their humanitarian dream. We learn from Shabbo that upon receiving a (false) report of Veer's death, Zaara divorced her Pakistani husband, with support from her parents, and subsequently moved to Veer's village to fill his place.

The complication in this seemingly radical move by the women is that, while it causes one set of social relationships to come unglued—namely, the differential relationships identified with Pakistan—it acts as emotional glue for another set of family feelings identified with Indians' flexibility and humanity. In effect, the tropes of the border-crossing woman and unregulated feminine friendship are used to organize a higher narrative of difference between friendly and unfriendly nations and manhoods. The source of the false report of Veer's death turns out to be none other than Zaara's Pakistani husband. Portrayed throughout as a rivalrous and duplicitous man, Raza Sharazi (Manoj Bajpai) is the one who engineered Veer's arrest in Pakistan on a false pretext and caused the long separation of the cross-border lovers. These machinations of Raza are complemented by the self-serving xenophobia of Zaara's father, an unrelenting patriarch whose sentiments against Indians and designs for his daughter's life alike are tied to his political ambitions. Pitted against feelings such as these of alienation or menacing control evoked by the Pakistani men are the free-wheeling generosity and companionate attitudes of the Indian men. At the pivot of that narrative of human connectivity—and at the origin of Veer's embrace of Zaara's difference—is Veer's idealistic father Chowdhury Sumer Singh (Amitabh Bachchan), a landowner and a missionary educator who lives and bonds on an equal footing with villagers. This uniformly friendly father figure is the coherent embodiment of ties across differences of nation and religion, gender, social status, and age. As such, he satisfies the overarching Oedipal drive of the Indian film to end the narrative of border conflicts by superseding/suppressing difference.

How might feminist visions situated in postliberalization India disagree with such popular cultural strategies as these of suppressing difference and border violence in the name of enabling individuated relationships? And in what way could they be reconceptualizing friendship in staking the dissent? I conclude the chapter by speaking to these questions.

Friendships through Difference: Dissident Affect on the Feminist Indian Screen

In critical feminist stories, friendship is not an outgrowth of the affective habits of community and cohabitation (as it is with the relationships forged by Veer's father in the village, or by Zaara with Shabbo). For in the feminist eye, the sensorium of daily living in postcolonial India is rife with the divisions of gender, labor, health and ability, caste, class, religion, and nationalism. The value of friendship as a feminist metaphor for interpersonal bonding lies, instead, in delineating its process. Because the friendly bond has to be cultivated through the mutual appreciation and effort of two different individuals, it is a critically valuable way for feminists to explore how divisive or hostile feelings could be overcome through personal initiative. Thus friendship as a process works in Indian feminist portrayals by uncovering the feelings beneath habitual and seemingly natural relationships and by working through divisive attitudes to achieve a singular love. This also means that, in feminist narrative film, the friendly affect must work against the Oedipal drive for the standard family narrative, and unravel its cohesion. Friendships portrayed in the narrative cinema of Aparna Sen, India's most prolific woman filmmaker, work precisely in this way.

It is useful to juxtapose Aparna Sen's offbeat narrative cinema to industrial productions such as *Veer Zaara* because they grapple with some of the same gender issues and emotions in the context of postliberalization India while they alter the trajectories. Here I consider two films by Sen, which resonate with different aspects of the *Veer Zaara* narrative—respectively, the global politics of religious nationalism (*Mr. and Mrs. Iyer*) and the micropolitics of the propertied patriarchal family (*House of Memories/Paromitar Ek Din*). In the vein of the Bollywood production, both these (commercially successful) films by Sen evoke the sensory comforts and erotics of friendly proximity and mutual understanding. Yet their portrayals depart from the Bollywood one in at least two significant ways. First, the films show that this process of getting to understand the other is bound to fail off and on as the two individuals "work through" their institutional identities—that is, as they strive to "gain a measure of responsible control" (LaCapra 2001, 25) over their ingrained mentalities of coercion or hostility. Second, they demonstrate that these achievements of bonding with the other in a deeply sensory way have to remain as memorable episodes only of spectatorial comfort—outside of and at odds with spectators' general expectations about "what happens next" in the organization of the familiar family drama. As such, the stories of radical friendship explored by Aparna Sen refuse to cohere with the banal endings of the family films in which they appear.

Aparna Sen's critically acclaimed Anglophone film *Mr. and Mrs. Iyer* (2002), following on the heels both of the massacre of Muslim minorities in eastern India and of the 9/11 attack in the United States, portrays the blossoming of an unlikely solidarity between an orthodox Hindu woman and a Muslim man in the midst of Hindu communal violence in India. The film shows Meenakshi Iyer (Konkona Sen Sharma), a young high-caste Hindu woman, traveling from her parental abode in the hills to her marital home in the city of Kolkata. Raja Chowdhury (Rahul Bose) is a wildlife photographer who has been requested by Meenakshi's father to help her on the way. The unexpected bond that germinates between the woman and the man (who turns out to be a Muslim) at first glance might appear to be an intuitive outgrowth of the affective communion between different people brought together by the habitual circumstances of multireligious /multiethnic India—that is, by the habitual need of learning to live with difference. But both the nuances of Sen's storytelling and the turns of her camera clarify that, in fact, this is far from being the case. Group identities and hostilities, based on deep-rooted ethnobiological prejudices about pure and polluted kin lines, lurk just beneath the surface of Indian community emotions. Solidarities across difference have to be cultivated the hard way—by working through one's hostile drives and by learning to bear witness to one's own violent alliances. This theme of the film appropriately is encapsulated by a haunting refrain, "Don't look away."

Constituting a microcosm of the multireligious, multiethnic nation, the people on the bus traveling downhill with Meenakshi and Raja at first appear to embody Indian customs of cohabitation and affective patience with difference. While the soundtrack blares with an off-key chorus sung by a group of Westernized college-goers jumping around at the back of the bus, medium close-ups reveal the wry humor with which an elderly Muslim couple tolerates the noise while the two reminisce about the different norms of their tradition-bound youth. At another end, a group of young men carry on with a game of cards, working all the while on managing the space of their game as a mother attempts to feed and care for her disabled son on the next seat. Amidst these voices and bodies that differ as they get along, a "touchy-feely" (Sedgwick 2003, 17) bond begins to grow between Meenakshi and Raja as she involves him in the little tasks of feeding and caring for her infant. His sensitive reciprocity makes her notice his individuality with a new eye of fondness, as suggested by a medium shot of the woman looking with care upon the face of the man in repose as he dozes by the window in a fading ray of sunlight. The narrative logic up to this point would suggest that, when their bus is stranded on a border zone of communal uprising and then attacked by Hindu terrorists, the intuitive friendship born in Meenakshi through the affective communion is what impels her to protect Raja from the violence. Despite the fact that initially she had recoiled with prejudice upon learning that he is a Muslim, Meenakshi shields him from the terrorists by naming him as her Brahmin husband, Mr. Iyer.

However, we soon understand that the *telos* of Meenakshi's friendship for Raja exceeds the sporadic affect of intuition. A blending of individuated love for him with responsible control over her prejudice is what inculcates Meenakshi's solidarity for the man and eroticizes her attachment to difference. It is clear also that the woman is the agent of building and sustaining this solidarity. For she works through her own majority Hindu identity and his ethno-religious difference and thereby overcomes a communal barrier rooted deep in South Asia's imperial history of national-identity-formation and border conflict (during and after British colonization). We see Meenakshi learning to bear witness to history by arriving at a "broader understanding of the meaning of what has been done to [Muslim] victims" (Kaplan 2010, 299) and in what way her kind and she have to be held responsible for failures of community in the subcontinent. As briefly suggested earlier, Meenakshi's initially friendly appreciation of the tender man who helps take care of her infant ends in failure. Upon learning that he is a Muslim, her body language (specified through a medium close-up) galvanizes into loathing. She recoils from his touch with a hostility rooted deep in the Hindu sensorium, which divides pure from polluted bodies on the basis of a caste system inflected by race (De 2011b, 37, 182). This hostile libido is what she must work through and dissent with in order to reclaim the vitality of the bond.

After they have been put up at a forest bungalow by a protective police officer, Meenakshi and Raja watch from their window the slaughter of a Muslim man by the Hindu terrorists. Her visceral horror at this sight—making her cling to Raja for the rest of the night—throws into disarray her customary way of perceiving the other and building identification. In the clear light of the new day, Meenakshi stands before a mirror. At odds with the fragmentation of subjectivity associated with the mirror-image in the Lacanian tradition, this mise-en-scène of self-mirroring has the camera remain steady upon the thoughtful eye of the woman upon her own face. The reflexivity of this look implies the growth of a responsible dissidence with her prior sensory habits of kin relation. This realization is that she can belong and bond with others only if she chooses to take corporeal victimage "in her stride" (Spivak 2002, 30)—whether this victimage stems from her own custom of defiling the other or from the way her particular habits come to be generalized in imperial history's alienation and carnage. Subsequently, Meenakshi enacts her way of loving and relating to the other by choosing to demolish Hindu nationalism's fundamental ethnobiological barrier, that between the pure and the polluted/alien body. She elects to sip water from Raja's bottle, whereas precisely this act on his part had earlier signaled to her Raja's alien descent and made her recoil (since orthodox Hindus view sipping water directly from the bottle as the alien's typical way of polluting the body). Through this dissident touch, the woman sets the seal on the fundamental egalitarian quality of the bond she has forged with the alien man.

The unregulated intimacy between the two—combining heterosexual attraction with a deep understanding of the other's perceptual inclinations—is encoded in the pleasant words and looks they exchange on their train journey to Kolkata after being able to escape from the riot-torn zone. Their arrival at the destination, and the ending of the narrative, are unsatisfying by contrast. The real Mr. Iyer awaits his wife and baby at the railway station, greeting them with the news of how distraught his father and family have been in not knowing where they were. Even though the film ends upon this banal storyline about the reuniting of a standard Hindu patriarchal family, the episode of the dissident friendship has interrupted that narrative and left an indelible mark on the normative emotions of family togetherness. In a subsequent film, Aparna Sen is to return to the theme of bearing witness to Muslim victimage through the portrayal of a schizophrenic CNN-news-buff's hallucinatory friendship with the face of a globally victimized Muslim man (Saddam Hussein before his death). Interconnecting global pathologies of victimage with the intimate violations of bourgeois Indian life, *15 Park Avenue* (2005) shakes the family narrative at its foundation. I round out my discussion by looking at an earlier family melodrama by Aparna Sen that paves the way to a work such as *15 Park Avenue*. It appropriates the emotions associated with daily life (weddings, funerals, motherwork) in the bourgeois Indian family film to delineate the process of a most unusual friendship—one that blossoms within and which radically displaces the daily desires of kin formation and the drive of alienation.

House of Memories/Paromitar Ek Din (2000) revolves around the day in the life of the title character Paromita (Rituparna Ghosh) on which she attends the last rites of her ex-mother-in-law and recalls her life as a housewife in this joint family (prior to divorce by her choice). We learn through flashback of the remarkable solidarity she had developed with the key authority figure of the patriarchal household, mother-in-law Sanaka (played by the filmmaker, Aparna Sen). We are taken to the moment when this extraordinary affective understanding between these unlikely companions first took root. We see Paromita in bridal wear being ushered in by Sanaka with the Hindu rites of bridal-welcome or *badhubaran*.

Deliberately saturating the frame with the fertility-coded colors of vermilion and yellow, while it combines fill and key lighting to lend a fiery brightness to the bride's face, this mise-en-scène easily unifies with the dominant Hindu Indian conventions of eroticizing the mother-to-be in patriarchal wedding representations. At the same time, the composition is in line with the new liberal culture of visuality in the way it individualizes the emotions of the bride, being not unlike *Veer Zaara* in this respect. The uniqueness of Sen's mise-en-scène, however, is that it personalizes not one individual but rather an interaction between two, shot at close range. The interaction displaces the authority structure built into the bridal-welcome ritual and conventionally so visualized. Mother-in-law Sanaka's triumphant remark about the beautiful daughter-in-law she chose, while still hierarchal, is personalized by a look of affectionate pleasure. Greatly heightening this individuation of a kin relationship, Paromita takes the step of breaking out of the deferential behavior expected of a new bride. Framed in a tight close-up, we see her eyes turn toward Sanaka with a "haptic" (Marks 2000, xi) look of intensely pleasant warmth. This reciprocity of affect sparks an intimacy between the women that thickens in course of their daily activities in the joint household and lends mutual support to the challenge they level at the demands of father figures and husbands.

The key struggle in which the mother joins hands with her daughter-in-law is against the patriarchal demand for an able progeny. This demand relates in the Hindu mindset to assumptions about the pedigree of the mother's sexuality rooted, in turn, in the idea of a high patriline or *kula*. While deriving from the Hindu caste system, such assumptions as these were reinforced by racial bias under the legal system of British India. Thus the friendly bond between these women is dissident to systemic borders of ethno-patriarchy and empire—that is, ideas about inclusion and exclusion which assume the purity of the family, nation, and race. When it turns out that the baby boy Paromita has given birth to—hitherto cherished as the only male heir of the *kula*—suffers from cerebral palsy, Paromita's husband Biresh (Rajatabha Dutta) becomes brutally abusive. He charges that because (orphaned) Paromita was brought into the family without a sufficient background check prior to the arranged marriage, her unknown bloodline is to blame for the birth of their disabled son. In a memorable mise-en-scène, mother Sanaka is shown to burst into the son's bedroom and intercept his abusive tirade against Paromita with the reminder that his own sister and daughter of the family is herself disabled, suffering from schizophrenia.

Following this, a good part of the storyline is devoted to showing how Paromita and Sanaka develop an intimate same-sex relationship through their daily practices of caring for their disabled offspring in the interstices of the patriarchal household. These cooperative caring practices allow the two very different women also to develop a deep sensitivity to each other's perceptual changes, and thereby to become mutually "oriented" (Ahmed 2006, 2–3) toward the other's corporeal needs and wants. Their appreciative orientation to the other's embodied subjectivity is as nurturing as it is erotic. Radically rupturing the narrative of heteropatriarchal desire, the two are portrayed together as they beautify bodies or take showers together. Moreover, the relationship is shown to breach patriarchal borders not simply within the boundaries of the home.

Deploying the new liberal cinema's tropes of public access and freedom, the film shows the friendship to be flourishing away from the home, on city roads that take the women to the fresh opportunities and attitudes emergent in a globalizing metropolis. Notable among these is the access they gain to a newly established school for spastic children and to the caring attitudes toward the disabled being fostered in this alternate public space.

Because the women relate to each other as friends—at odds with differential conventions—their mutual appreciation also is shown to be conditional, subject to failure and regression into the prevalent sensorium of difference. The monumental failure in understanding that erects a border between the friends has to do Paromita's disclosure that she has asked for a divorce from Sanaka's abusive and alcoholic son (following the death of her child from cerebral palsy). She tells Sanaka that she has found a congenial and companionate man and resolved to marry him, instead. Reclaiming her institutional identity of the patriarchy-driven mother-in-law, Sanaka reacts to this disclosure with acute hostility. She accuses Paromita of promiscuity, charging that she is about to defile the sanctity of the Hindu marriage (a national institution that imposes a severe monogamy on the high-caste Hindu woman as the condition of her purity). On her part, Paromita resolutely exits, leaving behind her isolated and aged "friend." At this moment, Paromita shows a callousness indexing the generational privilege of mobility and financial independence she commands as a modern-educated young woman. Thus this failure in the friendship should be understood in the context of a liberalizing economy, which provides able women with new opportunities for independent lives and incomes at the same time that it causes the disintegration of family support structures, including support for elder care and illness care. Precisely these failures alike of affective bonds and social bonds—within the history of change—are worked through in the story of how the women resume their friendship and individuate their dedication for each other.

Putting on hold the demands of her career and new conjugal life, Paromita voluntarily returns to care for her ex-mother-in-law on Sanaka's deathbed. She tends to the dying woman with untiring and intent sensitivity until her very last breath. The depth of Paromita's vital understanding of her traditional friend's inclinations is vindicated by her canny perception of Sanaka's inarticulate refusal to urinate. Paromita saves Sanaka's life at this point by creating a secluded space (a makeshift toilet by the bed) where Sanaka can urinate in private and maintain dignity while she performs her bodily functions. Vision and sound take on the attributes of touching and feeling in a series of tight close-ups that show the two women facing each other with utter satisfaction—Paromita holds Sanaka steady, the latter fingers Paromita's face with a wordless gratitude, and the faint sound of urination is heard in the background. In this riveting portrayal of mutually individuated love, we see how each has successfully worked through their respective institutional identities and alien feelings.

This affective achievement of a dissident friendship between two different women once again stands at odds with the predictable emotions ending the family melodrama. At the end of the narrative, Paromita resumes the customary track of married life and maternity. We see her sharing with her new husband the joy of feeling the movements of their unborn child within the expectant mother. Vindicating maternity, the narrative thus closes by suturing Paromita's drama to the glorification of Hindu-mother-centered family life common to Indian mass media. As we see in the discussion of *Veer-Zaara*, this vindication of Hindu-Indian family values in neoliberal media can also inflect to difference by showing the family to be open to adopting members from different social positions, ethnic, and religious backgrounds. Nonetheless, popular family narratives on the Indian screens invariably tend to drive toward a coherent subject position and an underlying patriline. The importance of exploring cultures of dissident friendships and individuated love lies precisely here. It helps us to discern where and how critical feminist approaches to social relationships unravel the normative views of bonding, individuation, and difference in our present day.

References

Ahmed, Sara. 2006. *Queer Phenomenology: Orientations, Objects, Others*. Durham, N.C.: Duke University Press.
Barthes, Roland. 1975. *The Pleasure of the Text*. Translated by Richard Miller. New York: Hill and Wang.
Berardi, Franco. 2008. *Felix Guattari: Thought, Friendship, and Visionary Cartography*. Translated and edited by Giuseppina Mecchia and Charles J. Stivale. New York: Palgrave Macmillan.
De, Esha Niyogi. 2011a. "'Choice' and Feminist Praxis in Neoliberal Times: Autonomous Women in a Postcolonial Visual Culture." *Feminist Media Studies* 12 (1): 17–34.
———. 2011b. *Empire, Media, and the Autonomous Woman: A Feminist Critique of Postcolonial Thought*. New York: Oxford University Press.
De Lauretis, Teresa. 1984. *Alice Doesn't: Feminism, Semiotics, Cinema*. Bloomington: Indiana University Press.
Deleuze, Gilles and Felix Guattari. 1991. *What Is Philosophy?* New York: Columbia University Press.
Gabriel, Teshome. 1989. "Third Cinema as a Guardian of Popular Memory: Towards a Third Aesthetics." In *Questions of Third Cinema*, edited by Jim Pines and Paul Willemen, 53–64. London: British Film Institute.

Gopal, Sangita. 2011. *Conjugations: Marriage and Form in New Bollywood Cinema*. Chicago: University of Chicago Press.

Hall, Stuart. 1994. "The Local and the Global: Globalisation and Ethnicity." In *Culture, Globalization, and the World System*, edited by Anthony King, 19–40. Minneapolis: University of Minnesota Press.

Heath, Stephen. 1981. *Questions of Cinema*. Bloomington: Indiana University Press.

Kaplan, E. Ann. 2010. "European Art Cinema, Affect, and Postcolonialism: Herzog, Denis, and the Dardene Brothers." In *Global Art Cinema: New Theories and Histories*, edited by Rosalind Galt and Karl Schoonover, 285–303. Oxford: Oxford University Press.

LaCapra, Dominick. 2001. *Writing History, Writing Trauma*. Baltimore, Md.: Johns Hopkins University Press.

Lugones, Maria, in collaboration with Pat Alake Rosezelle. 1995. "Sisterhood and Friendship as Feminist Models." In *Feminism and Community*, edited by Penny A. Weiss and Marilyn Friedman, 135–145. Philadelphia, Pa.: Temple University Press.

Manning, Erin. 2007. *Politics of Touch: Sense, Movement, Sovereignty*. Minneapolis: University of Minnesota Press.

Marks, Laura. 2000. *The Skin of Film: Intercultural Cinema, Embodiment, and the Senses*. Durham, N.C.: Duke University Press.

Mr. and Mrs. Iyer. 2002. Directed by Aparna Sen. Kolkata, India: MG Distribution, India. Film.

Naficy, Hamid. 1996. "Phobic Spaces and Liminal Panics: Independent Transnational Film Genre." In *Global/Local: Cultural Production and the Transnational Imaginary*, edited by Rob Wilson and Wimal Dissanayake, 119–143. Durham, N.C.: Duke University Press.

———. 2001. *An Accented Cinema: Exilic and Diasporic Filmmaking*. Princeton, N.J.: Princeton University Press.

House of Memories/Paromitar Ek Din. 2000. Directed by Aparna Sen. Kolkata, India: Rajesh Agarwal Productions. Film.

Ponzanesi, Sandra, and Marguerite Waller, eds. 2012. *Postcolonial Cinema Studies*. London and New York: Routledge.

Said, Edward. 1994. *Culture and Imperialism*. New York: Vintage.

Sedgwick, Eve Kosofsky. 2003. *Touching Feeling: Affect, Pedagogy, Performativity*. Durham, N.C.: Duke University Press.

Spivak, Gayatri Chakravorty. 2002. "Ethics and Politics in Tagore, Coetzee, and Certain Scenes of Teaching." *Diacritics* 32(3/4): 17–31.

Veer Zaara. 2004. Directed by Yash Chopra. Mumbai, India: Yash Raj Films. Film.

CHAPTER 7

The Space Between Us
Reading Umrigar and Sangari in the Quest for Female Friendship

ELORA HALIM CHOWDHURY

This chapter is an exploration of the idea of friendship between women across cultures as a basis for social and political transformation. Deploying a transnational feminist analysis, I enjoin Thriti Umrigar's novel *The Space Between Us* with Kumkum Sangari's essay "Consent, Agency, and Rhetorics of Incitement" to further a discussion on solidarity among women. The politics of marginal friendship is taken up by Leela Gandhi in her book *Affective Communities* where she draws attention to hitherto ignored individuals and groups who renounced the privileges of imperialism and allied with victims of their own expansionist cultures. Devoting attention to these presumed "nonplayers," Gandhi's work seeks to illuminate some "minor" forms of anti-imperialism that emerged in Europe, specifically in Britain at the end of the nineteenth century that took the form of what she calls "dissident friendships." Excavating such examples of internal expressions of anti-imperialism, Gandhi argues, complicates the common perspective on colonial encounters that overwhelmingly focus on non-Western oppositionality. Relationships between women can be seen in a context much more complex than a mere separation of colonized (anti-imperialism) and colonizer (proimperialism), particularly for women who were part of the imperialist project.

While Gandhi's purpose is in part historical redress, I am inspired by her impulse to unpack the politics of "dissident friendship" in order to think through relationships between women across differences, or more specifically between a lesser colonizer and the colonized. By "lesser colonizer," I mean those who were in some ways on the fringes of imperial society—women, gays, people of color. Uma Narayan has demonstrated the similarities between the ideology of sexism and colonial racism where physical and moral attributes were used to define women (of the colonizer society) and the colonized (men and women) as the weaker sex/race (Narayan 1995).

Despite being of the "weaker sex," colonizer women played vital roles in maintaining the colonial project and taking on the "white man's burden" that put them in paternalistic positions in relation to the colonized. Like their male counterparts, they replicated the colonial structure of at once oppressing the natives while couching that subjugation in the ethic of care. This system, which robbed the colonized of full humanity and rights, was justified by an ethic of responsibility and obligation of the oppressor to provide moral and cultural guidance to the less enlightened. Even within these hierarchical conditions, relationships emerged to varying degrees that hinted at affinity and friendship. In another essay, Narayan takes up the idea of dialogue between members of heterogeneous groups in encounters that can take the form of friendship or politics. She states that it is important to understand that "Working across differences is a morally and politically important enterprise in either context. Both in political contexts and in the context of friendship, such differences in elements of background and identity can be enriching resources, epistemologically, politically and personally. Learning to understand and respect these differences can make more complex our understanding of ourselves and our societies, can broaden the range of our politics and enrich the variety of connections we have as persons" (1995, 32). In this chapter, I enjoin Gandhi's insistence of paying attention to dissident friendships, and Narayan's urging that relationships between individuals of heterogeneous backgrounds with discrepant power positions in society can elicit a deeper understanding of human connection. I argue that Thriti Umrigar's novel, *The Space Between Us,* offers an example of such a dissident friendship between Sera, an upper-class Parsi woman, and her maid and confidant, Bhima, as both women experience transformations of consciousness through their contrapuntal struggles.

I find Umrigar's novel a significant contemporary text to engage the ideal of lasting social and political change through the practice of female friendship between women of differential gender positionality—however fleeting and difficult that may be. In *Politics of the Possible,* Kumkum Sangari traces the persistent reformulation of patriarchies in colonial male reformism to contemporary structures of labor, family, and women's consent and agency. Regulating gender difference, she posits, was/is an instrument of the construction and reproduction of "higher values" which functioned to obfuscate class, imperial, and patriarchal relations. According to Sangari, "The pastoralization of the home, the emergence of structures of surrogate power for women along each axis of social difference, and changes in notions of philanthropy were all part of a broader colonial process that inscribed gender inequalities in different registers for middle-class Indian and English women. And of course for laboring women below: low class/caste and tribal women (supposedly sexually unrepressed, free from patriarchal regimens) were objects of control or later, in a reverse move, absorbed into a quasi-anthropological version of authenticity as 'others' of schooled middle-class women" (1999, xliii). It is this continuation, (re)formulation, and (re)production of the colonial power relation between the middle-class Indian and the low-class women within the bastion of the domestic domain—purportedly "uncolonized"—that Umrigar is able to illuminate in deeply nuanced ways, leading this reader to theorize about the potential of conceptualization and enactment of marginal yet liberatory/decolonial friendships.

Leela Gandhi draws from the work of Edward Said who, in his book *Culture and Imperialism*, demonstrates that although colonialism was a hierarchically aligned system of division and binary opposition, this project of separation failed as imperial boundaries were often porous. Like Gandhi, I borrow Said's notion of the "contrapuntal perspective" that reveals the "overlapping" and "intertwined" histories and realities of colonial encounter. But, unlike Said, and more in the vein of Gandhi, I am more interested to go beyond the anticolonial nationalist critique—which foregrounds non-Western opposition—as well as the "contrapuntal histories" critique—which foregrounds the parallel yet integrated formations—to instead engage dissident cross-cultural alliances in metropolitan or peripheral sites, whether in the putative West or non-West and between oppressors and oppressed. Umrigar's text set in postcolonial, urban, modern, and domestic context offers precisely such an opportunity, especially because the relationship between the two women in question is indelibly framed as a colonial one. Arguably, it allows readers to consider the underside of the perhaps "incomplete modernity" of a specifically postcolonial, local context, and the kinds of social alliances possible within it, which are nevertheless deeply imbricated in older colonial histories. Moreover, the text illuminates what Raka Ray and Seemin Qayum demonstrate as the evolving structure of patriarchy from feudal, colonial, to contemporary urban contexts evident in employer-servant relations in South Asia where class domination is sustained by distinction (2009, 119). Intimate bonding of women is tested by the power of an idealized patriarchy that is elusive in providing protection and security (121) to women and between women.

While these alliances may be minor narratives, I believe they are significant for three reasons: First, they offer another instance of understanding the colonial encounter beyond its categorical West/non-West binary. Second, they illuminate ways in which the colonial power structure replicates itself even in marginal sites and relationships and allow us to think of friendship—at times clandestine, conflictual, even unacknowledged—as a mode for social and potentially political transformation for diffuse groups and individuals. Third, it takes as the premise of such transformation the desire to recognize a mutual humanity based on compassion and empathy. I use these terms with some caution here and do not mean to evoke romanticized nor cultural relativist notions of unity within diversity. Again, I refer to Uma Narayan who unequivocally states that empathic sensitivity in unions across differences do not simply hinge on "good will" (1988). Similarly, feminist theorist Jane Mansbridge defines empathy against such emotions as pity, condescension, or self-righteousness and instead as a gesture toward human connection. It is that which Adrienne Rich calls furthering "the conscious work of turning Otherness into a keen lens of empathy, that we can bring into being a politics based on concrete heartfelt understanding of what it means to be Other" (1995, 400). Alliance across differences for the purpose of this project, then, is a connection based on shared humanity across differences that has to be strived for. I would like to explore whether such alliances are inevitably crushed within dominant patriarchal colonial relations or whether they can cause a change in self-and-other-perception and potentially contribute to social and political transformation.

In this chapter, I have largely used the terms "alliance," "friendship," "community," and "solidarity" interchangeably. While alliance, community, and solidarity are generously discussed in literature dealing with social change, friendship is often believed to be outside the realm of social and political transformation. I intend to trouble that assumption to convince readers that friendship revisioned can be the basis of solidarity precisely because it is premised on a kind of human connection that other types of unions may not contain as explicitly. What makes friendship an interesting medium to discuss is that it allows for the expression of emotion, which in more formal political unions is more often than not dismissed. Instead of rejecting emotions, Narayan, in "Working Together across Differences," proposes that emotions can infuse our experiences and knowledge of reality in a way to expose the subtle workings of power more insightfully and intensely; hence, their role in explaining human connection should not be presumed to be outside of politics. An exploration of friendship allows us an understanding of power and oppression that is more immediate, complex, and subtle. In addition, following Gandhi's cue, friendship in this project refers to a collaboration between the "most unlikely of associates." It may take the form of minor or seemingly insignificant gestures of affinity to the other at the risk of endangering the self's security in her own community. I am particularly interested in exploring when and whether "dissident cross-cultural friendship"—sometimes between these unlikely associates of oppressor and oppressed communities—trumps, or is trumped by, other kinds of loyalties women might have, to family, community, or nation, in the pursuit of social justice.

Feminist theorist Maria Lugones has also talked about friendship as "bonding among women across differences." Such bondings do not presuppose unconditionality but do recognize the situationality of each person while being cognizant of their plural realities. According to Lugones, friendship can be based on "practical love" and knowledge of and commitment to the other person. She says, "Because I think a commitment to perceptual changes is central to the possibility of bonding across differences and the commitment is part of friendship, I think that friendship is a good concept to start the radical theoretical and practical reconstruction of the relations among women" (1995, 141). Understood as such, friendship recognizes the logic of plural realities and remains open to the possibility of self-reflexivity and transformation in perception. That is, instead of the impulse to make the other into an image of one's own, in friendship "one comes to see oneself as constructed in that reality [other's realities] in ways different from the ways one is constructed in the reality one started from. Thus pluralist friendship enhances self knowledge" (143). This enhancement is not merely a cooptation of the other in the service of self-actualization but involves a mutually meaningful and empathetic relationship with the other. It is an epistemically demanding position because one dislodges one's own centrality and strives to work across inequalities rather than simply acknowledging them.

This study employs a combination of literary and transnational feminist analysis. I share Shari Stone-Mediatore's definition of transnational feminism, which is an analytical and a political project that goes beyond unpacking gender ideologies to confronting far-reaching relations of domination spanning but not limited to political, economic, and cultural spheres. These relations of domination "cross over national boundaries and produce historically specific cooperative as well as hierarchical relations among women of different nations, races and classes" (2003, 129). A transnational feminist approach understands that women are part of various groups across communities and thereby part of different struggles. Additionally, this approach suggests that women's myriad struggles, whether individual or collective, are often inseparable from structural oppressions shaping their and their communities' lives such as globalization, patriarchy, and poverty. A transnational feminist lens in this chapter provides a way to understand the paradoxical dynamic of conflict and cooperation that shapes women's relations with one another. I read the novel *The Space Between Us* by Thrity Umrigar in relation to Kumkum Sangari's influential essay "Consent, Agency and Rhetorics of Incitement" to foreground the discussion about relationships between women through the medium of friendship, community, and solidarity and their social and politically transformative potentials. At the same time, Umrigar's book acknowledges the vast challenges of maintaining friendships across patriarchal colonial power structures.

These challenges are explored in the landmark feminist collection *This Bridge Called My Back*. In its foreword, Cherrie Moraga expresses the book's unique intention to create a space for dialogue among women as opposed to between men and women. She argued that understanding the specific conditions of oppression of women, be it for marginalized communities in the United States or outside, is key to building a more effective "Third World feminism," which she described as follows:

> In the last three years I have learned that Third World feminism does not provide the kind of easy political framework that women of color are running to in droves. We are not so much a "natural" affinity group, as women who have come together out of political necessity. The idea of Third World feminism has proved to be much easier between the covers of a book than between real live women. There are many issues that divide us; and, recognizing that fact can make that dream at times seem quite remote. (1983, n.p.)

Together with Stone-Mediatore, Moraga's vision is an effective medium to both illuminate and analyze the "internal differences" within groups, even women's groups, which feminist debates have shown are never coherent. When thinking about and organizing around women's oppression, the cooperative yet conflictual lens that transnational feminism provides is a medium that humanizes the suffering of others different from "us" even as it recognizes friendship, community, and solidarity not as natural alliances but as being sought for through active engagement and reflection. Such alliances can take on dissident forms across cultures and are steps to the realization of that remote dream Moraga talks about for feminism—human connection that nourishes self-growth as well as fosters community.

The Space Between Us, arguably, revolves around the challenges to and potentials of dissident friendship. Set in Mumbai, India, Thriti Umrigar's second novel is about class-differentiated patriarchal oppression, the difficult choices women make within it, and their uneven consequences. The novel traces the parallel yet intertwined lives of the two protagonists, Sera, an upperclass Parsi, and Bhima, her elderly maid. While the women share a genuine friendship, it is born and nourished within insurmountable inequality. Both women are survivors of troubled marriages and hopeful for the future of their progeny. The two women share a close bond, as evidenced through such events as when Bhima soothes Sera after beatings by her husband, Feroz, and the latter makes sure to arrange for medical care for Bhima's husband after a terrible accident in the factory where he works. This bond, however, is sutured by the paternalistic social contract of mistress-domestic servant, worldly "modern" patron and the serving classes. The failure of patriarchy is represented here by the dereliction of husbandly duties—whether financial or emotional by both women's partners—even as the structure continues to delimit the bond between the two women.

Nonetheless, Umrigar poignantly depicts the "space between" the two women. The women bond every day when they have tea and discuss their lives. Despite this clear indicator of friendship, the space between them is obvious. Sera sits at the table while Bhima squats on her haunches on the dining-room floor and sips from the stainless steel cup set aside for her sole use.

After a tragic accident at the factory where Gopal, Bhima's husband, worked, he lies in the general ward of a hospital ignored by the doctors. The mere arrival of the Dubashs alters the complexion of the ward. "To Bhima, it seemed as if the two of them, in their good clothes and their clean, glowing faces, were a splash of color against the black-and-white background of the dark, dingy room. They look like film stars compared to the rest of us, she thought, like gods dropped from the sky onto this mortal earth" (212). Feroz's commanding presence has the nurse, ward boy, even the doctor scurrying to oblige. He explains the relationship between the two families to the doctor:

> "You see, this fellow [Gopal] is important to our family." He leaned closer to the doctor, his black eyes scanning the man's face and his words slow and deliberate. "Anyway, what's done is done. It sounds like your hospital has made a major mistake here. But the question is, What can we do to fix this?" His voice dropped even lower. "May I speak to you a moment, man-to-man? Good. Now here's the thing. For some reason, my wife is very fond of our servant here. And if my wife is happy, then I am happy." He winked at the doctor. "If you are a married man, Doctor, then you know what I mean. For instance, today is our wedding

anniversary. I took the day off to be able to spend it with my wife. Believe me, the last thing I want to do is to be here, in this—place. But my wife insisted we stop here to check on things, and here we are." (213)

This passage is particularly poignant for understanding what Maria Lugones calls the colonial modern gender system, which she sees as a "worldwide system of power." This system relies on the construction and enactment of "heterosexualism as tied to a persistently violent domination that marks the flesh multiply by accessing the bodies of the unfree in differential patterns devised to constitute them as the tortured materiality of power?" (2007, 188). In the passage, Feroz emerges as the authority both in the domestic space of his household, even as he symbolically "grants" the realm to his wife Sera by alluding to her happiness being his paramount pursuit, and refers to his wife's unreasonable patronage of their maid. Furthermore, he conjures up an affinity with the doctor based on their gender, even when he deems him inferior, another enactment of heterosexualism, and although Feroz is clearly the one in control. He gets the lesser man, the doctor, to agree to personally administer Gopal's treatment and report back to Feroz on a daily basis. Within such a framework of heterosexualism, where genders are differentiated, where certain women's own social standing depends on their affirming the colonial modern gender system (Sera is empowered to "help" Bhima through her union to the Dubash family), and only certain men are able to reach the pinnacle of success (Feroz who is educated, wealthy, *and* of higher status), Lugones finds the ideal of solidarity among females nonconducive.

The illusory nature of cross-class solidarity becomes evident as Bhima's hopes for securing a better future are dashed when her beloved granddaughter Maya quits college because of an unexpected pregnancy and thereby abandons the education paid for by Sera. The father of the baby is Viraf, who is married to Sera's only daughter Dinaz. The theme of the contrapuntal lives of the two women is eminently clear since Dinaz is also pregnant with the couple's first child, Sera's much anticipated grandchild. Umrigar starkly measures the life of the privileged against the life of the powerless, yoking their relationships with empathy and compassion. Yet, the final choices the two women make bring into sharp relief the unacknowledged social contract that binds Sera to her family over Bhima, even in the face of egregious injustice. Sera breaks her contract with Bhima literally and figuratively by ending their decade-long relationship and with it Bhima's employment, as well as Sera's obligation of care and protection. While Sera ostensibly chooses security and family honor and Bhima chooses her own dignity over their relationship with each other, readers are left to ponder the women's choices—class over gender, family honor over friendship, security over solidarity—and their consequences.

Umrigar's novel provides an opportunity to read the complex machinations of class differentiated patriarchal oppression and capitalist exploitation, particularly as they operate between women of upper and lower classes, while exploring both the limits and possibilities of solidarity in spite of these forces. More specifically, it enables a discussion of circumstances where women's loyalty to family-, class-, and community-specific structures ostensibly trump an alliance based on a "common" gender-based oppression. It is an instance to test the ideas of contrapuntal histories of the oppressor-oppressed and the possibilities of cross-cultural dissident friendship within that context.

The two women share a "stout affection" despite their vast differences. While loyalty binds Bhima to Sera, the latter expresses gratitude to the former as the sole provider of a kindly "human touch" to her lonely and beleaguered life. After a particularly brutal beating by her husband, Bhima nourishes Sera's bruised body back to life:

> Sera recoiled. Bhima had never touched her before. She tried to muster some resistance but found that she couldn't come up with one good reason for why Bhima's hands should not touch her. The oil stung Sera into awakeness. Although Bhima's thin but strong hands were only massaging her arm, Sera felt her whole body sigh. She felt life beginning to stir in her veins and couldn't tell if this new, welcome feeling was from the oil or the simple comfort of having another human being touch her in friendliness and caring. Even at the sweetest moment of lovemaking with Feroz, it never felt as generous, as selfless, as this massage did. (108)

This passage is significant because it reveals that even though they are coming from opposite ends of the social spectrum, the two women share a bond greater than the one between Sera and her husband Feroz. Yet, this bond is also dictated by the terms of the contract between Sera and Bhima—it is distinctly one-sided in the sense Bhima is duty-bound to provide service to Sera. Similarly, Sera must fulfill her wifely duties to Feroz and the Dubash household for self-preservation. When she tries to break free of the marriage contract, her mother, who despite being aware of her daughter's unhappiness is still bound by patriarchal expectations, tells her daughter, "your place is not with us; it is with your husband and your in-laws" (189). It is the promise of protection and safety for her daughter Dinaz that ultimately convinces Sera of her place with Feroz.

Of course, Sera and Bhima's relationship is also defined by paternalistic inequality. Despite being sympathetic to her maid's plight, Sera does not make an alteration in the kitchen, which would make Bhima's daily routine infinitely more comfortable. Sera watches a tired Bhima scrub the dishes from the night before in her kitchen and dismisses her son-in-law Viraf's offer to buy a dishwasher to make the maid's chores less onerous. "'Go, go,' she [Sera] says. 'My Bhima can put your fancy dish-washers to shame. Not even a foreign-made machine can leave dishes as clean as Bhima can. Save your money, deekra'" (18). Hearing this exchange, Bhima thinks, "Sometimes she can't figure Serabai out. On the one hand, it makes her flush with pride when Serabai calls her 'my Bhima' and talks about her proprietarily. On the other hand, she always seems to be doing things that undercut Bhima's interests" (18).

This inconsistency in their relationship can be explained by the competing ideologies of rights and care furthered through colonial domination. Although there are instances of deep friendship between the two women, ultimately the master-servant relationship transcends Sera's goodwill. That is, the exploitative conditions of Bhima's work and the consequent diminishing of her humanity is unwittingly emphasized by Sera by invoking the proprietorial yet affectionate term "my Bhima" when talking about her. At the same time, Sera is subjecting Bhima to a standard she would not reduce herself to by alluding to an ethic of care often used by the oppressor to make their oppression more palatable.

Their relationship takes on deeper dimensions after the death of Feroz, Sera's abusive husband, as it transforms Sera's "tomblike" home to a more light and cheerful one. "And yet... The thought of Bhima sitting on her furniture repulses her. The thought makes her stiffen, the same way she had tensed the day she caught her daughter, then fifteen, giving Bhima an affectionate hug" (28). Jan Jindy Pettman (2006), in her article "Women, Colonisation, and Racism" talks about the racialization of colonized women as unclean in relation to the purity and cleanliness of colonizer women so as to facilitate the project of domestication. Here, the distance between the two women is maintained by the avoidance of physical contact even though at moments of intense vulnerability, Sera allows Bhima to massage her bruised body and heal her wounded spirit. Again, the diminishing of Bhima's humanity in one instance is counterbalanced by the rhetoric of care in another to make the oppression more palatable. For instance, it is Bhima that Sera turns to in her darkest moments, instead of women of her own class. These women marvel (if a tad disapprovingly) at Sera's generosity toward Bhima. One such friend praises Bhima's service to the Dubash family over the years, "That is truly exceptional, I have to say. No wonder you treat her like a family member. My Praful always used to say that you've made that woman sit on your head, if you don't mind my saying so." (44). The patronizing and downright hateful attitudes of the upper classes toward the poor and other minorities are expertly captured in various scenes and juxtaposed with

Dinaz's attempts to call out her mother's hypocrisy. The desire to maintain the sanctity of the family and the community is in no small way influenced by the anxiety of the Parsis about their shrinking numbers, and perceived "threatened" existence (it is estimated that in India and worldwide the Parsi population is witnessing a steady decline). The exchange between Sera and her friend serves as a reminder that the kind of relationship she has fostered with Bhima within the institutional structures of the patriarchal family and community is truly exceptional and mired in contradictions.

In her essay "Consent, Agency and Rhetorics of Incitement," Kumkum Sangari makes several important observations about patriarchies, which she defines as "system[s] of subordinating women." She argues that patriarchies are maintained and made more resilient through various degrees of coercion (the practice and threat of violence) and consent. Patriarchal contracts yield differential compensation based on diverse women's varied access to power, and consent can be measured "across a continuum from acquiescence or passive acceptance to active collusion" (1993, 868)—processes "to which women are subject but of which they may also be agents" (869). Although patriarchal systems are linked to other systems of oppression, and women's consent and resistance are simultaneously produced through and linked to other structures of inequality such as caste-class, it (patriarchy as a distinct form of subordination) is not necessarily collapsible into them. One can argue that Sera is an acquiescing subject of classic patriarchy living in an extended patrilineal family, including an abusive mother-in-law, Banu, who actively colludes in oppressing her. On the other hand, she negotiates within a set of constraints, particular to her location, to move her immediate family—husband and daughter—away from under the same roof of her extended family where the combination of her manipulative mother-in-law and obliging husband produces an extremely oppressive situation. Paradoxically, the contract to which she consents, that of being provided for and protected through marriage to Feroz, and of which she is at once resentful, offers only the illusion of protection.

In so many ways, the workings of this patriarchal contract (of which Sera is both a subject and agent) is replicated in the relationship between Sera and Bhima. For example, during her menstrual cycle, Sera is quarantined in her bedroom by Banu to maintain the purity and cleanliness of the Dubash family home. During the cycle, Sera is forbidden to make physical contact with her mother-in-law. Bhima's "uncleanliness"—associated with her low class-caste status—is repeatedly brought up by Sera and used as an excuse for separation (to not invite Bhima to sit with the family, or eat and drink from the same cutlery used by the family). Likewise, even when Sera brings a sickly Bhima to her own home to nurse her back to health—a gesture etched in Bhima's mind as reflective of Sera's boundless generosity—the older woman is given a thin mattress on the balcony on which to sleep. The only difference is that one woman's motives (in the case of Sera's mother-in-law) are driven by malice, the other's (Sera's own) maintain inherited traditions of separation between the classes. Arguably, both sets of relationship serve to (re)produce patriarchal power between women.

Sangari's work is further useful in analyzing women's complex agency and resistance in the novel. She works with the notion of "indirect agency" in its specific articulation of consent and resistance in individual and collective acts. For women, even within consensual contractual situations, consent can still breed resentment. Women's agency has to be weighed through this contradictory aspect within patriarchies and can be both complicit and transgressive. An example of this complicitous and resentful agency is Sera's continued care for her paralyzed mother-in-law, Banu—her tormentor in another life when she was still living with the extended family under the same roof. In an effort to save his son's marriage, Feroz's father, Freddy Dubash, a mild-mannered "patriarch" who prefers the company of talking birds perhaps to escape the steely domination of his wife, purchases a separate flat for Sera and Feroz. After the death of both Freddy and Feroz, Sera continues her duties by arranging for the best possible care for Banu, now a ghost of her tyrannical self as she lies paralyzed and unable to speak. Yet, Sera cannot resist pinching Banu's flaccid lifeless cheek between her fingers when no one else is looking. "It is her only way of chalking up a minor victory for the idealistic, hopeful girl who lies buried inside this graveyard of a house" (51).

Maya, Bhima's seventeen-year-old granddaughter, also exercises indirect agency in significant, though minor, ways in the novel. Orphaned at age seven when both parents succumbed to AIDS, Maya was raised by her elderly toiling grandmother. Sera's beneficence and Dinaz and Viraf's business contacts, Bhima believes, will help procure a job for Maya once she completes her degree in accounting. In a life that had seen more than its share of despair and menial, backbreaking labor, Bhima had allowed "a freckle of hope" to enter through Maya, who she believed could alter its course. She dreamed of a future for her granddaughter that would be different from hers, her mother's, and her grandmother's, where Maya would be "fat and content, busy in a kitchen with sparkling stainless steel pots and pans, frying puris for a rambunctious, dark-haired son and a father who came home each evening from his white-collar job" (21). Therefore, she feels utterly crushed and betrayed by Maya's pregnancy by what she considers the consequence of her granddaughter's feckless behavior. Bhima's heart swells with the conflicting emotions she feels toward her:

Bhima wants to take the sobbing girl to her bosom, to hold and caress her the way she used to when Maya was a child, to forgive her and to ask for her forgiveness. But she can't. If it were just anger that she was feeling, she could've scaled that wall and reached out to her grandchild. But the anger is only the beginning of it. Behind the anger is fear, fear as endless and vast and gray as the Arabian Sea, fear for this stupid, innocent, pregnant girl who stands sobbing before her, and for this unborn baby who will come into the world to a mother who is a child herself and to a grandmother who is old and tired to her very bones, a grandmother who is tired of loss, of loving and losing, who cannot bear the thought of one more loss and one more person to love. (11–12)

What puzzles Bhima further is Maya's reluctance to agree to a swift abortion and disinterest to continue her college education—both arranged and financed by the Dubash family. Even as Sera, Viraf, and Bhima "plotted" the "death" (94) of Maya's unborn child, they pampered and protected Dinaz, pregnant with Sera's first grandchild. Viraf is "proprietarial" in his declarations, "Maya needs to have an abortion, and the sooner it is done, the better off she will be. I'm just surprised that we've waited all this time, actually" (69). He then turns to his wife, Dinaz, to say smilingly, "Besides, it's so depressing talking about abortions and all when Dinaz is—when we are—pregnant. You know? It's like every time I want to just be happy about our good fortune, I feel forced to think about Maya's misfortune" (71). Even as he plans for the birth of his child with his wife Dinaz, Viraf tries to erase all traces of his other baby growing inside Maya.

When Maya finally agrees to the procedure, she sets the condition that Sera-bai (a term reserved for a woman of higher social status) must accompany her to the clinic instead of her own grandmother. Bhima accepts the condition thinking her granddaughter wanted to ensure superior care at the hospital that would surely come because of Sera's wealth and status. The cruel irony in the situation is that Maya wants to implicate the unwitting Sera in the murder of the baby whose father is none other than her own son-in-law even as they are poised to celebrate the birth of his "legitimate" child with Dinaz. Maya is at once a victim and reluctant beneficiary of the feudal and patriarchal power structure here, while her actions demonstrate her resistant and resentful complicity to it.

On the morning of the abortion, Sera picks up Maya at the bus stand and asks Bhima to continue on to the Dubash residence to get started on her chores. Surprised to learn that Sera has left the house keys with the neighbor instead of bringing them with her to hand over to Bhima in person, Maya makes a brittle retort, "She could've trusted you with them [the keys]. But she trusts the neighbor more" (118). Bhima and Sera are both shocked by the implied insolence and ingratitude in Maya's comment, and Sera chalks it up to the pregnancy. She thinks to herself, "The unwanted pregnancy had also cast a pall on the Dubash household, so that the baby growing like a weed inside Maya was smothering the happiness they should be feeling at the thought of the child flowering within Dinaz's belly" (119). At the hospital, the procedure is performed by a doctor friend of Viraf's, following which Maya flatly informs Sera, "all of you will be satisfied now. My baby is dead" (123). Sera provides for the provisions for Maya's recovery and buys her a new shalwar-kameez before dropping her back to the slum. It is ironic here that Sera compares the two pregnancies in the above-mentioned quote even though the line that separates the contrapuntal courses of Dinaz's and Maya's lives is the same one that maintains the space of difference between her and Bhima. One pregnancy and relationship is legitimate while the other is not, even though they might have shared a common lineage. In this instance, maintaining honor and power are greater than the ties of blood (Maya's baby), kinship (the relationship between the Dubash family and Bhima's), or friendship. The kin-like relationship between the two families is ultimately trumped by the patriarchal workings of power.

Although the Dubashs feel satisfied that they had helped Bhima by taking care of the "problem," Maya "sits stone-faced, as if the abortion doctor has killed more than her baby, as if he has also cleaned out her insides, has scooped out her beating heart just as Bhima scoops the fibrous innards of the red pumpkin that Serabai puts in her daal" (130). She is neither interested in returning to college, nor in anything else for that matter. She spends her days in the claustrophobic slum room waiting for her grandmother to come home at the end of the day so together they can walk by the ocean and eat pani-puri or bhel in Chowpatty. In a novel so attuned to class differences, Chowpatty is the great equalizer where men and women of all castes, classes, religions, and nationalities seem to partake of the "street foods" and revel in the fresh salty sea air. Despite the parallel worlds that Sera and Bhima inhabited, Chowpatty, as we shall see, was the site where they encountered each other outside the binding relationship of master-servant. It was also where Sera and Feroz, and Bhima and Gopal went for romance during their respective courtships, as well as in the loving phases of their marriage. For Sera, it also became a place to escape from Banu and their fort-like home after marriage. It is here that Umrigar stages the fateful encounter between the Dubashs, and Maya and Bhima, when the elderly woman becomes aware of the truth behind her granddaughter's pregnancy.

Upon spotting Maya and Bhima from their booth at an outdoor food stall in Chowpatty, Dinaz waves to the two women sitting nearby. Bhima and a reluctant Maya walk over to greet Dinaz and the Dubashs. The young and cheerful mother-to-be draws attention to her "swollen belly" by saying "Yah, I've probably grown like a fat pig since you last saw me, na?" In a manner uncharacteristically rude, Maya responds, "I was looking the same way, too. That is, until your mummy fixed me" (265). Bhima realizes the truth about Maya's pregnancy by observing Viraf's guilty and fidgety demeanor. He tries to "hide behind his wife and mother-in-law." Yet, she still blames her granddaughter for the "sin" and "betrayal." She accuses Maya for "Pissing in the pot you have been eating out of. Betraying the trust that the whole Dubash family had in you. That boy's wife, Dinaz, has been like a daughter to me. How will I ever face them again? Namak-haram, every letter that you know to read, every stitch of clothing that you wear, every grain of salt in your mouth, it all comes from Serabai's generosity" (269). Reminding Bhima that it was her labor that provided their food and clothing and not Serabai's unbounded generosity, Maya responds, "Why this rush to make your granddaughter into the only sinner here? . . . Why do you love their family even more than you love your own?" (270). Bhima's subservient loyalty to the Dubash family is striking here. Enraged by Maya's betrayal by shattering the hopes for a secure and protected future, Bhima seems to forget that it is her backbreaking labor that has sustained the Dubash family's physical and spiritual well-being at the cost of her own depleting energy—much like the "innards of the pumpkin" she scoops for the daal that nourishes Serabai. It is the risk of losing the increasingly elusive idea of protection, which Bhima believes will ultimately lead to a life of respectability for Maya that is at the root of her blinding anger toward her granddaughter and the exaggerated affinity toward her employer.

Ironically, it is this steadfast and unquestioning love for her patrons that also sows the seeds of ruin for Bhima's own family. Love and duty had compelled her to massage Sera's bruised body all the while as the paternalistic relationship they shared had grown roots and replicated over generations. Maya, the shining star of Bhima's life and her hope for a secure future, is put to work by the handsome and irresistible Viraf in Banu's flat where he stops by one afternoon to balance her accounts. As the paralyzed old matriarch lies unable to speak or move in her bedroom, Viraf sets the seduction stage in another room by asking Maya to massage his back. Maya both "protested; she did not protest." It did not matter either way because "it was inevitable what was about to happen." One can argue that Viraf carefully plotted his sexual encounter with Maya by arriving at a time when he knew she would be alone with Banu, praising her for being "sweet" and "loyal," and then playfully and teasingly drawing her out of her shy schoolgirl demeanor to apply Iodex and baby oil to his aching muscles. On the other hand, this relationship of unquestioned service—between Maya and Viraf, between Bhima and Sera, and among Maya, Bhima, and any member of the Dubash household, for that matter—was the bedrock of the contract between the two families. Maya sits on her haunches and weeps as Viraf cleans himself off and orders her to do the same and get rid of all "suspicious" signs. Finally, he extracts the promise of her silence by referring to their contractual family relationship: "If you tell anybody what happened, who do you think they're going to believe? You or me? First of all, I'll deny everything. Be sensible and don't do anything to jeopardize either your education or Bhima's job" (279).

True to Viraf's words, that is exactly the outcome of Maya's confession to Bhima, who is outraged and hurt at this betrayal by a member of the Dubash household. Even as she continues to blame Maya, she also begins to see Viraf in a new light during their weekly journey together to the market. She watches how comfortable he is in exercising his status-related power as he interacts with the lift-boy, the beggar-woman with the two children in the streets. He admonishes one for daring to want to sully the image of the nation by throwing banana peels on the cricket ground when India takes on West Indies and shouts at the other, "How you going to raise those children if you can't even look after yourself?" When Viraf asks Bhima about Maya's well-being, she feels the weight of the crushing poverty that generations of women in her family had faced stifle her answer. She is unable to carry out her plan to remind him "that his thoughtless pleasure has derailed her Maya's life, has blocked the path that would've taken the girl out of the slum. What she and Serabai had built together, Viraf has destroyed. Women create, Bhima thinks, men destroy. The way of the world" (283).

Bhima, however, faces the greatest betrayal from none other than her ally Sera when in the moment of revelation her friend/employer chooses to align herself with her son-in-law. Thus she chooses honor vis-à-vis the terms of her class-specific patriarchal contract to family while breaking the one with her lower-class female confidant. Viraf, not wanting to risk Bhima revealing the truth to Sera, orchestrates her dismissal by alluding to Sera that her elderly maid might be responsible for swiping 700 rupees from Banu's cupboard. Bewildered by the ugly exchange of words between Viraf and Bhima, Sera demands the truth from Bhima. Unable to control her fury that strikes at the heart of her dignity for being accused of stealing from the Dubashs when she had been nothing but loyal to them, an enraged Bhima blurts out to Sera, "Ask him what he did to my Maya if you want the truth . . . Ask him what guilt he is trying to hide. He thinks he can buy my silence with his seven hundred rupees? If he builds me a house of gold I won't forgive him for what he has done to my_" (302). A shattered Sera's final words are, "I can excuse you stealing from me, but to challenge my son-in-law's honor, that I can never forgive you for" (303).

According to Sangari, women's acceptance of the social contract evoked by patriarchy is lodged within at least two contradictions: the economic and ideological assurances of family and the "myth of the responsible male protector-provider," which men are either unable or unwilling to fulfill. Even though Sera has been repeatedly victimized by the illusion of protection through family, it is to this institution that she ultimately turns for security. She exercises her agency, not on behalf of justice or care, but by severing the contract with the lesser compatriot in her life who had been her greatest ally. Sangari notes, "Women from the propertied classes or the upper layers of social hierarchy should especially be looked at in the full range of complicities and extracted compensations ... Does their consent rest on the pincer logic of bondage produced through caste-class affiliations and privilege or power exercised over others?" (1993, 869). In other words, the agency and consent of women of upper and laboring classes are produced and nuanced differently as per their gender positionality.

Sera's choice nevertheless begs the question that Sangari poses in her article about "the cost of such power or of subsistence within compensatory structures for women" (871). She asks, "Are the rights or compensations on which consent rests structurally available to all women of that group or to some? ... How far do contractual and consensual elements persist because of the absence of external support structures for women and how far do they actually inhibit their formation?" (871). One could deduce that the cost of Sera maintaining her status, and through that power, is the loss of the possibility of a meaningful even dissident alliance between her and Bhima. Sera's power here is self-serving and self-preserving, the means to which are not available for someone in Bhima's position. The illusion of security through male association within family structure trumps the possibility of solidarity, justice, and a kind of freedom, which risks the breakup of the family and threatens the tarnishing of honor, status, and social acceptance.

Bhima too exercises agency in choosing dignity over silence, but of course with very different consequences. If she had not spoken the truth, Sera would not have terminated the contract. But to not speak the truth would have left her bereft of dignity and respect, the very attributes—social capital for someone in her position—that she aspired to above all, and the ticket to which was held by her employer. But, once the truth had been uttered it had to be covered up at all cost in order to preserve the fragile patriarchal contract of which Sera was an agent. Ironically, Bhima is set "free" by Viraf's deception: "She is almost grateful to Viraf baba now, for his treachery has been the knife that has cut the thread that kept her bound for so long" (315). Nevertheless, her freedom is borne out of terrible circumstances and with abject consequences. As Sangari notes, the divisive nature of patriarchal distribution of power leads to both tensions between women as well as the disenablement of collectivity, at best the fleeting possibility of an "uneasy collectivity" (1993, 871).

Sera's choice also has to be considered within what Sangari calls the notion of "female incitement"—women calling upon men (as provider and protector) to act on their behalf. We have already established that the (patriarchal) contractual relationship between Sera and Bhima replicates that of Feroz and Sera with the illusion of protection as its cornerstone. It is also pertinent here to recall Lugones's notion of the colonial modern gender system discussed earlier to illuminate the functioning of multiple and differential gendered positionalities through the structuring of heterosexualist power arrangements. When Bhima reveals the truth, she calls upon Sera (her provider and protector) to act justly on her behalf. "Incitement exists at the intersection between the 'political' and 'domestic,' between gender relations and other power relations, occupies an uneasy boundary between the respective logics of women's consent and resistance rearticulating their relationship in different ways." For incitement to beget the desired results, it has to reflect a set of conditions. "First, women must share the values for which men are being incited and have a stake in the social relation which is sought to be preserved" (Sangari 1993, 872). Are these reflected in the contract between Sera and Bhima? Yes and no. Here, the critical question is whether Sera and Bhima—differently gendered and receiving asymmetrical rewards of the colonial gender system—share these values and are equally committed in preserving the social relation that is being called on to be defended.

The second condition for incitement is that women cannot act independently and directly but must act through men or the person who is being incited to defend social values. That is, women can be "the active custodians of those values and social relations but they cannot usually take action (generally militant or public) themselves" (872). With regard to this condition, Bhima needs Sera's acknowledgment of the wrong that has been done for any justice to be meted out. She cannot possibly act on her own behalf and get the kind of result she desires. It is Sera who has the power to acknowledge the wrong and ensure the just outcome.

Third, "if incitement is to carry an inspirational connotation, women must never name the social relation they are trying to preserve or present it as a personal or material interest; they can only name the abstraction—family, honour, religion, nation—to which the social relation is either directly attached or which mediates it. If women name it (or rather give it no other name?) and/or state their own personal stake in it, then it acquires a malignant connotation: they become status conscious materialists, conniving intriguers, women leading men astray, wicked manipulators. In the naming and the not naming resides the distinction between villainous and heroic inciting women" (873). Bhima cannot name the intimate relationship she shares with Sera. It has to be an abstraction that motivates Sera to act in the interest of justice. Indeed Sera, the provider, does exactly that, not for Bhima but on her own behalf for self-preservation and security, and names honor as the reason for her choice in denouncing Bhima. What is interesting here, however, is that Bhima gains "temporary control over male sexuality" because this moment of revelation reveals that the Dubash family honor is tied to a deceptive male sexuality, which has to be preserved even at the face of injustice. In the elaborate theater of Sera's abdication of care of and responsibility, Viraf's outrage belies this deeper reality.

Sangari further notes that, "Since men are usually perceived as having both rights and duties, while women as having primarily duties, any claim to 'rights,' unless effectively disguised, becomes a sign of women's evil nature." The same situation that enables Sera to have a "convoluted agency" concomitantly produces "misogyny" and "characterizing that agency as malignant." Sera has rights and duties, the right to self-preservation, the duty to preserve her family and the lesser duty to Bhima. The lesser Bhima is absent rights in this relationship, and her claim to it makes her a pariah. Female incitement does not work in producing the kinds of results that would serve justice to Bhima and enable an enduring alliance between Sera and Bhima in this instance because it would also expose "a large number of social values, endangering the entire dense imbrication of patriarchal structures with the other related social structures" (873). What it hints at, however, is a fleeting bond across differential positionalities that women occupy within patriarchal power structures and the affective relationships that are momentarily forged despite the contradictions.

If Sera had taken the challenge of incitement and chosen to act on her duty to Bhima, it would have elicited an outcome irreconcilable within the patriarchal contract. Yet, women suffer from both the successes of patriarchy and from its breakdown. Sera suffers from her silencing choice: she is left with social guilt, which ultimately will turn her home once again to the tomb of deception and lies and denial from which she had been temporarily freed.

Ultimately, the final choice that Sera makes should not entirely determine the limits and possibilities of the affective bond—within and external to the contract—shared by Sera and Bhima. What this choice illuminates rather is the fragility of the patriarchal contract without diminishing the depth of the relationship between Sera and Bhima. Here Umrigar's comment is instructive: "as human beings we share experiences that can connect us profoundly, in spite of differences in social class, gender, and culture; but those differences can also create unbridgeable spaces between us, persisting in spite of what we may need or want." In this interview with Cheney, Umrigar talks about the impulse behind her writing as "looking for how humans connect, how people cross class lines, the difficulties they have communicating with each other, where communication breaks down and why relationships fail" (2008, 1).

I would like to return here to the question of dissident friendship, community, and solidarity between women and explore further the circumstances in which these are or are not trumped by loyalties women have to their families, communities, or nations. Of course, the idea of friendship and community in feminist discourses are contested. In the collection of essays *Feminism and Community*, the contributors make the distinction between "traditional" and feminist communities. In traditional settings, they argue, significant relationships of female support and acts of resistance can coexist with hierarchical and exploitative ones, whereas internal struggles can also inhibit feminist communities from achieving the desired political transformation on behalf of women. The point is that these two settings are neither mutually exclusive nor completely antithetical to one another. Rather, the authors suggest that, "Both can be the sites of genuine friendship, social support, and collaborative political activism among women" (Weiss and Friedman 1995, xii). The arenas Umrigar highlights in *The Space Between Us* are arguably traditional—the upper-middle- and working-class patriarchal families and the feudal household where neither women are motivated by political activism. Yet within these settings also exist collaborative relationships among women who come from opposite ends of the spectrum forming unexpected alliances. At the same time, it is useful to keep in mind Penny Weiss's cautionary note to not engage in uncritical celebration of women's agency and resistance within traditional communities but instead to listen carefully to women in all of these contexts in order to learn the specific insights women as women have to offer in the larger struggle for social transformation. While Sera and Bhima may not have achieved much through their sometimes dissident alliance, readers come to learn how the identities—or positionalities—of each are constituted through their specific class and gender locations. These positionalities dictate the limits of their agency and the risks each can take on behalf of women's freedom.

Ironically, Sera's inability to transcend the norms of her middle-class existence ultimately offers Bhima a kind of freedom from the subservient loyalty through which she had come to constitute a class- and gender-specific identity. When Bhima says her final goodbye to Sera, raising her employer and confidante's hands to her eyes, "Even in the dim light of the evening, she notices the teardrop that glistens on Sera's fair-skinned wrist" (305). Bhima describes the world outside Serabai's "protection" as "hell," where readers are left to only imagine Sera's own hell as her front door slams shut, foreshadowing her return to the tomblike fortress full of guilty secrets. The bond the two women shared, however, signified by the single merging teardrop (the origin of the teardrop is left ambiguous by the author), cannot be denied. Feminist political theorist Iris Marion Young has argued for the need to broaden an understanding of individuality and community that does not pit one in negative relation to the other. *The Space Between Us* then allows us to expand this debate and to recognize when striving for solidarity that women's relationships are heterogeneous, complex, and conflicting. Solidarity is a demanding ideal to strive for. Moreover, the attainment of it can be ambiguous and fleeting. These ephemeral moments nevertheless allude to "disruptive possibilities" (Friedman 1995, 200) and can lead to important transformations in female consciousness in the broader and ongoing struggle to create more enabling conditions of care.

References

Friedman, Marilyn. 1995. "Feminism and Modern Friendship: Dislocating the Community." In Weiss and Friedman 1995, 187–208.

Gandhi, Leela. 2006. *Affective Communities: Anticolonial Thought, Fin-de-Siècle Radicalism, and the Politics of Friendship*. Durham, N.C.: Duke University Press.

Lugones, Maria. 2007. "Heterosexualism and the Colonial/Modern Gender System." *Hypatia* 22(1): 186–209.

Lugones, Maria, in collaboration with Pat Alake Rosezelle. 1995. "Sisterhood and Friendship as Feminist Models." In Weiss and Friedman 1995, 135–146.

Mansbridge, Jane. 1995. "Feminism and Democratic Community." In Weiss and Friedman 1995, 341–366.

Moraga, Cherrie. 1983. "Refugees of a World on Fire: Foreword to the Second Edition." In *This Bridge Called My Back: Writings by Radical Women of Color*, edited by Cherrie Moraga and Gloria Anzaldúa, n.p. 2nd ed. New York: Kitchen Table: Women of Color Press.

Narayan, Uma. 1995. "Colonialism and Its Others: Considerations on Rights and Care Discourses." *Hypatia* 10(2): 31–47.

———. 1988. "Working Together across Difference: Some Considerations on Emotions and Political Practice." *Hypatia* 3(2): 133–140.

Pettman, Jan Jindy. 2006. "Women, Colonisation, and Racism." In *Beyond Borders: Thinking Critically about Global Issues*, edited by Paula S. Rothenberg, 142–149. New York: Worth Publishers.

Ray, Raka, and Qayum, Seemin, eds. 2009. *Cultures of Servitude: Modernity, Domesticity, and Class in India*. Stanford: Stanford University Press.

Rich, Adrienne. 1995. "If Not With Others, How?" In Weiss and Friedman 1995, 399–406.
Said, Edward. 1993. *Culture and Imperialism*. New York: Vintage.
Sangari, Kumkum. 1993. "Consent, Agency and Rhetorics of Incitement." *Economic and Political Weekly*, May 1, 867–882.
———. 1999. *Politics of the Possible: Essays on Gender, History, Narratives, Colonial English*. New Delhi: Tulika.
Stone-Mediatore, Shari. 2003. *Reading across Borders: Storytelling and Knowledges of Resistance*. New York: Palgrave Macmillan.
Umrigar, Thrity. 2005. *The Space Between Us*. New York: William Morrow.
———. 2008. Interview by Jean Cheney. *Human Ties: Utah Humanities Council Newsletter* Fall/Winter: 1–2.
Weiss, Penny, and Friedman, Marilyn, eds. 1995. *Feminism and Community*. Philadelphia, Pa.: Temple University Press.
Young, Iris Marion. 1995. "The Ideal of Community and the Politics of Difference." In Weiss and Friedman 1995, 233–258.

CHAPTER 8

Who Are "We" in the Novel?

SHREEREKHA SUBRAMANIAN

Introduction

Arundhati Roy's documentary film, *We* (2006, 64 minutes), offers significant ideas for breaking down global polarizations—North and South, capitalists and impoverished, status-bearers and the protesters, and also what I see as the yawning divide between the academic and the popular. Roy's take on the world of corporate greed and nationalist wars, the remapping of world powers in the wake of 9/11, and the condition of the hundred million poor of the world, offers a way of bridging the binary she raises in her opening, "fiction and non-fiction, power and powerlessness," alerting us to a way of seeing without which it becomes impossible to locate the "We" of her title. Interpreting modern history through Roy's "physics of power" renders visible the intersections of race, class, nation, ethnicity, and gender imbalances that turn the "haves" into blind amnesiacs unable to understand what the Other bears to maintain the standard of life for the privileged few of the Global North. My examination of Roy's ever-shifting "We" will illuminate the questions at the heart of dissident friendships that can be, in Leela Gandhi's terms, between the "most unlikely of associates" and also "trumped by other kinds of allegiances individuals might have to family, community, or nation," as Elora Chowdhury and Liz Philipose caution us in the introduction.

In her literary imaginary, Thrity Umrigar, a contemporary Indian American novelist who writes primarily about the Parsi community in Bombay and its diaspora, meditates repeatedly on female friendships that cross cultural, national, and class differences. Transnational feminism informs Thrity Umrigar's narrative praxis. She is committed to exploring friendships that Maria Lugones has described as being founded on "coalitional communicative gestures" (2006, 81) grounded at once in memory and resistance that are mutually meaningful, empathetic, and transformative. In her novel *The Space Between Us* (2005), Umrigar presents the complex and ultimately failed relationship between the wealthy widow, Sera, and her domestic servant, Bhima. Bhima labors for decades before being dismissed in ways that deem her, in Ranjana Khanna's (2009) psychoanalytic term, as disposable. Another Umrigar novel, *If Today Be Sweet* (2007), charts the metamorphosis of a recently widowed woman, Tehmina, who joins her son and family in the USA and slowly finds her own voice, autonomy, and strength in a novelistic frame of a solid friendship with an American friend, Eva, who emerges as her steadfast ally. Umrigar's latest novel, *The Weight of Heaven* (2009), gives a grim account of the costs of globalization wherein perennial wanderers (arch-signifier in the history of the Western novel) choose India as part of their personal catharsis. An American couple, Frank and Ellie Benton, relocate to India after surviving the tragedy of the death of their child due to an illness. It is useful here to be reminded of Ashis Nandy's (1989) psychoanalysis of asymmetries in psychic power relations between the white colonizer and native subject. Frank and Ellie's catharsis relocates the intimate enemy in neocolonialism.

The complex milieu of this novel is marked by a tragic resolution in that Ellie does not return home with Frank. Her murder reveals how unchecked imperial power turns to wreck Frank. This element of poetic and social justice is framed by the unlikely friendship of Ellie and Nandita, raising critical questions about the possibilities of dissident transnational sisterhoods. Who are "We" in Umrigar's novel? Maythee Rojas's (2009) elucidation of Inderpal Grewal and Caren Kaplan's transnational feminism charts a transnational feminist project founded on radical love, loving across borders, territories, and walls, loving without colonizing, loving against form, and loving as the alphabet in the discursive order of transnational solidarity. In bringing together the theoretical lesson in Roy's distillation of "We" with Umrigar's novelistic fabric, this chapter reconfigures questions of transnational feminist possibilities into a new trajectory apart from "Us'" and "Them" wherein the third world female is always already an occupant, an Other.

Theorizing the Liminal and the Subjective Other

Roy's narrative film, just over an hour in length, speaks of her relationship to fiction in a world divided between the powerful and the powerless, where she seeks to speak on the paranoia and physics of power.[1] Speaking over images of war tanks, advertising, and simulacra, Roy ranges across the subjects of nuclear race, war against terror, and the many 9/11s that preceded the one in the United States, concluding with an emphasis on the depredations of corporate privatization. It is critical in the theoretical framing for the purposes of this chapter to concatenate Roy's prolificity of essays and collections such as *The Cost of Living* (1999) and *Listening to Grasshoppers: Field Notes on Democracy* (2009) with the metaphors for ontology offered in her visual essay, *We*. Hard times demand concrete adjustments. The novel cannot be studied through words alone. As a pedagogical practice, Charles Lawrence (1992) indicates how the word is forever subjective, multiple, and substantial because of the dream. Reflecting on the ontological foreclosures entailed at the beginning of the third millennium, Julia Kristeva succinctly summarizes the perniciousness of our moment because we are "in a world subject to the automatization of minds by technology and to wars of religion that encourage archaism and terrorism" (2006, 13). I suggest that the novels produced in the third millennium can be addressed through the multiple registers of our historical transition from the written to the visual that some forecasted as the death of the novel.

Roy's advocacy and solidarity on behalf of the subaltern people of the world, who shoulder the burden of "development" in the Global North (not a geographic north but multiple locales within cities and nations), provide critical balance to the literary imaginary offered by Umrigar, especially in her novels *The Space Between Us* and *The Weight of Heaven* that address the intersections of race, class, and nation. Roy's prophetic fist shaking at capitalism, a few years before the protest fevers spring around cities and nations as far apart as Santiago, Chile, and Tokyo, Japan, along an arc of disaffection in the Middle East and sites in the Global North, raises questions that Umrigar addresses in her quiet novelistic reflections on the Parsi community in India and abroad. Just as the music of Dead Can Dance, Nine Inch Nails, and Amon Tobin vibrate in the background as Roy fulminates against the American regime of International Monetary Fund, World Trade Organization, and World Bank, which dominates the global order, Roy's measured vocabulary resonates in the back chambers of the postcolonial contemporary novel. The novels' aporetic endings raise the very question of the shelf life of power upon which Roy concludes, pleading with her viewers to "read." In the end, the video archive returns its spectator to the page, and Roy returns us to the traditional text or else, as she cautions, "we're all screwed."

Inderpal Grewal and Caren Kaplan's feminist manifesto leaves its mark on the postcolonial feminist novel. Deeply aware of the "new forms of colonialism" that pervade local and global spaces, they articulate a feminism that speaks to and against the reigning order of imperialism, vis-à-vis globalization, development projects, and internationalism. "Emphasis on the history of modern imperialism has helped feminists look at race, sexuality, and class not only as bounded categories but as concepts that 'travel'—that is, circulate and work in different and linked ways in different places and times" (2000). In destabilizing monolithic categories of oppression and working off the model of intersectionality, Grewal and Kaplan complicate the category of "woman" itself, attending to multiplicity in gender alongside exploitation. Leela Gandhi's (2006) careful and systematic construction of the worlds of friendship that question the veracity of standard ideological apparatuses such as nation, capital, race, religion, is crucial to unpacking the possibilities of cross-national, cross-cultural, and cross-racial friendships being imagined in Umrigar's novelistic landscapes. Gandhi argues for plurality of identities, echoing Grewal and Kaplan's declaration against binarism. Friendships, based on trust and loyalty, supersede other value systems and augment a politics of the disappearing present. Maria Lugones's formulations of the liminal space—arising out of her close reading of Gloria Anzaldúa's *Borderlands*—illuminate cross-cultural affective circuits that might attempt friendship. In the practical materiality of our own multiplicity, Lugones's vision synchronizes with Grewal, Kaplan, and Gandhi as she argues toward a complex communication generated out of a "coalitional limen" (2006, 78). In her argument for disrupting domination and deciphering resistant codes, Lugones theorizes nodes of resistance across patriarchal ossifications. What conversations are possible when the liminal becomes semiotic and transparent? Umrigar's novels narrate such conversations wherein women's friendships stretch across material restrictions and ideological formations, hypothesizing an intimacy that transgresses the symbolic, and enter the imaginary of transnational feminist alliances. Veena Das's (2006) devastating reading of quotidian forms of violence helps us approach and discern fragments of structural violence evinced in the lives of women.

The Space Between Us (2005): Contesting the Divisions of Class

Umrigar's novels, despite their setting in the modern world, remind us of classic medieval morality plays and inverted convention: the virtuous protagonists, generally distanced from capital and power, enter into conflict with the powerful, lose the battle, and learn deep truths about their own selves. *The Space Between Us* (Umrigar 2005) centers on friendship between women of two different classes, Sera, a rich Parsi housewife in Bombay and her maidservant of several decades, Bhima, who dwells in slums Sera dreads to even enter. In a relationship that spans decades, wherein their friendship bubbles through the domestic space they share as they learn of the most intimate troubles each faces, Bhima is the one who helps heal her mistress's blistered back after an evening of abuses heaped on by her husband, Feroz. Sera maneuvers the hospital bureaucracy when Bhima's husband has an accident in the factory where he used to work. The novel opens and closes at a more recent stage in the women's lives when twin pregnancies are augured—Sera's daughter, Dinaz, is pregnant with her first child and is giddily awaiting her future alongside her husband, Viraf. Bhima's granddaughter, Maya, a college student, is suddenly home with a pregnancy resulting from a tryst Maya refuses to disclose. Bhima's life is full of hardship and strife as she suffers a husband who loses his humanity along with his health after a workplace accident. With the loss of her son, daughter, and home, Bhima is perched at the abyss with a sliver of hope, her educated granddaughter who might work her way up the socioeconomic ladder with her merit. However, the pregnancy and ensuing abortion throws the young woman into deep depression. The novel's conclusion reveals that the unnameable subject of paternity was Maya's attempt to protect everyone—Bhima, Sera, and herself—from the truth. The father is in fact, Viraf, the golden son-in-law who can do no wrong, according to Sera. When he tries to have Bhima fired after she finds out by charging her with theft, she speaks the truth. Upon hearing the accusations against Viraf, Sera immediately ejects Bhima from her household as Viraf shuts the door on Bhima's protestations. The final chapter shows Bhima straddling the waters of the Arabian Sea, with a bouquet of bright balloons she lets drift off into the dark night sky as she promises herself a new dawn. "Feminist theory must be temperate in the use it makes of this doctrine of 'double vision'—the claim that oppressed groups have an epistemic advantage and access to greater critical conceptual space. Certain types and contexts of oppression certainly may bear out the truth of this claim. Others certainly do not seem to do so; and even if they do provide space for critical insights, they may also rule out the possibility of actions subversive of the oppressive state of affairs" (Narayan 2004, 223).[1]

Shoshana Felman's concept of competing pregnancies critiques Freud through Juliet Mitchell. Felman raises questions that have haunted twentieth-century psychoanalysis: male insight, anxiety of paternity, and competing pregnancies. In decoding Freud's dream discourse, Felman politicizes male insight to arrive at new paradigms. At the seashore, Bhima is poised at the limen where the earth and sky are both present and absent, where all emotions dissolve. As Felman writes, "Irma's dream is a dream of pregnancy," and it is pregnant with "the pregnancy of dreams" (1993, 109). The novel pits Bhima's rebirth against the earlier aborted pregnancy of her granddaughter—wish fulfillment as joke in the psychoanalytic sense, then. Together the two women laughed at the seashore as Maya heals and Bhima reconstitutes herself. Bhima remembers the absent signifier that threads her life story together, the *pathan*[2] who comes back to her like a dream and compels her to buy all the balloons from the vendor. Rather than the solution offered in male discursive order, we end at the knot of female pain, "a dream about a knot of irreducibly resistant women; a dream about a knot of feminine complaints" (118), we are left with at the navel of the novel, at the unknowable of Bhima who, in the ultimate daredevil stunt of her life, centers her own pleasure and dares to dream of a better tomorrow after enunciating to the vendor, "I have no mistress," repeated for emphasis, "Hah. No mistress" (Umrigar 2005, 318). With the balloons floating away, as are her moorings and troubles, she recollects the *pathan*, her absent double whose face is "sad and pensive but also dignified and courageous" (320), as are the faces of the teeming subalterns of the Global South connected by the invisible threads that hold aloft rays of hope and dreams of a new dawn. In psychoanalytic terms, then, the dream disengages from reality and presents the unknowable as an entryway into the real. The limen is the only place that matters for the subaltern who has otherwise been wrested of speech.

Bourgeois hegemony (Williams 1977, 108–127) is the framing device for this novel, which hints at the emergent of dissident friendship of these two women who represent the elite and the proletariat in Sera and Bhima. While the emergent is configured in the possibility of a dissident friendship between two women who are each other's moorings, signposts, healers, the hegemonic ideal is firmly the irreconcilable class difference that marks the two. On one hand, Sera cannot wait because her day does not begin until Bhima comes; partly, it is to chop the onions she cannot bear to chop but the undercurrent is to begin their daily conversations, which are updates on each other's lives. At one point, Bhima spreads a secret ointment to heal the bruises on Sera's lacerated back, but yet, over the years of their relationship, the space between them remains implacably in place. Sera cannot bear to offer Bhima tea in anything other than the cup reserved for her or furniture to sit on. "Part of it is the damn tobacco she chews all day" and the conditions of the slum that make it questionable "how effectively she is able to clean her nether regions" (Umrigar 2005, 29). On the day of revelations, as Sera recedes "like a moon that climbs higher and higher into the night sky," Viraf scolds his mother-in-law for making the mistake of "turning a stray dog into a family pet" (302), thereby returning Bhima to the place beyond marginality from which she enters their bourgeoisie domestic order. Viraf's ontological regime does not allow for Bhima's entry into the human for she remains in an aporetic misidentification between a stray dog (wild, diseased, uncontrolled, dangerous) and a family pet (cute, tractable, dependent, clean), both abject at the threshold of signification.

If Today Be Sweet (2007): Race, Nationalism, and Diaspora

Omar Khayyam's eleventh-century rubaiyats interrupt the novelistic discourse with this novel's title drawing from his famous quatrain that is at once an ode to intoxicants and the celebration of the fleeting present, "Ah, fill the cup:—what boots it to repeat / How Time is slipping underneath our Feet:/ Unborn TOMORROW and dead YESTERDAY, / Why fret about them if TODAY be sweet!" (Umrigar 2007, 277). *If Today Be Sweet* is a novel centered on love, family, and friendship with its protagonist, a sixty-six-year-old newly widowed Parsi woman who travels to Cleveland, Ohio, to spend some time recovering with her son, Sorab; his wife, Susan; and her grandson, Cavas, or Cookie, as he prefers. Tehmina, also known as Tammy in her American context, is deliberating throughout the novel whether she should return to her apartment in Bombay albeit without her late husband's presence, a partner she misses so intensely that he appears and converses with her when she needs him. Her son, who is negotiating corporate troubles at work with a female boss, Grace Butler, who rankles him, finally wrestles with this enemy through his mother's help, as the novel's plot reveals in its denouement. Tehmina, despite differences over her Indian habits and distaste for American suburban sterility, is tugged between her children's wishes to stay in the USA with them and her own wish to return to the teeming streets of her beloved Bombay. Alongside her husband's ghost, her corporeal companion is Eva Metzembaum, an older Jewish neighbor who quickly becomes her confidante, a woman in whom she is able to confide, a woman she can also comfort, and theirs is the dissident friendship that anchors the novelistic logic.

Tehmina intervenes in the lives of two abused children, Jerome and Joshua, who live next door. She protects them from their mother, Tara, and rescues them on Christmas Eve by climbing the fence in the backyard and bringing them over to her side. The rescue soon involves police, reporters, and her chagrined son and daughter-in-law. She emerges as the Christmas angel for the children, rescues her son out of his troubles at work, earns the respect of her daughter-in-law, along with the entire community where the daily newspaper travels, and reaches a state of self-autonomy that helps her decide to start a life in the United States, but on her own terms. Her literal moment of fence-sitting symbolizes the border crossing that helps her finally migrate. She will have her own apartment, and with Eva's help, she will learn to drive. By novel's end, a sweet past with Rustom and a partially sweet present with her son is balanced with the promise of a sweet future for Tehmina, who chooses to be addressed as Tehmina by Eva in her journey to selfhood.

At the heart of this novel lies a realigning of the deconstructive postcolonial feminist paradigm proposed by Spivak, a signatory of a new era in the U.S. academy in the 1970s to 1980s—the ideological social function of colonialism was for the white man to rescue the brown woman from the brown man. Here instead, the brown woman rescues the white children (future white men) from the abuses of the white woman. In the newer paradigm proposed herein, the white woman is hypervisible, the white man recedes, and the brown woman is given primacy. In overturning the deconstructive critique of the previous century, Umrigar's work rests in the humanist feminism articulated most explicitly in Chandra Mohanty's collaborative work with Biddy Martin, where they read Minnie Bruce Pratt closely and define the implications of home, diaspora, and community. Mohanty writes at the intersections of projects of feminism, anti-racism, and anti-Semitism that at once helps to unsettle normative notions of home and community. Both are shifting signifiers that remain unstable, negotiable, and contextual. Mohanty writes: "'Being home' refers to the place where one lives within familiar, safe, protected boundaries; 'not being home' is a matter of realizing that home was an illusion of coherence and safety based on the exclusion of specific histories of oppression and resistance, the repression of differences even within oneself" (2003, 90). Mohanty complicates standard notions of home within diaspora studies and speaks to Tehmina's journey of selfhood and agency within the novel. She realizes that she too has brought home with her in her travels. Alongside loss, central to the discourse on diaspora studies, she gains a deeper understanding of her own strength, wit, endurance, and humor, necessary Benjaminesque traits in surviving the odds of time and space. She clearly prefers downtown Cleveland to the suburbs where her son lives because downtown promises the life she misses from Bombay. It is possible she will choose to find an apartment populating the forbidden city spaces her son cautions her against. She is ready to let go of a nostalgic past in order to construct a new future that is inclusive, self-generated, and based on people totally unfamiliar to the heteronormative order of her Bombay life. Even Rustom's ghost insists it is time for her to regain her dignity and stop meeting him furtively in the dark. This new life promises the fullness of dissident friendships rather than the heteronormative ideal of her past that constituted all her moorings. Her friend, Eva, the humorous foil to her own melancholy, signifies the many Americans she will rescue from their own alienating suffocations and disempowerment. Tehmina is more at home in the foreign land than her son and daughter-in-law, who were well-prepared to continue to turn a blind eye to the troubles brewing in their neighbor's home. In many ways, Tehmina learns to negotiate her own distance from a static home, the city of Bombay, through the affect of friendship and the politics of a new community she has founded through new forms of kinship that revises static notions of home.

Tehmina is given grounds to maintain her own rationale of differences and logic of perspicacity that is at variance with the dominant ethos of corporate leadership, democratic systems, and free market flow of capital. Ultimately, the ghost requires another leave-taking so Tehmina can prosper on her own and let go of her anxiety of indecision, "She would stay. But on her own terms. And the main thing was that she had to have her own apartment . . . she felt daring, excited at the prospect" (Umrigar 2007, 293). The woman finds her agency, and in contexts provided nearly a century ago by Virginia Woolf, a room of her own. However her source of income is left ambiguous. Is Tehmina a woman of independent wealth from which she can draw such autonomy in her lifestyle, or does she plan on starting some form of occupation that will provide her an income, or will she be dependent on her well-to-do son, who is climbing the corporate ladder thanks to the boost he receives from his mother? The capitalist logic remains undisturbed in the plot; Sorab climbs, and Tehmina's altruism has material repercussions in his world. Her "good deed" is turned into corporate merit; the semiliterate, ambitious, and uncaring Grace Butler is fired from her position as lead, and Sorab is knighted officially for his long years of dedicated service, while his mother is now a celebrated American hero. Heroism has material ramifications; celebrity brings monetary remuneration. Just as Sorab is now able to dream big, Tehmina can entertain thoughts of independence thanks to her celebrity as the Christmas angel. Dissident friendship arrives at the heels of obeying the rules and adhering to the logic of free market capitalist imperialisms that come at a cost to other worlds, other ways of thinking and living. The American dream is indeed real and proceeds undeterred no matter what its cost might be to the lives of others.

The Weight of Heaven (2009): Intersectional Globalizations

Umrigar's most recent novel, *The Weight of Heaven* (2009), is a classic moral tale spun out of the postcolonial novel. The novel details what happens when the privilege of the first world traveler encounters third world impoverishment and degradation; all that is free and available is not for purchase or easy pickings. Instead, the wandering corporate citizen of the Global North loses everything in his quest for a reasonable and healthy life.

Frank and Ellie Benton, young parents who find love in their happenstance romance spawned in Ann Arbor, Michigan, in the early 1990s, lose their young seven-year-old son, Ben, to an illness. Grieved and split apart, the two decide to relocate to a small town in India, Girbaug, the fictional setting for much of what transpires in this novel, the plot of which remains deeply invested in the cost of living, the weight of losses, and other lives that burden and mark the lives of those who carry on. In charge of the India wing of a multinational company, Frank's company, Herbal Solutions, pockets the profits from its monopoly of natural forest products, from which its native occupants have been disbarred and, in many ways, disenfranchised from their lives as Indian subjects. Being in India precipitates a new range of crises—with unionizing disgruntled workers at the factory and a little boy of their servants, Prakash and Edna, Ramesh, with whom Frank develops a fatherly attachment. The larger troubles of the factory floor combined with pressures from the U.S. boss cause Frank's personal world to cave in around him, resulting in Frank's destructive act of smashing all that is fragile and beautiful in his world. Ellie, who works her way through the all-consuming grief for her child, chooses life over mourning. She does so by participating in a march in honor of Cindy Sheehan, the real-world mother who stands for her vociferous opposition to the Iraq war, and then, her decision to return to therapy so that she can use her healing of others as a balm to heal her own broken self.

Frank's excessive attachment to the preternaturally bright Ramesh alarms his father Prakash, a drunk and dissolute man, struggling with his own inadequacy as an illegitimate citizen in his personal life. He is an orphan, a Hindu married to a Christian Goan woman cast out of her own family, a physically weak man abused by the bullies in Girbaug such as Gulab, Frank's head of security and chief executer of all orders, including the order to take care of things. Anxious that he might lose his son to the glitter and privilege of an affluent American upbringing, Prakash disappears one fine morning with his son on a failed secret mission to unite Ramesh with his erstwhile maternal grandparents in Goa. Though the father and son return in a week, Frank ages overnight and his rage never abates. He hires Gulab as a hit man and together they devise a plan to murder Prakash so that all paths are clear for Frank to adopt Ramesh and take him back to America. However the plot runs afoul. Ellie never leaves as expected with her dear friend, Nandita, for Delhi and instead helps out Edna in her hut with stomach pains. Thus, the murderer finds the two women in Prakash's home while Prakash sleeps in the large Benton home the night Gulab arrives and shoots in the dark finding the perfect mark thinking he has done away with both of the child's parents. Remembering his own grandmother's words of wisdom that the only man to watch out for is the one who is truly free, Frank is bound back for America, marked like Cain to wander with his crime and punishment for eternity, now truly "free and dangerous" (Umrigar 2009, 363).

The novel's fast-paced tragic conclusion drowns out Nandita's sober reflections on the rights of the indigenous, and what multinationals owe the natives. Instead it is the material consequences of their pleasure trip coming askew that sentences Ellie to death. The more invisible friendship, that of Edna—the domestic servant figure caught in her unhappy marriage with Prakash, the mother of the desired child, Ramesh—with Ellie comes to play an even larger part in the tragedy that unfolds. Edna's abdominal pain leads to Ellie's kind ministrations, and thus the strange bedfellows pass off as the spousal pair when the murderer comes armed to kill. These friendships that defy class, race, and nationality are doomed to failure, barely rising up to create a dent in the plot of Frank's descent into the wilderness of Cain. These friendships, especially the intimacy and shared solidarity of Ellie and Nandita, are marked by what Leela Gandhi terms "affective cosmopolitanism, the ethico-political practice of a desiring self inexorably drawn toward difference" (2006, 17). In charting the affective ontology of friendship that ranges from Derrida, Blanchot, Bataille through Kant and Marx to Hardt and Negri, Leela Gandhi names the politics of friendship as "the co-belonging of non-identical singularities" (26). Friendship is in some ways a contrastive communing that belongs against normative patterns of belonging; the nonidentical singularities bring together a figure in mourning, a first world sojourner in the rural hinterlands of the third world with a third world educated elite, located ideally at the cusp of worlds ready to critique Western hegemonic practices carved out of the new global order of late-twentieth-century capitalism. Yet, the novel raises the question on what plane can these nonidentical singularities coalesce, and for how long?

Looking back at the anticolonialist symbolism of friendship acts performed by Charles Freer Andrews (1871–1940), which includes touching M. K. Gandhi's feet on South Africa's docks, Leela Gandhi extrapolates the difficult polarities of distancing and intimacy, symbolism and contrapuntal closures that are evidenced in acts of friendship reflected in the undertext of Nandita's playful banter with Ellie. At one point, when the Europeans and Americans mingle with villagers during the Diwali celebration, organized at the clinic Ellie volunteers at, and Ellie is joking with her British friend, Richard, about the historicity of their relationship to India, Nandita quips, "Nice to hear you two imperialists arguing about your claims to India," and Umrigar writes, "Her tone was bemused, her eyebrows raised, and they all chuckled" (2009, 226). Leela Gandhi's conclusions on the limitations of cosmopolitanism is deeply relevant: "cosmopolitanism may well be the means to puncture those fantasies of security and invulnerability to which our political imagination remains hostage. It might, for instance, teach us that risk sometimes brings with it a profound affirmation of relationality and collectivity" (2006, 32). The novel introduces Frank as a figure condemned to eternal wandering in the wilderness. In an ironic twist, the person who does the appropriate final ritual and thus farewell to his wife's presence by scattering her ashes is Nandita, her bosom buddy and consolation during her days in India. Dissident friendships are possible and radical in their potential; even at the moment of annihilation, they draw meaning from redrawing the map of the family, community, and nation. Ellie and Edna, in their violent finale, embody the cost of radical compassion—Edna, in allowing Ellie to engage with her son, Ramesh, and Ellie, in aiding Edna in the primal condition of humanness, the event of extreme bodily pain consequent to mortal wounding.

The elimination of the Ellie-Edna duo literally and figuratively ends a significant female friendship and makes way for the survival of the key male figures of the text—Frank, Prakash, and Ramesh, who augurs the future. Exorcizing the females from the text also makes way for the uninterrupted flow of phallogocentric logic to envelop the text in entirety. Insuring Ramesh's future with the "blood money" returned by the hit man, Gulab, furthers the corporate logic that rests undeterred at the crux of this novel. While one can chalk up the murders to a mistake, they are an insistent reiteration of violence against women, especially in the gruesome witness paid to the dead bodies of the two women: "In place of the red bindi she always wore on her forehead, was a bullet hole, the size of a rupee coin. Her eyes were closed" (Umrigar 2009, 349), sums up Edna's fetal position in death. Ellie is similarly bloodied after being shot in the head, her insides oozing outward down the wall where she is slumped. The female forms have been eviscerated from the discursive order of the novel. The symbolic replacements in the imagistic description signs toward the phallogocentric global market order that reigns supreme—the "bindi" is replaced by the patriarchal stamp of modernity, the bullet hole that is equal in size to a rupee coin, returning us to the circuit of capital in which the narrative is strictly enmeshed.

While friendship might bring together nonidentical singularities, the regime of phallogocentrism governed by capital is never displaced. A form of pessimistic humanism does away with the radical potentialities of dissident feminist alliances. In many ways, the discursive domain shifts away from entangling with the dominant theoretical and activist work of the past few decades wherein South Asian feminists have allied themselves with third world and women of color feminisms to find both home and community apart from the limiting binaries of nation (us vs. them, citizen vs. alien). Chandra Talpade Mohanty writes: "Home, not as a comfortable, stable, inherited, and familiar space but instead as an imaginative, politically charged space in which the familiarity and sense of affection and commitment lay in shared collective analysis of social injustice, as well as a vision of radical transformation. Political solidarity and a sense of family could be melded together imaginatively to create a strategic space I could call 'home.' Politically, intellectually, and emotionally, I owe an enormous debt to feminists of color—especially to the sisters who have sustained me over the years" (2010, 84). Reflecting on genealogies of community, home, and nation, Mohanty brings back the theoretically and emotionally charged cartography of homemaking that emerged in South Asian diasporic feminist discourse by the 1990s and into the new millennium. Umrigar's novel presents an older dialogue between the second wave white feminist represented in the figure of Ellie with third world feminist, Nandita, whose lives meld together in bourgeois capital order rather than "differences" that mark the schisms of second wave feminisms. The latter movement points to the particular flags of "women of color" and brings a motley range of themes to the table from race, sexuality, and nation to question the stable figure of "woman" as an identifier.

Mohanty's personal reflections are an ode to her solidarity with a corps of sisterhood, sustained over the years, across racial lines, which discuss and reflect upon difference that constitutes the remaking of home in the world. Umrigar's discursive order remains firmly ensconced in an earlier era, where the most important conversations occur with the hegemonic, white women, or the help, or the domestic servants. In many ways, the novel can thus be reduced to a recycling of clichés from an era that was revamped and interrogated by Mohanty's generation of cross-racial sisterhoods and coalition-building. Furthermore, the aberrancy of the white woman stepping down to help the "help" is unsustainable and punished through the denouement where the women, who had stepped out of their logical domestic realms, consorting at night when they were meant to be in their own beds, pay for radical compassion, and of course, even in this instance, the agential figure is the white woman, who is coming down from her tower to the poor woman's simpler home. Thus, the "We" of the novel is the sublimated subject that remains outside its discursive order, and the nonidentical singularities of the female figures remain nonidentical and apart from one another. The narrative fails in the project of radical imagination that might conjure another form of social justice to dismantle the law of the father.

Possibilities: Transnational Feminist Friendships

On the genre of romance, theorists note that romance reaffirms as well as resists heteronormative patriarchy in ritualistic repetitive ways, and as noted by Alison Light, "The reader is left in a permanent state of foreplay, but I would suggest that for many women this is the best heterosexual sex they ever get" (1984, 23). The impossible realm of femininity offered in gauzy silhouette, in this genre, in many ways, makes painfully apparent the difficulty of heteronormative climax for the woman, who is left in a state of inarticulate quivering desire. I argue that the Umrigar novelistic landscape appropriates in many ways the formulae and momentum of the romance genre but performs a radical appropriation because it propels us toward the distillation of a female-female friendship as the height of the novel's discursive domain. The dissident friendships paired in these texts—Bhima-Sera, Tehmina-Eva, Ellie-Nandita, and Ellie-Edna—stage conversation and intimacy as foreplay, with Tehmina and Eva coming to the happy conclusion of an ordered world, whereas, the others dissipate or dissolve because the literary novel does not have to follow the regulatory mechanism of the romance novel's cheery conclusion. The pleasure of foreplay, staged most poignantly in the intimacy revealed between Bhima and Sera, when the domestic servant helps heal her mistress's wounds with herbal remedies, transforms into the *jouissance* that is beyond patriarchal decipherability/disciplinarity in Julia Kristeva's logic: "And Sera was fading now, caught in the undertow of an ancient, primal memory, drowning in a pool of sensation and feeling, old hurts and fresh wounds being exorcized from her body, leaving her feeling as bright and new as the day she was born" (Umrigar 2005, 109).

Kelly Oliver's reading of Kristeva is of import here. Kristeva's theoretical modality offers a channel for our psychic lives, for understanding our vulnerability, and the impulse for violence in worlds we live with. The spectacles of violence act as a counterbalance only when the interpretation is sublimatory. As Kelly Oliver puts it, "Moreover, this sublimatory interpretation should also be a source of a jouissance that takes us beyond the realm of finite sensuous pleasures and puts us in touch with the realm of infinite meaning or what Kristeva might call 'psychic rebirth'" (2009, 56). We are witness to the psychic rebirth in the narrative arc followed by Tammy, who emerges as Tehmina, ready to effectively say her own name, articulate her identity, exercise agency, and rely on her friendship to carry her forward; in some ways, she chooses kith over kin, as she readies for her new life in America. She undergoes the psychic rebirth that allays her own fears about losing Bombay, her husband's ghost, and her own past as she finds a multiplicity of meanings surrounding her one act of heroism.

In Umrigar's *The Space Between Us* and *The Weight of Heaven*, the psychic rebirth remains interrupted. Sera's efforts to channel her own distaste for the other and any proximity to the dirt symbolized in her intimacy with Bhima surfaces at the first finger-pointing concocted by her son-in-law in his machinations to oust the servant from the household. Sera remains enmeshed in the sensual and the visceral, but she is unable to transcend to "a realm of infinite meaning," and the ensuing violence ejects Bhima from the bourgeois domestic order that she had served dutifully for decades. *The Weight of Heaven* presents the rupture of dissident friendships; precisely at the moment Ellie descends from her house on the hill to the hut below to aid Edna, the narratological impulse of violence is aimed at the pair, who reach the "realm of infinite meaning" in the noncorporeal form.

The competing pregnancies in *The Space Between Us* between the wealthy mistress's daughter, Dinaz, and the servant's granddaughter, Maya, create the tension and also mark and measure the space between the bourgeoisie and the proletariat. In the class differential that is at stake and aborts the poorer fetus out of Maya's womb, Shoshana Felman's point is quite useful: "this sexual separation—this mutual discontent of the sexes toward each other within the normative prescriptions of a patriarchal social structure—may be seen as the very issue of the Irma dream" (1993, 87). Felman reads the aporia in Freud's psyche between his condition of being pregnant with psychoanalysis versus his own wife's impending pregnancy alongside the patient, Irma's dream of being cured, as a method to rewrite the question, "What do women want?" to "What does Freud want, especially of women?" It is the irreducible difference of class and her vulnerability that makes her granddaughter, deeply aware of the politics of power, unable to point fingers at the perpetrator of sexual violence. Felman's deft deduction that Irma's dream posits the undecipherability of a woman's wants in patriarchy is also the way into woman's resistance of the patriarchal cure. Veiled underneath the more obvious cross-class impossible friendship of Sera and Bhima is the more powerful emergent relationship between Bhima and Maya, which involves mourning, melancholy, bringing pain into language. Bhima's resistance comes upon the heels of her constant memory of the aging balloon seller, the *pathan* who frequented the familiar Bombay shores. Built into the novel's discourse is a subaltern solidarity that makes possible dissident friendships between the disenfranchised. The competing pregnancies of the text make room for a transcendental jouissance that is beyond the "We" of the novel; instead it is a "We" that is exterior and still in progress.

This is why, I believe, the most recent novel forecloses any feminist transnationalist friendship—because it cements phallogocentrism in the shooting death of its central female figures. The earlier novel, *The Space Between Us*, despite its record of capsizing the female friendship of Bhima and Sera, is pregnant with radical possibility because, as Toril Moi points out, "Kristeva's emphasis on marginality allows us to view this repression of the feminine in terms of *positionality* rather than of essences" (1985, 166). Bhima exits the hegemonic order of the novel, bourgeois domesticity, and stands half-submerged in the wildness of the sea, deliberating a new beginning. Her position, exiled and determined, is neither inside nor outside and is capacious as all frontiers. She refuses to abide by the linguistic novelistic order that relegates her to abject submission; instead she enters the semiotic (marginal to language as feminine is marginal to patriarchy, as Moi points out) by standing at the edge of infinity and letting her enormous bouquet of balloons drift skyward. In her singular separateness from the paired possibility of dissident friendship and a psychic mapping that has her remembering the aging balloon seller from another time, perched on the edge of wilderness, she is at once antiessentialist, intricately woven into a web of the familial, and unmoored from the heteronormative. The novel's aporetic conclusion suggests that it is not Bhima who has been ejected, but rather she has ejected the hegemonic and stands poised at the limen emboldened: "It is dark, but inside Bhima's heart it is dawn" (Umrigar 2005, 321).

Conclusion

"Transnational feminism is haunted by this puzzle concerning the relationship between the messianic and the pragmatic, and how to understand the relationship of ethics to politics, law, justice, and the ontology of the Other as much as that of the self" (Khanna 2003, 211). Women contend with the anxiety and haunting of specters of patriarchy and patronage when it comes to the gift of sisterly solidarity offered across borders to the Other. In the chasm between the messianic or the visionary ideas and the pragmatic or the daily to-do of feminist labor, transnational feminism collapses and ossifies into first world patronage and third world suspicion or bourgeois distaste and working-class consciousness. Rather than allocate ethics to the litigious or the juridical, it is critical to draw on ethics to speak toward a transnational solidarity that actually works toward sisterhood that is also aware of the psychic history of colonialism, feminist maternalism, and first world materialisms.

For the failed dissident friendships enacted within the literary imaginaries of Umrigar, the pragmatic overwhelms the messianic, and the vision of a borderless friendship is subsumed under the larger material forces that complete the story. Ethics is abrogated to the realm of law and politics, though Frank, as murderer, and Viraf, as sexual assailant and perjurer, never pay for their crimes in knowable ways. Ethics, within the realm of female friendship, no longer stays anchored to notions of justice; instead it is the escapability of ethics to invisibility within the regulatory domains of law and politics and nationhood that keeps the novel mired in the impossibility of dissident feminist friendship. Furthermore, the unknowability of the crime at the heart of these texts—Frank's plan to murder Prakash, or Viraf's plan to remove Bhima from her premises to cover his own trespass—is crucial to the continuation of hegemony past the novel's duration. Nandita, Ellie's close friend whose ethics are always articulated in her honest conversations, is never allowed full knowledge of how her friend's life ends. She is left sputtering consolations to Frank and remains outside the narratological momentum of the text. Although Bhima's crime is never clarified and her name remains sullied within her mistress's household, she is standing tall at novel's end, and thus her character is allowed the narratological transcendence that makes room for the messianic alongside the pragmatic. Elizabeth Povinelli's astute self-reflections of her sixteen years of ethnography in Northern Australia's indigenous communities provide apt direction to understand the triangulation through what she terms as the intimate event caught between the autological subject and genealogical society. For Povinelli,[3] her reflections complicate the critiques of liberalism through her emplacement in white settler nations and indigenous communities wherein she participates as an outsider/insider for years. The cartography of intimacy offered pushes toward more constitutive interrogation of liberal imaginaries of the self and the Other.

And here I think it is critical to connect the polemics surrounding third cinema to the discursive order of the novel. In the way that third cinema (Chanan 1997) functions as a method of radicalizing its audience, who are in some ways the invisible subjects/subtexts of the cinematic text, I argue, through Arundhati Roy's vision of the constitutive global collective where she leaves her spectator with an urge to "read" that within Umrigar's literary imaginary, the reader is a critical orchestrator of meaning and sisterhood. "We" are the readers located within the interstices of the text, some diasporic, some not, located in the *untext* and dreaming of difference alongside sisterhood, coalitions, activism, poetry. "We" are the liminal of the novel, and we are the ones who make possible the road map to dissident sisterhoods in reading that is as much about the text as the world. Edward Said's (1994) traveling intellectual connects nodes of location articulated herein through Adrienne Rich via Caren Kaplan, Maria Lugones, and Chandra Talpade Mohanty. Leela Gandhi's cobelonging of nonidentical singularities is enacted in the literary and the liminal. The novels function as provocateurs in raising consciousness toward *feminism without borders*, friendship across lines so that the cobelonging is also in the bridge between the text and the reader.

Radical labor is performed under the guise of romance, the heady romance of friendship through difference—race, class, nation, religion, age. Romance novels provoke anxiety in precisely a hyperfeminine espousal of the hypermasculine, bringing into relief the politics of gender and power many feminists rally around. Here, the ardor of the romance novel that has been often constructed as extended foreplay works in turn to heat up the possibility of an intimacy where the self recognizes the Other, acknowledges difference, accords respect, refutes distance, comingles in the context of anti-imperial, anticapitalist imaginaries, and works out the possibility of dissident friendships. "We," located in difference, reside unequivocally outside the text and its discursive domain, and thus can address its aporetic foreclosures and anti-hegemonic awakenings. "We" are the free radicals of feminisms unbound.

Notes

1. Uma Narayan's caution in reserving our judgment about the epistemic privilege of the oppressed bears reckoning here; nevertheless, Umrigar's discursive order is weighted toward an epistemic privilege afforded Bhima that has her rejecting the hegemon and finding a countervision to the ontological truths about the working poor.

2. Afghani migrant balloon vendor she remembers from her youthful days.

3. Povinelli writes, "intimacy is, among other things: an intensification of enduring social relations of kinship, ge-ontology, and ritual, themselves anchoring and anchored by institutions of everyday life; a means of building collectively oriented and materially anchored socialities; and a manner of securing the self-evident social roles of men and women" (2006, 179).

References

Arundhati Roy film, *We* (2006). Accessed December 16, 2011. http://www.weroy.org/watch.shtml.

Chanan, Michael. 1997. "The Changing Geography of Third Cinema." *Screen* 38(4): 372–388.

Das, Veena. 2006. *Life and Violence: Exploring Violence and the Descent into the Ordinary*. Ewing: University of California Press.

Felman, Shoshana. 1993. *What Does a Woman Want? Reading and Sexual Difference*. Baltimore, Md.: The Johns Hopkins University Press.

Gandhi, Leela. 2006. *Affective Communities: Anticolonial Thought, Fin-de-Siècle Radicalism, and the Politics of Friendship*. Durham, N.C.: Duke University Press.

Grewal, Inderpal, and Caren Kaplan. 2000. "Postcolonial Studies and Transnational Feminist Practice." *Jouvert: A Journal of Postcolonial Studies* 5(1). Accessed April 4, 2012. http://english.chass.ncsu.edu/jouvert/v5i1/grewal.htm.

Khanna, Ranjana. 2003. *Dark Continents: Psychoanalysis and Colonialism*. Durham, N.C.: Duke University Press.
———. 2009. "Disposability." *Differences: A Journal of Feminist Cultural Studies* 20(1): 181–198.
Kristeva, Julia. 2006. "Thinking in Dark Times." *Profession*, Modern Language Association, 13–21. Accessed January 15, 2012. http://www.jstor.org/stable/25595824.
Lawrence, Charles R. 1992. "The Word and the River: Pedagogy as Scholarship as Struggle." *Southern California Law Review* 65: 2231.
Light, Alison. 1984. "Returning to Manderley—Romance Fiction, Female Sexuality and Class." *Feminist Review* 16: 7–25.
Lugones, Maria. 2006. "On Complex Communication." *Hypatia* 21(3): 75–85.
Mohanty, Chandra Talpade. 2003. *Feminism without Borders: Decolonizing Theory, Practicing Solidarity*. Durham, N.C.: Duke University Press.
———.2010. "Genealogies of Community, Home, and Nation (1993/2003)." In *Women's Lives: Multicultural Perspectives*, edited by Gwyn Kirk and Margo Okazawa-Rey, 81–88. New York: McGraw-Hill.
Moi, Toril. 1985. *Sexual/Textual Politics: Feminist Literary Theory*. New York: Routledge.
Nandy, Ashis. 1989. *The Intimate Enemy: Loss and Recovery of Self under Colonialism*. New York: Oxford University Press.
Narayan, Uma. 2004. "The Project of Feminist Epistemology: Perspectives from a Nonwestern Feminist." In *The Feminist Standpoint Theory Reader: Intellectual and Political Controversies*, edited by Sandra Harding, 213–224. New York: Routledge.
Oliver, Kelly. 2009. "Meaning against Death." In *Psychoanalysis, Aesthetics, and Politics in the Work of Julia Kristeva*, edited by Kelly Oliver and S. K. Keltner, 49–63. New York: State University of New York Press.
Povinelli, Elizabeth A. 2006. *The Empire of Love: Toward a Theory of Intimacy, Genealogy, and Carnality*. Durham, N.C.: Duke University Press.
Rojas, Maythee. 2009. *Women of Color and Feminism*. New York: Seal Press.
Roy, Arundhati. 1999. *The Cost of Living*. New York: The Modern Library.
———. 2009. *Listening to Grasshoppers: Field Notes on Democracy*. New Delhi: Hamish Hamilton, Penguin.
Said, Edward. 1994. *Representations of the Intellectual*. New York: Vintage.
Spivak, Gayatri Chakravorty. 1988. "Can the Subaltern Speak?" In *Marxism and the Interpretation of Culture*, edited by C. Nelson and S. Grossberg, 271–313. Chicago: University of Illinois Press.
———. 1999. *A Critique of Postcolonial Reason: Toward a History of the Vanishing Present*. Cambridge: Harvard University Press.
Umrigar, Thrity. 2005. *The Space Between Us: A Novel*. New York: HarperCollins Publishers.
———. 2007. *If Today Be Sweet: A Novel*. New York: HarperCollins Publishers.
———.2009. *The Weight of Heaven: A Novel*. New York: HarperCollins Publishers.
Williams, Raymond. 1977. *Marxism and Literature*. New York: Oxford University Press.

PART FOUR
Friendship across Borders

CHAPTER 9

A Spirit of Solidarity

Transatlantic Friendships among Early
Twentieth-century Female Peace Activists (Wilpfers)

LAURIE R. COHEN

> No person is an island complete of itself.
> —Stanley, *The Auto/biographical "I"*

On January 21, 1893, Hedwig von Pötting (1853–1915), an Austrian canoness (nun), wrote one of her very first letters to fellow Austrian feminist writer, peace advocate, and baroness by marriage Bertha von Suttner (1843–1914). Theirs was to become an enduring friendship:

> Most esteemed and dearest Baroness,
> Are you going to cry out in anger "What, again!" as soon as you recognize my handwriting? Or will you rather laugh at me? I hope the latter. Being laughed at by others and by myself has done me only good until now. So laugh away, and please don't be angry with me. I'm ever so pleased to busy myself with you, to catch a glimpse of your writings, which I then absolutely have to read. . . . Some obstreperous people made some classically idiotic judgments about you in my presence, esteemed Baroness, and about your strivings and work—without any of them having read a word of it. It's unbelievable! . . . What I wanted to say to you today with these lines has to do with egoism, of which you are no fan. But I simply needed to write to you again, since you allowed me to, because I would like so much, esteemed dearest Baroness, that you become better acquainted with me and that I can win back a very very tiny bit of love. . . . Forever yours sincerely, H. Pötting (1893).

At the time of this letter, Bertha von Suttner's name and image—mainly caricaturized in satirical German-language monthlies—was just becoming identified with the universal peace movement of the late nineteenth century (Cohen 2005). Suttner was author of the internationally bestselling antiwar novel *Lay Down Your Arms!* (1889), president and cofounder of the first Austrian peace society (1891), and coeditor with Alfred Hermann Fried of a new peace monthly, *Die Waffen nieder!* (1892). Hedwig von Pötting, whose letters suggest she was a progressive outsider in her conservative community, clearly admired Suttner's independence, her clarity of vocation, her principled commitment to peace, and not least her sense of humor.

A friendship—understood and used in this chapter as "a distinctively personal relationship that is grounded in a concern on the part of each friend for the welfare of the other, for the other's sake, and that involves some degree of intimacy" (Helm 2013)—quickly arose between these two middle-aged women, despite their different backgrounds and life experiences. Both inexperienced politicians—at that time, how could it be otherwise?—they nonetheless shared a political stance that prioritized peacemaking and social solidarity over warmongering. Such positions went visibly against the grain in a period of rising Austrian-Hungarian nationalism and militarism. Furthermore, Suttner and Pötting developed a relationship that was not untypical among politically minded women: between a rising star and an adoring admirer.

Bertha von Suttner, charismatic and cosmopolitan, stood in the limelight and left a public record, including her own memoirs. In addition, her life—especially after she was awarded the Nobel Peace Prize in 1905—then as now has inspired biographical (including cinematographic) investigations as well as streets, schools, and buildings that carry her name. Pötting, by contrast, remains much more of a historical mystery. Aside from a short mention in Suttner's autobiography, most of the little that we know about her is drawn from roughly a hundred pages of correspondence, with Suttner, dating from 1893 to 1904 and archived at the United Nations Office of Geneva (Fried-Suttner Papers). These letters provide, however, only a glimpse of Pötting and of the vibrant friendship that was integrated into their everyday lives (Manges 2011). From an asymmetrical acquaintanceship between an anticlerical baroness and a canoness who aspired to be a writer, there developed a friendship of trust as if among equals. Symbolic for this transformation, Pötting ceased her initial formalities and began addressing Suttner as her dear "*Löwos*"—Suttner's invented and playful word, which deviates from the grammatical gendered German rule of male or female and which we may today render as a queer word for "lion"—and signing off as "*Hexe*" (witch).

The common themes addressed in these letters are feminism, politics, and pacifism. At times, akin to entries in a diary, they also disclosed self-reflected vicissitudes of their daily private lives. Theirs was a friendship based on mutual respect and support for the contrarian cause of universal peace. Pötting's and Suttner's written (but undoubtedly too their in-person) communications enormously influenced and shaped their personal and world outlooks.

It was, however, a private friendship: one that Suttner mentioned but did not address in her well-publicized memoirs. Nor was it a relationship directly linked to the organized Austrian Peace Society, although Pötting became a somewhat active member. Rather, what these letters from Pötting to Suttner convey (most of those from Suttner have never been recovered) is a friendship between two conational though heterogeneous women drawn together not least because of the isolation late-nineteenth-century activist-oriented European women experienced, especially those pursing their political ideals before women even had the right to vote. Suttner appears to have had many colleagues and acquaintances, but few friends—aside from her husband—and much public scorn. For instance, according to Austrian writer Stefan Zweig, Suttner was medially categorized as a "good woman" in a pitying way such that "good" really meant "stupid"; likewise, "her passionate monotony" (i.e., her decades-long theme of disarmament) was taken as "weakness of thought" (1918, 2). Tellingly, Pötting's letters are almost exclusively supportive of Suttner: emotionally and in terms of Suttner's approach to pacifism. Indeed, throughout the next decade, Pötting was consistently and enthusiastically approving of her friend and never uttered (in writing at least) the slightest criticism. No doubt Suttner valued this seemingly unconditional love as a counterpoint to the endless hostility and ridicule she received for her peace efforts from society-at-large. For her part, Pötting, because of such ideas, became ever more marginalized from her social class. It appears that her normative "cultural mode" (fitting in) began to differ from her "lived mode" (deviance). Indeed, based on her correspondence in these years, Pötting's close friendship circle, apart from Suttner, was limited to a sister and a married male (pacifist) interest. Due to Suttner's friendship, Pötting eventually became more independent and self-confident, left her convent, and took up residence in Austria's capital.

The rest of this chapter concentrates on a next generation of transnational feminist pacifists. I first provide a brief overview of feminist-pacifist transnational dissidents and the origins of the Women's International League for Peace and Freedom (WILPF), for which Suttner was a beacon, and then a selection and a more in-depth analysis of a few examples of personal-political and dissident friendships that developed among leading, high-profile transatlantic women peace activists.[1] It is a topic (one of many) that has received little historiographic attention. I also examine certain tensions at play throughout the interwar period. My investigations show that it was a political und ultimately life commitment to the institution (WILPF)—which included regular face-to-face meetings and a joint multilingual journal (*Pax International*)—that helped keep these friendships from breaking up irrevocably, despite changing interpersonal relations, diverging political or ideological agendas, and entering activists who had grown up in a new century and/or culture, all of which caused a series of disruptions and some shifting of alliances and allegiances.

By comparing a few diverse friendships between committed German, Austrian-Hungarian, and British feminist peace activists on the one hand and American counterparts on the other (all associated with WILPF), highlighting the Sameness between them as well as the Otherness (see Narayan 1998, 89), I will show how these relationships not only empowered these women but also made visible barriers or vulnerabilities that divided them, including the power of disappointed expectations. Ethnicity, cultural milieus, political leanings, a sense of social justice, affluence, and personality all played a role. Specifically, I examine the enduring transatlantic relationship between founding WILPF members Rosika Schwimmer and Lola Maverick Lloyd. Next I explore Madeleine Zabriskie Doty's growing wartime friendships and interwar fall-outs with several European activists, and I conclude with some reflections about the significance of transnational female friendships in the peace movement as a whole.

Transatlantic Friendships and the Origins of WILPF

A generation of female friendships based on a political commitment to universal peace, democracy, and women's rights arose at the start of World War I. Unlike in the case of Suttner and Pötting, a new element to this friendship became central: transnationalism, or the rejection of narrow nationalism, which allowed relationships to form between women who neither shared the same mother tongue nor the same nation-state culture. Transnationalism, Patricia Clavin writes, "is first and foremost about people: the social space that they inhabit, the networks they form and the ideas they exchange" (2005, 422). Many of these early-twentieth-century pacifist feminists were "New Women," whose roots lay in the organized international feminist movement: the International Council of Women and the International Women's Suffrage Association.[2] In 1915, these individuals bravely forged a new and unique organization, one that linked women's enfranchisement with stopping World War I and preventing other large-scale wars. Upper- to lower-middle-class white women from different religious backgrounds, ethnicities, nationalities, and sexual preferences found common ground. Indeed, the greater "total war" conflictual context inspired them to define the term "internationalism" anew: no longer was it based on national citizenship or traditional patriotism, party politics, or even so-called free trade, but rather on human (particularly female) cross-border solidarity. As one leading German member, Anita Augspurg, characterized the term: The goal was "not the interests of a country, not a national policy, but humanitarian aims and world reconciliation."[3]

Many excellent histories have been written about WILPF's origins. Ironically, however, they are largely limited to national perspectives, especially American or British ones (e.g., Alonso 1993, Blackwell 2004, Early 1997, Foster 1995, Klapper 2010, Liddington 1989, Schott 1997; for exceptions, see Rupp 1997, Suriano 2012). That essential transnational (including transatlantic) relationships in fact grounded the organization—after all, during the war the organization's headquarters were in Amsterdam, the Netherlands, and after the war they were (and still are) in Geneva, Switzerland—and were fostered during international conferences and executive board meetings, is a topic that is all too often marginalized in its (U.S.-U.K.-centered) historiography.

Modern technologies (e.g., Skype, iPhones) might encourage one to assume that such personal interactions have always been commonplace, but at that time, they took a great deal of personal (including physical) effort and commitment. Indeed, consider how Anita Augspurg critically and poetically alluded to this in her reflective analysis of the ten-year evolution of the organization: "[League members now] prefer to substitute safe navigation close to land instead of courageous diving through storm and waves to faraway aims and beautiful new countries."[4] For transnational relationships to succeed, costs, time, and even possibly danger or risks had to be taken into account as well. This day-to-day perseverance of individual Wilpfers proved invaluable to WILPF's survival.

Despite bumps in the road—sometimes these transatlantic friendships were lost and sometimes then regained—the organization grew in particular as new menacing international interwar conflicts emerged: for example, dictatorships, National Socialism (Nazism), fascism, and Stalinism threatening European democratic stability. Significantly, some of the female peace activist friendships formed during World War I became actual lifesavers for European Wilpfers twenty years later, from 1933 to 1945. Their convictions, their fundamental "idealist" resistance to authoritarianism and militarism—idealist meant here in the positive sense of living and acting out of and for recognized values and ideas, in spite of overwhelming opposition—is the dissident if opaque glue that united them. These women, not least through their common strivings against enormous displays of nationalism during World War I (as well as the passivity of the general public and the irresponsibility of the state leaders in thwarting the welfare interests of the majority of their citizens), perceived the value of the role of organized international social networks and the sense of the political being the personal.

ROSIKA SCHWIMMER AND LOLA MAVERICK LLOYD

Rosika Schwimmer (1877–1948), born in Budapest and the daughter of Jewish-Hungarian parents, was one of the first of the organized and politically active feminists (among other things she had founded the first Hungarian society to promote the rights of so-called low-skill women workers) to recognize the humanitarian turmoil that Austria-Hungary's ultimatum to Serbia ("July Crisis") had caused. Just as the war was about to start, she outlined her arguments in the international suffragist journal *Jus Suffragii*. This article, titled "The Bankruptcy of the Man-Made World War," foresaw the imminent war as "the greatest tragedy," an "hour of disaster, greater than any imagination." She bluntly accused the Western male population for having "maintained that spirit of hatred and destruction as an inextinguishable human instinct, and hav[ing] incessantly nursed it by organising human society in every respect as an immense attacking body." But she also charged the Western female population of having "watched that anti-social course without using all our constructive forces to counterbalance the fatal spirit of destruction" (1914, 2). Her solution: to inspire as many women as possible to overcome their apathy and forge organized protests against the war. Indeed, Schwimmer aimed at stopping the war—or recalling Bertha von Suttner, at convincing world leaders to immediately disarm.

By October 1914, when Schwimmer arrived in the United States for the first time and started giving lectures on the actual effects of the war and why it thus had to stop (she had had to flee her residence in London to avoid being possibly interned as an "alien enemy"), her mostly female audiences overfilled the halls. Yet U.S. peace leaders, including feminist, peace activist and Quaker Jane Addams, were sceptical of "Frau Schwimmer's" peace plan. As Addams wrote to Paul Kellogg in September 1914, "I have signed it reluctantly as a member of the National Suffrage Board, simply because I don't like to damp any plan which is so widespread, but it doesn't seem very feasible."[5] Furthermore, much of the organized U.S. feminist leadership (mostly white, upper-middle class, and Christian), worrying that their struggles for suffrage would be railroaded by a new enthusiasm and engagement for peace activism, took up even more oppositional stances toward Schwimmer, her work, and her growing number of U.S. suffragist-pacifist followers (e.g., Ada James of Wisconsin[6]). Indeed, Schwimmer would encounter strong resistance to her pacifist ideas from within the feminist movement even after the war and after she (reluctantly) took up residence in the United States (as of 1921). As one of her biographers (a woman who had worked for and with her) put it: "Rosika Schwimmer was a mover and a shaker. Many people swore by her, many swore at her, some did both at different times" (Wynner 1985, 864). Denied citizenship by the U.S. Supreme Court in 1929 for refusing to take up arms to defend her new homeland (!), Schwimmer, childless and unmarried, remained in Chicago, relatively poor and legally "stateless"—though still politically active, such as founding in 1933 a campaign named World Citizenship for the Stateless—until her death (Cohen 2012, 73–75).

One adherent of Schwimmer's was the Texan Lola Maverick Lloyd (1875–1944), an independently wealthy suffragist and socialist and, in 1916, a divorced mother of four living in Chicago. Lloyd and Schwimmer developed a close and long-lasting relationship, not least solidified by their commitment to universal peace. Paralleling in part the origins of Suttner and Pötting's friendship (also initiated when they were already near or over the age of forty), Lloyd attended one of Schwimmer's antiwar lectures. This took place in November 1914 at the Chicago College club which, according to Schwimmer, social reformer and schoolteacher Florence Holbrook had organized. After her speech, Lloyd (together with Holbrook and Mabel Sippy) "were at my heels all the time and I was nervous when I saw them"[7] (Schwimmer 1944, 5). Lloyd, profoundly inspired by Schwimmer—she heard Schwimmer speak at least seventeen times in the course of a few months (ibid.)—spent much of her remaining life participating in the feminist peace movement, including, during the war, cofounding the Women's Peace Party (January 1915), representing its Chicago branch at the Women's (Peace) Conference in The Hague (April 1915), and participating—with three of her children—in Henry Ford's "Peace Ship" Expedition (November 1915), initially run by Schwimmer. "Peace agitation had become a duty," Lloyd affirmed (Gustafson 2001, 518, quoting a letter from Lloyd to her mother). Indeed, Lloyd even came close to succeeding Anna Garlin Spencer in 1920 as president of WILPF's U.S. section.

Schwimmer and her "dear friend Lola" continued their peace activism after the war and closely collaborated on the Chicago-based Campaign for World Government (coauthoring a brochure of the same title). Theirs was a friendship and collaboration between a charismatic dissident leader (Schwimmer) and an admiring, ever loyal, yet independently minded follower (Lloyd). Both remained committed suffragists as well. Alice Paul (founder of the U.S. National

Women's Party), and a close American friend of Lloyd's, recalled in her eulogy seeing Lloyd probably in the early 1930s "in Geneva at the League of Nations and I remember Mrs. Lloyd going in this delegation, to one of the leading men in the League, and explaining to him with much earnestness and her rare sense of humor, that there could never be a League that would endure, there could never be any World Government that would endure which was made up of the men of the world only, and not made up of men and women alike."[8] On the same occasion, Schwimmer honored her talented friend as follows: "Lola Lloyd, the peace hero, the woman with courage, with moral courage—the courage that does not count while we admire only physical courage—but she had both."[9]

However, as feminist sociologist Liz Stanley points out: "Once friendship is admitted to be an important aspect of biographical investigation, unresolved issues remain concerning how this investigation should be carried out as well as the significance that should be accorded to its textual product" (1992, 233). Indeed, determining the exact extent of Lloyd and Schwimmer's transatlantic friendship from the existing documents is problematic. What is clear is that Lloyd immediately belonged among the so-called intimates of Schwimmer's first inner American circle. Furthermore, when Schwimmer ultimately moved to the United States, she initially settled in Lloyd's home. Thereafter, with both living in the Chicago area, correspondence (and everyday evidence) drops off, and one only has correspondence mostly from third parties (their associates and mutual friends) to rely on, supporting the idea that their close friendship continued.

Schwimmer formally left WILPF in 1921, scarred by what she perceived as an unwillingness of the WILPF's U.S. section to treat her with the respect she deserved: she was erroneously accused in the press of being a German spy and of taking money from Henry Ford earmarked for WILPF, defamations that WILPF's membership did not (or not enough) formally reject. Moreover, she had her own reservations about the section's pacifist convictions, and in this she was not alone. Fanny Garrison Villard (1844–1928), who was a committed feminist and a Tolstoyan pacifist, had already resigned from WILPF's U.S. section on these grounds and founded the international Women's Peace Society (1919). Last but not least, Schwimmer seemed to prefer her independent, if often impoverished, and in the United States at least, dissident status as an international peace activist. Lloyd, however, remained an active WILPF member and served Schwimmer as WILPF liaison throughout the interwar period. For instance, she would send on WILPF newsletters and suggest to the WILPF leadership that Schwimmer should be invited as speaker at international and regional congresses, which she sometimes was. Lloyd also spearheaded a successful international campaign (which included many U.S. section Wilpfers) that awarded Schwimmer the World Peace Prize in 1938.

Lloyd's own interest in certain European perspectives and her willingness—as well as having the means—to travel to Europe on political business was certainly conducive to winning over Schwimmer's friendship. As was her burning commitment to absolute peace. Shortly after Schwimmer wrote to her (in October 1930) that "It is the same old thing. The militarists act and prepare for war by their actions, and pacifists sit at pink teas, and study books and plans. That is why we are going to have another world war and a worse one," Lloyd actively attended WILPF's international congresses and several executive board meetings in Europe (until 1937) (quoted in McFadden 2011, 538).

Schwimmer left a legacy of writings and work, which peace and women's historians especially in Hungary, Austria, Germany, and in the United States have recently begun unearthing. Of Lloyd's long life and courageous work there remains little interest, despite numerous boxes of diaries (up to 1933), correspondence, and documentation: for example, of her participation on the international Ford Peace Expedition in 1915, a life-changing milestone, which she was asked to talk about at an event arranged by WILPF's New York branch in 1941, shortly before the United States entered World War II.[10] It was also at this time that she mutually and satisfyingly reunited with cofounding German Wilpfer, journalist, and feminist Helene Stöcker (1869–1943), who had recently found refuge in the United States.

MADELEINE ZABRISKIE DOTY AND EUROPEAN FRIENDSHIPS

At the end of April 1915, a historic three-day international Women's (Peace) Congress at The Hague took place. One participant, New York lawyer, feminist, and writer Madeleine Zabriskie Doty (1879–1963), representing the Woman's Lawyer's Association, wrote about the general inspiration for attendance: "The women knew they could not stop the war, but they decided to register a protest against the slaughter of man and lay plans for a future permanent peace" (1917, 3). This extremely significant Congress drew together for the first time activist feminists from both belligerent and neutral countries. (There were many more participants here, for example, than at a groundbreaking Socialist women's antiwar conference in Switzerland two months earlier.) Few of the nearly four dozen Americans who crossed the Atlantic together—largely members of the newly founded Women's Peace Party—had previous experience either in peace advocacy or in traveling to Europe.

The congress of course did not "stop the war," but it did result in setting a precedent for women to enter the public space of international diplomacy: On

Schwimmer's initiative, small official delegations visited eighteen European capitals and actually had audiences with prime and foreign ministers to discuss negotiating a peace settlement. At the same time, a cohort of attending pacifist feminists formed life-long friendships. Eyewitness Doty wrote: "Newspapers ridiculed the women; they call them 'peacettes' bound for a tea party at The Hague. But, as usual, opposition only strengthened the cause. We grew fearless and united" (12). Similarly, Professor of Economics Emily Greene Balch, who had done field research comparing Slavic populations in Austria-Hungary and in the United States and who in 1919 would become WILPF's first international secretary, recalled: "When I sailed in April with the other 42 American delegates . . . it looked doubtful to me, as it did to many others, how valuable the meeting could be made. I felt, however, that even a shadow of chance to serve the cause of peace could not today be refused. . . . [In retrospect it] repaid all that it cost us a hundredfold" (1915, 39). Doty herself become WILPF's third international secretary, serving at the Geneva headquarters from 1925 to 1927; she was also editor-in-chief of WILPF's monthly *Pax International* (1926–1932). In 1930, having long considered the necessity of highlighting internationalist aims, "of allowing new solutions to be born out of pooled transnational intelligence," she tried (and failed) to start up a World Section of WILPF (Rupp 1997, 120).

Even after war broke out in Europe, Doty specifically reached out to a number of Europeans from belligerent nations. British suffragist-pacifist leader Emmeline Pethick-Lawrence, for example, fondly recalled their first meeting: "Miss Ward of the famous Henry Street Settlement [Lower East Side of New York] gave a reception and many gathered to welcome me [October 1914]. It was on this occasion that I met Madeleine Zabriskie Doty, whose life from that moment, for the next 22 years until the present time, has been closely interwoven with mine. *We fell for each other at once.* She asked me to stay with her in her apartment in Greenwich Village [Manhattan]" (1938, 307, emphasis added). Pethick-Lawrence then joined Doty and the rest of the American Hague delegation crossing the Atlantic in April 1915. For her part, Doty described Pethick-Lawrence (for whom she had the nickname "Malini") as someone who "would go singing to death to rid the world of war" (1917, 5).

Doty also became close to German feminist and peace activist leaders Anita Augspurg (1857–1943), a lawyer, and especially her companion (as of the 1890s) Lida Gustava Heymann (1868–1943), who had joined the German Peace Society in 1897. Such was the relationship between Augspurg and Heymann (a type of "Boston marriage") that their friends commonly addressed them as "AniLid." Doty initially met up with them at The Hague (April 1915) and twice again as she traveled through Germany: first in 1915 to Berlin; then in 1916 to Bremen,

Hamburg, Heidelberg, Baden, Stuttgart, Nuremberg, and Munich as well. Heymann, shunned by other leading German feminists for attending the "Peace" Congress in The Hague (Wilmers 2008), was particularly touched by Doty's sincerity and her refusal to pigeonhole Germans as victory-oriented Prussian warmongers and militarists (cf. Newman 1915). In other words, Doty displayed her U.S. dissident traits by seeking out individual human beings rather than the collective "they" ("the bad Germans"). Indeed, Doty's account of wartime Germany's plight, published in the United States in 1917, portrayed rebellious German feminist pacifists explicitly and sympathetically (in spite of the fact that Doty hardly knew any German). Recalling her first encounter with Augspurg and Heymann and their commitment to peace and justice, Doty wrote: "On one occasion Mr. and Mrs. Pethick Lawrence of England invited Dr. Augspurg and Fräulein Heymann of Germany to dine. A gasp went 'round the dining-room as this little group entered.... For hours those amazing people talked in great friendliness.... They readjusted the world" (1917, 18). Several years later, Jane Addams (WILPF's international president) would freely write to another Wilpfer, without betraying any confidences, that Doty is "a great friend of Miss Heymann."[11]

Among Doty's most fulfilling experiences in Germany in 1915 was observing a few secret feminist antiwar gatherings in Berlin, also attended by Heymann, who was "received with open arms by the rebel women, and at once nick-named the 'criminal.' In them I find the Germans I sought. Free, fearless people, *whose love for the Fatherland is so great that they dare protest!"* (Doty 1917, 35, emphasis in original). Traveling to Munich (Heymann and Augspurg's home base), Doty attended further peace meetings. She also witnessed what it cost to be a (female) peace activist in wartime: the police arrived at Heymann's home, forbade her to "speak in public, have more than five people in her house at a time, or send any telegram or letter outside the country" (218; cf. Heymann 1992, 153–154). She was told that all her correspondence would be inspected as well. Nonetheless, Doty explained:

> We four spent absorbing days together. If it had not been for the streets filled with soldiers and sorrowing people and the shortage of food, I should have forgotten where I was. These women loved the same books, the same pictures, the same works of art as corresponding groups of women in England and America. Language was the only difference.... To suppose that Germans are born of an alien strain is an absurdity. If anything these German women were superior to any I had known. They had sounded the depth of emotion, had more passionate energy, and were less conventional than the same group in my country. (1917, 218–219)

Shortly thereafter, Heymann was ordered out of Munich altogether.

Doty then highlighted Heymann's admirable appearance at the conclusion of a local peace meeting: "[Heymann] turned upon her tormentors. She had been powerless in the meeting, for the police had ordered her not to speak, but in the open she risked it. She is a tall, slender woman, with golden hair and blue eyes—a Madonna woman—but in her burns white heat. Turning on the crowd and shaking her fist, she hurled at them: 'I want peace, but I want a real peace. I am more radical than you'" (222). In 1921, Doty was among the first to suggest that WILPF's U.S. section invite women from former "enemy" countries such as Germany to give lecture tours to American audiences. They did come, but it was a young Gertrude Baer and not Heymann who was sponsored to represent Germany, against Doty's fierce protest.

In summer 1921, following the Third WILPF congress (in Vienna), Doty found herself in a closer relationship with another German-speaking feminist: horticultural school founder and Austrian WILPF's section president (Mrs.) Yella Hertzka (1877–1948), whom Doty called "Birderly." Writing to Hertzka from Berlin, Doty expressed her newly won feelings:

> I want only to bring you happiness and I bring you unrest. What shall I do? I would like best to lie in the sunshine with you, and only to love you and talk to you. As it is my days are one long struggle to accomplish what must be done + I have no time to think of what I would like ... *Lieb, es ist gare keiner Krankheit für mir, es ist lieb—lieb immer die selber, bin ich mit Dich oder ohne Dich.* I long to be with you, but *wirklich* [truly]. I love you so much that if you could more easily become well and happy without seeing me, I could give up seeing you. Please love me with a love that will not make you unhappy. My arms are always about you near or far—always I shall love you.[12]

Hertzka's response is unknown, but not long afterward she takes up with a woman closer to home: her chauffeur Maria Hofer (1894–1977), who was also a renowned pianist and composer (Oesch 2010). Hofer lived in Hertzka's house until Hertzka's forced flight from Vienna in 1938, following Austria's *Anschluss* with Nazi Germany. Among other things, Hertzka encouraged Hofer in pacifist thought, which led in 1925 to Hofer composing a *Friedenshymne* (Peace hymn), which WILPF distributed. (Helene Scheu-Riesz, another Austrian WILPF member and one of Austria's first Quakers, wrote the text.) By the time Hertzka and Doty meet up again in the mid-1920s, their intimate friendship had seemingly cooled off: Hertzka now communicated with "Fräulein Doty" in a more neutral, collegial manner.[13]

Doty's close relationship with Heymann, who had become an active International Executive Board member of WILPF since its beginnings, also soon experienced a (rocky) transition. Heymann, highly supportive at first of Doty replacing Hungarian Secretary Vilma Glücklich at the league's headquarters in Geneva in 1925—Heymann, for instance, writing to Jane Addams immediately that "Doty enormously improved the work of our League"[14]—within months of her arrival began complaining to WILPF members about Doty's unsuitability. As concerns the failing friendship, the reasons seemed similar to the split with Hertzka: a matter of expectations and Doty's failure to deliver on them. The French and German WILPF board members, frustrated with Glücklich for being too meek and reserved but also too partisan to the more conservative (policy-oriented) British and Scandinavian colleagues, expected more deviance from the "American" Doty: they wanted her to rock the boat. When she did precisely that, however, it was not in the way they anticipated. Doty tried not to take sides (northerners vs. southerners/southeasterners) and expressed concern with the organization as a whole. Heymann (and Augspurg) considered this a betrayal of trust. Furthermore, Heymann did not much appreciate Doty's analysis of WILPF's internal international difficulties from the perspective of a theory of childhood: "As I see it the sections are like children in different stages of development, some enthusiastic, some indifferent and knowing so little about each other that there is not only no common program but even misunderstanding and dissatisfaction with each other. As I see it, we need to try and find two or three things on which all our sections can agree and get everyone taking vigorous and active part. I'd like the official representative of each section to spend a week with me here."[15] By early 1926, Doty too became deeply discouraged by the bitterness and hostilities openly expressed among her friends (that is, the board members) and also toward herself. Soon, Heymann wrote Addams: "I know that she [Doty] is more and more engaged in supporting our League's work; I notice, as time goes by, however, that I become more and more convinced that she is unfortunately failing. Her personality is not appropriate."[16] She explained to others that what was desired was a "professional," not an amateur child psychologist. Furthermore, according to Heymann "a secretary must be neutral and discrete. [Doty] was too much of a journalist and had not the slightest idea of politics—or at least of European politics."[17] This assessment echoed usually unspoken stereotypes about Americans among (not only) feminist pacifist Europeans: that they took political issues and organizational work too lightly or too superficially. (Another was that they were overly concerned with financial aspects and not enough concerned with explicit political objectives.) Heymann, for example, accused Doty of being more interested in using WILPF's journal *Pax International* (with some twelve thousand copies, around seven thousand of which were distributed in the United States) to propagate "useful information" to the public, rather than to use it as a forum for (especially so-called radical pacifist and anticapitalist) WILPF membership debates.

Mary Sheepshanks from England was persuaded to take up the position, and Doty was forced out. Yet Doty fought for and succeeded in continuing to edit *Pax International* and remained, with Addams's support, a WILPF board member. This kept her often in Europe and ultimately facilitated the resumption of a close friendship with Heymann, who eventually turned against Sheepshanks (who soon resigned). On the eve of World War II, then, Doty was back in Europe, living for a time in Italy, then Geneva, and working for WILPF. Her friendship with Heymann, who had had to flee Germany on both political and "racial" grounds (with her Jewish partner Augspurg) once Hitler took power in early 1933, remained strong. The German women resettled in Switzerland and kept active as WILPF's German branch-in-exile. Eventually all three would live together in Geneva, until Augspurg's and then Heymann's death (both in 1943).

The Significance of Transnational Female Friendships in the Peace Movement

Soon after World War II began, WILPF International President Emily Greene Balch wrote to her colleagues and friends on the International Executive Board:

> This little note is only to assure you again of what you already know—that I think of each one individually with every good wish, *and with personal love to each of my old friends among you*. Ringed around by a wall of violence, we draw closer together, more than ever determined that the present method of conducting public business by wars and rumours of wars, must be superceded by reasonable methods on a basis of friendly relations of reciprocal help. Men must outgrow the fatal idea that the way to advantage one's own group is to injure others.[18] To end the war, as soon as may be, with a settlement such that peace can develop from it is our goal, and in every country we have to work all we can to educate our own people toward the necessary changes and sacrifices that a world organized for cooperative international life implies.[19]

The message she conveyed could have been spoken by any of the transnationalist WILPF members discussed here. Many of those brave Hague 1915 women (including Balch), who had actively protested together against World War I on rational, pragmatic, and humanitarian grounds, were well aware of the extent of Hitler's danger to world peace. These women, in spite of the frequent worldwide ridicule and disdain tossed up at them, had for decades developed close political networks, had interacted on different continents, and had learned to trust and mutually respect one another. Moreover, their commitment to urging and forging peace together had not waned. Unfortunately, their voices as peace activists—shunned as dissident idealists—were all too seldom heard.

In 1918, Austrian novelist Stefan Zweig (1881–1942), on the occasion of an address to the Second Socialist Women's International (Peace) Congress in Bern, Switzerland, analyzed the silencing of pacifism which, he claimed, Austrian peace advocate Bertha von Suttner, "knew, better than any other." Suttner, who died five weeks before the outbreak of World War I, knew "about the deep tragedy of the idea that she held, about the almost destructive tragedy of pacifism; that it never appears at the right time. In peacetime it's superfluous; in war it's insane. In peacetime it is without force, and in wartime it is helpless." Zweig paid tribute to Suttner, forty years his junior, whom he now admitted, to his shame and regret, that he had not respected enough as a person, nor valued her writings as they deserved, nor befriended her in their shared mutually loved city of Vienna. Suttner, Zweig concluded, with admiration, "lived her conviction and her conviction was her life" (1918, 4). Just over two decades later, in the midst of the Holocaust, Zweig, in exile in Brazil, would take his own life.

This brief survey of transnational (transatlantic) friendships among female peace activists (e.g., Schwimmer, Lloyd, Doty, Heymann, Hertzka) suggests the significance of taking the crossing of borders into account in (auto)biographies of political actors and also in evaluating more generally successes (or failures) of international relations and the peace movement as a whole. Transnationalism is a category of analysis as relevant as others such as class, ethnicity, age, and gender. The more transnational friendships—on an individual but also on an organizational basis—are ignored or undervalued in our attempts to understand critical social movements, the more likely we are to overlook key and inspiring elements of global human history.

WILPF as a transnational feminist peace organization somehow held together during World War II, with many Wilpfers doing what they could to prevent more deaths and provide aid to fellow international members in these new times of trouble. Naturally they were hindered in manifold ways, and what they achieved was not really enough. Nevertheless, they did save lives and restore personal dignity. Ruth Gage Colby (1899–1984), a WILPF U.S. section leader in Minnesota, for example, sponsored seventy-year-old German WILPF leader Helene Stöcker's affidavit to the United States in 1942, and in one of her last letters to Stöcker, she captured the transnationalist spirit of friendship and solidarity among Wilpfers: "Wouldn't it be grand if you and I could go back to the OTHER GERMANY together? There is so much to do. And you are no older than the men that are running the war. We need women, wise in ways of peace, to plan and administer the peace. So rest all you can."[20] We do not know if these two intergenerational women would have become closer friends, since Stöcker passed away shortly thereafter. But Colby went on to attend the charter U.N. conference in San Francisco in 1945, became a leader of the antinuclear peace movement in the 1960s, and served as WILPF representative to the United Nations in the mid-1970s. Like Suttner and the other women highlighted in this chapter, Colby lived her transnationalist pacifist conviction, and her conviction was her life. The chances of "winning the war on war" may well have moved a step forward because of it.

Notes

1. In April 2015, WILPF celebrated its centenary in The Hague. Over a thousand women from around the world, including a handful of Nobel Peace Prize and Right Livelihood Award (the so-called Alternative Nobel Peace Prize) laureates were present (WILPF 2015).

2. For excellent histories of these international women's organizations, see Bosch (1990), Rupp (1997), and Wilmers (2008).

3. Anita Augspurg "Neither Philosophers nor Martyrs." In *Pax International* (April 1926), reprinted in Jane Addams Papers microfilm (hereafter JAP microfilm), reel 44, 1–4, here 3.

4. Ibid., 1.

5. JAP microfilm, reel 7. Letter from Jane Addams to Paul Kellogg dated around September 15, 1914.

6. See, for example, the Ada James Papers, Wisconsin Historical Society Archives.

7. University of Illinois at Chicago, Women Building Chicago Records, box 34, folder 238. Speech by Rosika Schwimmer dated 1944.

8. Ibid., speech by Alice Paul dated 1944.

9. Ibid., speech by Schwimmer dated 1944.

10. In a similar vein, Lola Maverick Lloyd's granddaughter presented Lloyd's life work at the above-mentioned WILPF centenary in The Hague in April 2015.

11. JAP microfilm, reel 15. Letter from Jane Addams to Alice Lachmund dated November 26, 1923.

12. Universal Edition Archive, Vienna. "Yella Hertzka. Persönlicher Briefnachlass," Madeleine Doty, Letter to Yella Hertzka, undated [1921?]. The German excerpt (smoothing over the grammatical errors) reads: "I do not believe that love is any kind of sickness; it is love, always, whether I am with you or without you."

13. Cf. Women's International League for Peace and Freedom Papers microfilm (hereafter WILPF microfilm), reel 56. Memo from Yella Hertzka to Fräulein Madeleine Z. Doty dated August 29, 1927.

14. JAP microfilm, reel 17. Letter from Lida Gustava Heymann to Jane Addams, dated November 28, 1925.

15. Ibid., letter from Madeleine Doty to Jane Addams, dated October 28, 1925.

16. Ibid., letter from Lida Gustava Heymann to Jane Addams (in German), dated April 8, 1926.

17. Ibid., reel 19. Letter from Lida Gustava Heymann to Jane Addams, dated September 18, 1927.

18. Within this sentence lies a fundamental critique, by the way, of a "number one" obsession—competition—which Alfie Kohn, among others, has thoroughly deconstructed (Kohn 1992).

19. WILPF microfilm, reel 4. Letter from Emily Greene Balch, dated November 21, 1939 (emphasis added).

20. Swarthmore College Peace Collection, DG-35. Ruth Gage Colby's letter to Helene Stöcker dated February 4, 1943.

References

Alonso, Harriet Hyman. 1993. *Peace as a Women's Issue. A History of the U.S. Movement for World Peace and Women's Rights.* Syracuse, N.Y.: Syracuse University Press.

Balch, Emily Greene. 1915 (2003). "Journey and Impressions of the Congress." In *Women at The Hague. The International Peace Congress of 1915*, edited by Jane Addams, Emily G. Balch, and Alice Hamilton, 39–49. New York: Basic Books.

Blackwell, Joyce. 2004. *No Peace without Freedom: Race and the Women's International League for Peace and Freedom, 1915–1975.* Carbondale: Southern Illinois University Press.

Bosch, Mineke, ed. 1990. *Politics and Friendship. Letters from the International Woman Suffrage Alliance, 1902–1942.* Columbus: The Ohio State University Press.

Clavin, Patricia. 2005. "Defining Transnationalism." *Contemporary European History* 14(4): 421–439.

Cohen, Laurie R., ed. 2005. *"Gerade weil Sie eine Frau sind..." Erkundungen über Bertha von Suttner, die unbekannte Friedensaktivistin.* Vienna: Braumüller.

———. 2012. "Courage, Conflict and Activism. Transnational Feminist Peace Movements, 1900 to the Present Day." In *Gender and Conflict since 1914*, edited by Ana Carden-Coyne, 69–82. Basingstoke, U.K.: Palgrave Macmillan.

Doty, Madeleine. 1917. *Short Rations: An American Woman in Germany, 1915–1916.* New York: The Century.

Early, Frances H. 1997. *A World without War: How U.S. Feminists and Pacifists Resisted World War I.* Syracuse, N.Y.: Syracuse University Press.

Foster, Carrie A. 1995. *The Women and the Warriors: The U.S. Section of the WILPF, 1915–1946.* Syracuse, N.Y.: Syracuse University Press.

Gustafson, Melanie. 2001. "Lloyd, Lola Maverick." In *Women Building Chicago 1790–1990: A Biographical Dictionary*, edited by Rima Lunin Schultz and Adele Hast, 517–519. Bloomington: Indiana University Press.

Helm, Bennett. 2013. "Friendship." *The Stanford Encyclopedia of Philosophy*, June 21. Accessed July 4, 2015. http://plato.stanford.edu/entries/friendship.

Heymann, Lida Gustava. 1992. *Erlebtes-Erschautes: Deutsche Frauen kämpfen für Freiheit, Recht und Frieden, 1850–1940*, edited by Margrit Twellmann. Frankfurt: Helmer.

Klapper, Melissa R. 2010. "'Those by Whose Side We Have Labored': American Jewish Women and the Peace Movement between the Wars." *Journal of American History* (December): 636–658.

Kohn, Alfie. 1992. *No Contest: The Case against Competition (Why We Lose in Our Race to Win)*. New York: Houghton Mifflin.

Liddington, Jill. 1989. *The Long Road to Greenham: Feminism and Anti-militarism in Britain since 1820*. London: Virago.

Manges, Johanna. 2011. "Fragmente einer Frauenfreundschaft: Die Briefe Hedwig von Pöttings an Bertha von Suttner." Unpublished Diplomarbeit, University of Innsbruck, Austria.

McFadden, Margaret H. 2011. "Borders, Boundaries, and the Necessity of Reflexivity: International Women Activists, Rosika Schwimmer (1877–1948), and the Shadow Narrative." *Women's History Review* 20(4): 533–542.

Narayan, Uma. 1998. "Essence of Culture and a Sense of History: A Feminist Critique of Cultural Essentialism." *Hypatia* 13(2): 86–106.

Newman, A. Evelyn. 1915. "Three Days in Berlin." *Survey* 34(10): 226–227.

Oesch, Corinna. 2010. *Die Komponistin Maria Hofer (1894–1977): Frauenzusammenhänge und Musik*. Vienna: Strasshof.

Pethick-Lawrence, Emmeline. 1938. *My Part in a Changing World*. London: Victor Gollancz.

Rupp, Leila. 1997. *Worlds of Women: The Making of an International Women's Movement*. Princeton, N.J.: Princeton University Press.

Schott, Linda K. 1997. *Reconstructing Women's Thoughts. The Women's International League for Peace and Freedom before World War II*. Stanford, Calif.: Stanford University Press.

Schwimmer, Rosika. 1914. "The Bankruptcy of the Man-Made World-War." *Jus Suffragii* 8(12): 2–3.

———. 1944. Speech by Rosika Schwimmer. University of Illinois at Chicago, Women Building Chicago Records, box 34, folder 238.

Stanley, Liz. 1992. *The Auto/biographical "I": The Theory and Practice of Feminist Auto/biography*. Manchester, U.K.: Manchester University Press.

Suriano, Maria Grazia. 2012. *Percorrere la nonviolenza: L'esperienza politica della Women's International League for Peace and Freedom (1915–1939)*. Rome: Aracne.

Wilmers, Annika. 2008. *Pazifismus in der internationalen Frauenbewegung (1914–1920). Handlungsspielräume, politische Konzeptionen und gesellschaftliche Auseinandersetzungen*. Essen, Germany: Klartext.

WILPF. 2015. *Conference Summary*. Accessed July 2, 2015. http://www.womenstopwar.org/wp-content/uploads/2015/06/Conference-Summary-Final.pdf.

Wynner, Edith. 1985. "Rosika Schwimmer." In *Biographical Dictionary of Modern Peace Leaders*, edited by Harold Josephson, 862–865. Westport, Conn.: Greenwood Press.

Zweig, Stefan. 1918. "Berta v. Suttner (Eine Ansprache anläßlich der Eröffnung des Internationalen Frauenkongreß für Völkerverständigung in Bern)." *Neue Freie Presse* (Vienna), June 21: 1–4.

CHAPTER 10

The Dissidence of Daily Life
Feminist Friendships and the Social Fabric of Democracy

LORI E. AMY AND EGLANTINA GJERMENI

Tina

I could not call myself a "dissident." I was born in 1968 in Kruja, a small town in northern Albania. My mother was only nineteen years old when I was born. I was trained early by my family, in school, by the state media, to be a "good" girl, a good Albanian, the state's version of a "good" person. Albania was the most isolated communist country in southeast Europe, and the government drummed the same message into everybody in the country: that Albania was the best country in the world, that we were the luckiest people. This message was spread on the only state-owned television station that broadcast from 6 P.M. to 10 P.M. It was spread on the radio, in all of the youth groups, at all of the cultural events. It was spread through art and literature: socialist realism told us that communism was the beautiful spirit saving the world from the ugly brutality of the capitalist West. The propaganda presented Enver Hoxha, Albania's dictator, as our father, our uncle, our God. With no other models available to us, most of us believed the state propaganda. Some families figured out how to tune radios and television into Italian and Yugoslavian stations, but this had to be done in secret as we could be accused of being decadent, an enemy of the state, if we were caught with these forbidden signals.

My father worked for the Foreign Trade Ministry, so he sometimes traveled abroad. In my third year of high school, my parents moved to Greece, where my father was appointed to the trade office in the Albanian Embassy. At the time, my brother and I were living with my parents in Kruja; when my parents moved to Greece, we were sent back to live with my grandparents in Lushnja and visited our parents in Greece during summer vacations. Very few people had the opportunity to travel outside of Albania at this time, so we were very privileged to be able to travel in the summer to visit our parents. It was such a shock to see this other world! For the first time, I started to question what we were taught by the state. Some people had small, close groups of people that they could talk to about things that were forbidden. But my parents were so careful, and taught us to be so careful, that I never had contact with people who would speak openly against the regime. It was not possible for me to talk with anybody about the questions I was having, and we were all very careful not to talk about what we had seen in Greece.

The questions I was having remained in my mind, unspoken, for many years. When it was time for university, I was sent to study at the Faculty of History and Philology. At that time you had to have very good results in high school and a very good family biography in order to have the possibility of studying at university. The state decided what we would study, and it was decided that I would complete my undergraduate degree in history. The history we learned was very politicized. We studied the literature of Marx, Engels, Lenin, and Stalin, as well as the writings of Enver Hoxha. The entire curriculum was dictated by the communist party in power. When I graduated from university in 1990, I was instructed to remain in Tirana and wait to be placed in a job. I remained at home with my parents, which is where I was in 1990–1991 when students from the generation after mine began demonstrating and brought change to Albania.

I was at that time very confused, scared, not completely understanding what was happening. My life had been very sheltered and I had not seen the things from which many people suffered.

The rest of the communist governments in Southeast Europe had already fallen and, for the first time in Albania, I could see and feel people's anger toward those that had held power and to all members of the communist party. I could feel the rage of a people betrayed by communism and desperate for freedom. In this rage, people wanted to throw away everything from the past. Farms were burned, public offices were looted, buildings were stripped for construction material, and state infrastructure was destroyed. The need for freedom came out as a big explosion. We went from one extreme to the other: hating everything that symbolized the brutal, oppressive regime that had cut us off from the rest of the world for almost fifty years, Albanians destroyed the material and symbolic fabric of the state, ripped apart its physical as well as its ideological foundations. We did not know what "democracy" meant, but we threw away everything from the past in order to chase it.

As change was sweeping the country, I began to reflect on the history I had learned, the new world to which I was being exposed. At the same time, our media opened up. The rest of the world was being beamed into us through television programs that we were hungry to watch. To Albanians, the United States seemed like a paradise, and we idealized it. It is impossible to explain how poor we Albanians were. We could go more than twenty-four hours without drinkable water, and, because of strict food rationing, people would line up at food distribution centers as early as 3 or 4 A.M. Meat and dairy products were extremely scarce, and, in the 1980s, after Hoxha broke off relations with China, many people lived at near-starvation levels. America, which we had grown up believing was the imperialist threat, became the things we dreamed of—being like America, going to America, living like Americans. American television shows like the soap opera *The Bold and the Beautiful* and *Santa Barbara* were famous in Albania—we all wanted *that* life, a dream of wealth and comfort that we could not even have imagined in our years of poverty and isolation.

While thousands of Albanians learned about American culture through television, some of us benefitted from American educational and development programs that helped us make new lives after the fall of the communist government. The School of Social Work in Tirana was established with the support of a U.S. Government Grant and Bethany Christian Services. This grant allowed an exchange program between Albania and Grand Valley State University (GVSU) in Grand Rapids, Michigan. I went on this exchange program for the first time in 1995. Slowly, I began to understand the words "democracy" and "human rights," began to see that the history that I had studied was manipulated history, in the service of a regime.

Lori

I came to Albania, and hence to my friendship with Tina, via America's "war on terror." After finishing my first book, *The Wars We Inherit: Military Life, Gender Violence, and Memory*, I wanted to write something that could make Americans see the daily, horrifying effects of the global violence we had unleashed. Initially, I wanted to go to Pakistan to research and write a materialist feminist analysis of the effects of war on women's lives. Through a series of chance meetings and uncanny intersections, I came to Albania instead. I knew very little about

Albania before I arrived, and I did not realize that, in this small country, I would find a direct link between the war on terror consuming us now and the Cold War that has become an amnesiac blur in Western consciousness.

The explosion of an old army barracks in the village of Gerdec, just outside of the capital city, Tirana, provides a glimpse of the intricate web of global finance and arms trafficking connecting the Cold War to America's wars in Afghanistan and Iraq. Albania has over one hundred thousand tons of military stockpiles—communist-era weapons and munitions—deemed a public hazard and proliferation threat (Likmeta 2012; USDOS 2012). A decommissioning operation in Gerdec that was supposedly extracting scrap metal and destroying unsafe explosives blew up in March 2008. The resulting fire caused a series of smaller explosions that continued for another fourteen hours. Twenty-six people were killed, 302 injured, and 5,500 homes damaged or destroyed. For miles in all directions, houses burned, and windows were blown out of cars and buildings. The explosion was heard over a hundred miles away in Skopje, Macedonia.

Investigations into the explosion uncovered the involvement of AEY Inc., a U.S. arms trafficking organization run by Efraim Diveroli. AEY was awarded a multi-million dollar defense contract to supply 7.62 mm automatic rifle and machine gun ammunition for the Warsaw Pact model weapons used by the Afghan forces (USAO 2010). AEY is one of the many previously unknown defense companies to have thrived since 2003, when the Pentagon began dispensing billions of dollars to train and equip indigenous forces in Afghanistan and Iraq. Its rise from obscurity once seemed to make it a successful example of the Bush administration's promotion of private contractors as integral elements of war-fighting strategy (Chivers, 2008).

According to Tristram Korten (2009), an investigative journalist specializing in armed conflict, "Diveroli and his crew" procured the required munitions through Evdin Ltd., "a shell company connected to a Swiss arms dealer, Heinrich Thomet, whose name was on a U.S. arms-trafficking watch list. Acting as broker, Evdin bought" the forty-year-old Chinese ammunitions "from Albania's national arms-export company"—munitions that were supposedly to be decommissioned.

The United States' primary interest in this explosion was *not* the life, integrity, loss, grief of the Albanians, not the obscenity of the wars in Afghanistan and Iraq or the underworld of gun running and organized crime these breed. The United States was interested only in the quality of munitions received and the fact that forty-year-old Chinese-made munitions were repackaged and sold as Albanian. AEY, Inc., and codefendents Efraim Diveroli, David Packouz, Alexander Podrizki, and Ralph Merrill, were prosecuted for defense procurement contract fraud (Markus 2011). At the 17 December 2010 conviction of Ralph Merrill, U.S. attorney for the Southern District of Florida, Wifredo A. Ferrer, proclaimed the conviction reaffirmed the message that "defense contractors are responsible for the effectiveness and safety of munitions they provide to our troops and allies" (USAO 2010). Of all of the "crimes that led up to this explosion, in exchange for all of the lives lost and ruined, a conviction for 'defrauding the US government' is what counts as justice?" (Amy 2010c). "Justice" was as muddied on the Albanian side. In March 2012, Albanian investigations into the explosion resulted in a conviction of nineteen people on charges of "gross mismanagement and other related offenses" (Likmeta 2012, online). For the United States, the crime is fraud. In Albania, it is management. The truth of the relationship between the United States and Albania, between the Cold War munitions being trafficked to feed the death and destruction of the war on terror, fall into this gap between what counts as "crime" and "justice." To enter Albania is thus to enter the still bleeding, raw wounds of the Cold War—wounds that are simultaneously bound up with the "War on Terror."

In *The Three Guineas,* Virginia Woolf says: as a woman, I have no country. As the child of a military family, with a father who brought home the violences of the wars he lived in Korea, in Vietnam, in his own tortured psyche, I know, intimately, the destructive effects of twentieth-century nation-making. But I know these from one specific location: the child of an enlisted army man, born on an army base in the former West Germany (my birth country no longer exists), a target of family violence, lower socioeconomic bracket. I also know the privileges of U.S. citizenship: the wealth of a country whose science, technology, and money accrue in relation to the wars from which it emerges as a super power; a university education and job as a professor that give me access to funding for my research in Albania; a passport that lets me move with relative ease across borders that are closed to many others. In America, my life began as disadvantaged (a euphemism for poor, family uneducated, military meager wages, domestic violence). My state-school education got me through a PhD and into a tenure-track university job. In middle age, I have a lower-middle-class academic life—all, within American measures, relatively small-scale social and cultural capital. In Albania, an American identity brings me the unearned privilege of social capital through which, *as American*, I have greater social status than most Albanians. A foreigner, educated, researching a book, I slide into the category of the agents of "development" that measure Albania's progress on the transitional scale from "developing" to "developed" country. The implication, always, of inferior, of less-than . . . an implication internalized by so many in the country.

Tina

In 1995, before I went to the United States for the first time, I started working as a lecturer at the Social Work Department. In 1996, I became involved with the first Counseling Center for abused women in Albania. Several professional women were trained by Dutch and Irish domestic violence trainers, and, in October 1996, we established Albania's first counseling center for abused women. At that time, there were no master's programs in Albania, and those of us working in social work and counseling had only the skills and knowledge available through international organizations providing training in the country. In order to receive advanced professional training, I had to leave my husband in Albania and take my son, then five years old, with me to America. This was during one of the most difficult times in Albania and my life: the economy had collapsed, Albania was in a state of anarchy, and I felt as though I was escaping from a war situation in my own country. I was constantly worried about my husband, parents, and everybody else in Albania while caring for my son—who had not a word of English—and completing the Advanced Standing Program at GVSU. I also worked at GVSU as a teaching assistant in order to pay part of my tuition. I carried twenty-one hours per semester that year and did my internship in home-based center therapy.

I came back to Albania as soon as I graduated at the end of April 1998. I was flying with ideas—I wanted to practice all of the things that I had learned! But it was impossible. I had changed, but the structures in Albania had not. The school system, the people in charge—these were all the same. The "best practices" and theories I had learned in the United States were ideals that I had no opportunity to implement in Albania. In order to do something of value with the things that I had learned, I took the job of executive director of the Women's Center (later renamed the Gender Alliance for Development Center). While directing the Gender Alliance for Development Center, I also completed my PhD in social work at the University of Tirana.

I returned to GVSU in January 2007 for four weeks, on the last visit financed by the U.S. Government–Bethany Christian Services exchange program, and there was not any doubt that I would stay with my American family, Julie and Dave. I lived with them for six weeks on my first exchange program and they remain dear friends to this day. When I left, they gave me a key to their house as a symbol that I was welcome back anytime, that they had taken me into their family and that I would always find "home" with them. All of my American friends—Esther, Casey, Jesse, the many people who opened their homes to me—supported me and made it possible for me to develop myself and my thinking.

Lori

I came to Albania circuitously, compelled by a desire to understand the global consequences of America's war on terror. Albania showed me that I had to go deeper, take a longer view—that I had to trace the violences rupturing us now to the traumatic repetitions of the Cold War. My perspective on this research shifted partly in relation to Tina. When I came to Albania in February 2009, the woman I met was the executive director of the Gender Alliance for Development Center. By April, Tina had been placed on the Socialist Party (SP) ticket and was thickly embroiled in the bitter, adversarial world of politics. More than anybody I know, Tina hates the angry, aggressive nature of political rhetoric, the culture of accusation and confrontation that dominates the public sphere. The thought of being engaged in this terrain was a physical pain to her, even in May 2009. So many of her friends (especially her ex-students) counseled her against entering politics because they were concerned about the toll it would take on her physically and emotionally. As a trauma theorist, I see party politics in Albania as both repeating some of the most destructive aspects of the totalitarian regime and trapped by pernicious aspects of capitalism masquerading as democracy. Nevertheless, I supported Tina's decision to enter politics. I believed that Tina embodies the intellectual and ethical virtues of "good government," and that she could bring these things to the political sphere in Albania.

The June 2009 election was so close, so controversial, so heavily contested, that, at the end of July, it still was not clear which party had won the majority and would take political control of the country. Ultimately, the Socialist Movement for Integration brokered a deal with the incumbent Democratic Party, using their four seats in parliament to give the Democratic Party continued control of government and gain 20 percent of the government's top positions. The SP claimed that the vote count and electoral process were corrupted. In this hostile political sphere, characterized by opposition protests and personal attacks from all parties, a major news network aired video in January 2011 of two Socialist Movement for Integration deputies in the Ministry of Economy negotiating a 700,000 Euro kickback for a hydroelectric plant in the north of Albania. Protests against corruption in government followed, and, on 21 January, four protesters were killed.

Watching Tina struggle through this shift from civil society (a phenomenon about which I knew very little when I arrived in Albania) to the political world made me want to understand the things with which she was struggling. When I first got to Albania, the world of "development" was only an abstract idea for me. I had read many feminist critiques of the structure of international aid, but my understanding of this world was theoretical—and, I will confess, in some ways ideological. The practical round of meetings, lunches, coffees, functions, activities that formed Tina's world was at first a confusing whirlwind for me. I could not keep all of the embassies straight—was it the Dutch or the Spanish that funded x or y or z conference? The Swiss or the Americans? Working with which U.N. agency—U.N. Educational, Scientific, and Cultural Organization, U.N. Development Fund for Women (then known as UNIFEM, now known as U.N. Women), the U.N. Development Programme? And was the World Bank or the Organization for Security and Co-operation in Europe behind the Women's Network? Or was it the National Democratic Institute? Or Soros? Or U.S. Agency for International Development? When I first met Tina, this whirl of embassies and international organizations constituted the daily fabric of her life, and, through her, I learned to appreciate the specific, concrete help that many international organizations are providing to individuals and social groups. At the same time, my research shows me the link between development agendas and the political turmoil in the country (Krasniqi 2012; Gjipali 2011). The global infrastructure of "development" has imposed international policies, mandates, and legal frameworks in Albania, such as the shock therapy doctrine of "transition." Many of the social problems that nongovernmental organizations must tackle are thus related to the economic ravages of privatization under the International Monetary Fund policies of structural adjustment that compelled the state to abandon social services and welfare and drastically cut funding for education, health, and social protection. Paradoxically, then, nongovernmental organizations have been dependent on international donors to confront social problems that exist *in relation to* the development paradigms they impose (Amy and Gjermeni 2012; Zarkov 2008).

As I write this, I imagine Tina's gentle voice, reminding me of the many good things that crucial human rights and democratization organizations have done in the country. Without discounting the importance of this work, we also have to recognize that, around the world, "democracy" has become a euphemism for capitalism—a capitalism that, in Albania, "leaves schools and hospitals in devastating conditions, abandons social services, and cannot employ half of the working-age population in the formal economy" (Amy 2010a, 205). I am implicated in these structures, too. As Rey Chow so compellingly argues in *The Age of the World Target*, area studies programs in U.S. universities have developed in relation to military and global security nets interested in gaining sociological and anthropological knowledge about countries that may potentially pose security threats. In the event of war, this research becomes important to military analysts (Chow 2006).

Negotiating Differences

What began as a predictable working relation between two feminists, each concerned with the structural and cultural violences impacting women, turned into a strong emotional bond between women confronting, from different perspectives, the ways in which "social, economic, and political institutions produce unjust structural inequalities" (Young 2001, 675). As a U.S. citizen critical of U.S. economic and foreign policy and the ways in which a global war on terror is devastating the lives of so many around the world, Lori feels a primary obligation to produce research that can hold her country and government accountable for their complicity in the political and economic problems people such as Tina confront. As a woman who lived her first twenty-four years under a brutal communist dictatorship, at the forefront of trying to build a country in a post-communist reality scarred by the tremors of neoliberal shock therapy as well as the brutality of totalitarian repression, Tina needs the resources, support, and networks of the international community—including U.S. institutions, the institutions in which Lori is implicated.

In addition to different (trans)national stakes, Lori and Tina have very different ways of entering the political domain. Lori comes to Albania as a feminist activist. After seven years of directing the Women's and Gender Studies Program at Georgia Southern University, where she developed curriculum for Feminist Social Action as well as transnational feminist courses studying gender, war, and cultural violence, her first impulse was to bring the activist strategies with which she was familiar from United States' contexts to her work in Albania. Indeed, her first year in Albania, Lori found herself, quite by chance, organizing a production of the *Vagina Monologues* in Albanian. Tina, on the other hand, has to navigate the high-stakes political realities of Albania. In certain respects, these different relations fall along the lines of academic-politician. But Tina, who has a PhD in social work, is deeply committed to her intellectual and academic life. Indeed, despite the demands of the Albanian Parliament, she continues to teach in the Faculty of Social Sciences at the University of Tirana in Albania. Lori's academic work feeds Tina's own intellectual desires, and, rather than being a source of tension between theory and practice, academia is in fact an important glue in this relation.

From these different national and practical locations, then, we would like to consider the complexity of friendship and dissidence between women who, though both deeply committed to social change, bring very different skill sets and agendas to their shared work. Properly speaking, neither Lori's U.S.-university brand of local activism nor the harsh constraints of the terrain Tina navigates positions either of us as "dissident." While "dissidence" invokes for Lori a larger-than-life specter that overshadows her baby-steps activism, it in some ways negates Tina's work in a world that, were she to be openly oppositional, could easily crush and then discard her. We would thus like to reframe dissidence in a way that can account for the daily labor of confronting the long-term effects of histories of fear and silence and recognize the complex realities in which "resistance" must work its way through overdetermined layers of "complicity" from which few of us can ever be totally free. Indeed, both Lori and Tina struggle, daily, with this problem of complicity.

Grappling with this problem of complicity, we are inspired by Saadawi's eloquent argument that we "must cooperate with all progressive democratic social forces and above all promote solidarity among women who everyday and all over the world are proving their courage and resilience in the struggle against war and for peace, against oppression and for freedom, and against patriarchal culture and for a new culture built on equality and respect for human—and womankind" (2006, 32). The question for us is how to do this. Coming out of a brutal totalitarian dictatorship, Tina inhabits a political sphere still dominated by a totalitarian mentality that sees any criticism, much less open opposition, as a direct threat from an "enemy" that must be annihilated (Kajsiu 2010; Eyal 2004; Gillis 1996; González-Enríquez 2001; Amy 2011a,b). Lori, on the other hand, comes out of a U.S. academic framing of feminist activism on university campuses and in local communities. Participating in marches, organizing peace vigils, developing women's and human rights initiatives for a university program—these are a far cry from the high stakes of Tina's political world. As an American academic, Lori had not grown up under a brutal dictator or lived through the chaos of "transition" or the collapse of the economy from pyramid schemes and the ensuing months of violence, the chaos of the government failing. At the same time, her life on military bases and the violence she lived with through her father, a soldier in America's Cold War army, allows her to recognize both American complicity in shaping global Cold War politics and the long-term emotional effects of a life lived in fear, under the threat of violence. While Tina is taking up the overwhelming, seemingly impossible, labor of trying to build a country, Lori is struggling to understand the forces that keep us silent, complicit, and the processes through which we come to voice, define, and stand up to the oppressive powers working on us.

While we thus feel ourselves to be quite a distance from any larger-than-life "dissident" action, we both strongly believe in an ideal of social justice, in working to transform the structures and practices of oppression, exploitation, violence, and war from which so many on our planet suffer. Our daily struggle with *how* to take up this work is one of the things that bond us. In our struggle with the *how* of forging a transnational solidarity that can sustain a vision and give us the energy for this work, we find Iris Marion Young's analysis of the difference between the deliberative democrat and the activist especially useful. To shift the discussion from "dissidence" to activism versus deliberative democracy allows us to consider in a more manageable way both our practical, daily labor and the ways that we find to support each other.

As Young describes the activist—deliberative democrat poles, both are concerned with the fundamental question of what constitutes responsible citizenship, and both have a legitimate claim to political virtue (2001, 673). For the activist, the structural inequalities of a radically unjust political and economic sphere require citizens to call attention to the workings of power (676–677). Because structural inequalities limit participation in the political and economic spheres to elites who know the rules of the game and whose access to these spheres already constitutes an exercise of power, it is not possible for real social justice to come from participating in structures that are themselves constitutive of violence (677). Indeed, since participating in the institutions structuring oppression may in fact "confer undeserved legitimacy on them and fail to speak for those who remain outsiders," responsible citizens should "remain at least partially outside, protesting the process, agenda, and outcome of these proceedings and demonstrating against the underlying relations of privilege and disadvantage that condition them" (680).

The deliberative democrat, on the other hand, believes that those who believe "change is necessary must enter deliberative proceedings with those indifferent or hostile to them in an effort to persuade a democratic public of their rightness" (681). The responsible citizen should "engage and argue" with and within institutional structures in order to make them "more inclusive and representative of all the interests and perspectives potentially affected by the outcome of policy discussions" (681). While the activist makes use of tactics such as "picketing, leafleting, guerilla theater, large and loud street demonstrations, sit-ins, and other forms of direct action, such as boycotts" (673), the deliberative democrat believes that "protesting and making demands from the outside may be an effective way to bring attention to injustices that require remedy . . . but on their own they do not propel the positive institutional change that would produce greater justice" (681). In contrast, the activist assumes that to the extent that entering into deliberative discussion in policy arenas fails to question "existing institutional priorities and social structures, deliberation is as likely to reinforce injustice as to undermine it" (685). Without massive, concentrated action, it will not be possible to "shift priorities and goals," and "politics will continue to support structural inequalities" (684).

Lori

I find the activist—deliberative democrat pole a useful way of thinking about how Tina and I negotiate our relation. I supported her going into politics precisely because I thought she was capable of helping to change political structures. At the same time, I also enter my relation to Tina as a feminist critical of the ways in which women are appropriated into political structures dominated by men as well as a trauma theorist who sees all of Albania's existing political parties as engaged in a battle over what to repress and what to remember of the communist past (Stan 2006). Not only do I not have a "side" in the partisan fight, I see all of them as equally culpable—this brings me from time to time into a conflict with the ways in which, as a member of parliament for the SP, Tina, of necessity, is positioned differently.

I also struggle with my own sense of what "right" action is. In the United States, I do not think twice about organizing a peace vigil, driving to D.C. to participate in a march, coordinating speak-outs—these are such standard practices: necessary and important consciousness-raising strategies, on the one hand, and community-building steps, on the other. Until we started a chapter of the National Organization for Women on our college campus, young women had no recognizable, organized social space for challenging the patriarchal structures affecting them, supporting each other in their efforts to survive and transform those structures, or collaborating on social actions. But the first year I was working in Albania, the U.S. Embassy organized the first breast cancer walk. I of course told my students in the Department of Public Health and encouraged them to go. Only one young woman came, and, before she could come, I had to meet with her and explain what a "walk" is. This was a general election year and the political parties were all organizing marches, demonstrations, and flinging words like weapons. She could not distinguish between a "walk" and a political protest, and the idea of the walk triggered for her the problems of party politics.

In addition to the "walk" triggering contemporary problems with a rhetorically—and sometimes physically—violent political sphere, the idea of public demonstration of any kind triggered the fears she inherited from her parents' lives under the dictatorship. She had been raised with their stories of brutal oppression, where political dissent brought punishment. Public demonstrations against the party or its policies were unimaginable. What is more, in a country in which one in five people were in one capacity or another informers for the secret police, people learned to be very secretive, not to trust anybody, and not to risk speaking things that could be interpreted as criticism, much less dissent, for fear of being investigated by the sigurimi and exiled or imprisoned

(Krasniqi 2012). A very simple walk to show solidarity with victims of breast cancer, raise awareness about the problems women in Albania face with this disease, and encourage early diagnosis and treatment was thus so imbricated in an oppressive political history that only one of my eighty public health students participated, and her participation required extensive reassurance beforehand that this was not a politically organized event, there would be no police surveillance of the crowds, and that she would suffer no repressive repercussions. This experience has made me much more careful, now, about throwing around ideas for marches and "political actions"—the possibilities for effective activism in Albania are different than in the United States, and I am of no use to anybody in Albania if I try to sell a brand of American activism that plays into divisive party politics or compounds traumatic histories.

These internal struggles and the ways that our friendship helps us to rethink and resee ourselves highlights how fundamental friendship is "to the ways in which we conceive of the bonds that shape the possibilities for politics and the political" (Devere and Smith 2010, 351). In fact, Sibyl Schwarzenbach argues that civic friendship is the forgotten problem of modern democratic theory (2005, 239). While a comprehensive review of the literature on feminist politics and friendship is beyond the scope of this chapter, we want to close with a consideration of how our individual friendship illuminates some of the recent thinking about friendship as constituent of the political. In Schwarzenbach's analysis, the three necessary traits of all friendship—reciprocal awareness, goodwill, and practical doing—are integral to both personal friendships and civic friendships. While individual friendships are based on "personal liking, intimate knowledge and close emotional ties," civic friendships are structured by the "intelligent and orderly construction of political institutions, rights, and social practices [which] become embodied in public institutions and laws, which institutions in turn educate and encourage others, and are willingly upheld by the everyday habits of the citizenry" (2005, 235).

As Schwarzenbach sees it, friendship, far from being merely a conception of political care or a naïve or essentialist form of feminism, can in fact "help determine the limits of legitimate freedom and equality in a genuine democracy" (233). Following Aristotle's notion of friendship as *philia*, she argues that "friends must be aware of and *recognize each other* as some form of moral equal ... they must reciprocally *wish each other well* for the other's sake, and not merely for their own ... [and] importantly (because repeatedly overlooked) they must *practically do* things for one another" (234, original emphasis). In the political realm, however, reciprocal recognition, wishing each other well, and practical doing operate by way of the constitution, the public laws, and the social habits of the citizenry. That is, these traits work via institutionally recognized norms concerning the proper treatment of persons in general, what is concretely due them in a particular society, their recognized duties, etc., together with the knowledge and willingness of the citizenry to uphold these same norms in practice. Political friendship is thus the general and public concern citizens reveal for one another by way of both the form and content of a society's laws, its public institutions and its everyday customs (235).

This analysis of the foundational relationship of *philia* to a democratic political sphere is an especially important context for thinking about transnational friendship and dissidence from the point of view of Albania. A convergence of phenomena makes it extremely difficult for many Albanians to trust each other: the lingering effect of an exceptionally high degree of paranoia under Hoxha's regime; the duration and degree of persecution; the extreme poverty of much of the population and the inevitable position of dependency this creates; the system of clientelism under communism—these have evolved both small- and large-scale corruption at every level (Freedom House 2012, Gjipali 2011). From the expectation of "gifts" for services rendered (including to professionals such as doctors, lawyers, and teachers) to the cronyism through which public sector jobs are awarded only to loyalists of the party in political power, the concept of "friend" is tainted by perverted relations of power and fear. Gestures of friendship are thus suspiciously perceived as utilitarian, as the survival gesture of trying to benefit from a relation.

From this perspective, to open oneself to friendship is to take a risk; it requires confronting the fear that the other is interested only in using you, will betray or hurt you, will want to own you or to milk you. The harsh realities of both the communist past and the capitalism-gone-wrong present make the simple act of extending and opening to genuine friendship a specifically *political* act in that it insists on the possibility of forging a democratic sphere in which just, caring, and egalitarian relations are possible. As Schwarzenbach argues, a decent functioning state *requires* a "minimal reciprocal awareness, concern, and practical doing between citizens"; in fact, it is only through "a high degree of civic friendship" that genuine justice is possible. Without the "general good will and flexible 'give and take' that a civic friendship entails, citizens will be . . . unwilling to yield regarding their own interests when necessary, or forego their special privileges when called up. The requirement of a friendly background in order for parties voluntarily to yield ground must be among the most elementary facts of human psychology" and is absolutely necessary for citizens to "accept in practice the burdens of justice required in any particular case" (2005, 236).

If we can think of friendship as the ground of a democratic sociality, then how can we engage a notion of dissidence as a component of this sociality that moves us beyond oppositional political resistance to creative political transformation?

Lori

I worry about the risk Tina takes in exposing herself in this writing; I know that the political opposition will look for any reason to attack her and that she is making herself vulnerable by writing about her life under the regime, a relatively privileged member of a family that belonged to the communist party. This is a significant risk in a country still suffering from the open wounds of an unresolved totalitarian past, where to call somebody a "communist" is to invoke images of prison, exile, execution—to reinvoke a victim-perpetrator bifurcation that positions all members of the communist party as "bad" and responsible for the suffering of those who were persecuted. I am particularly sensitive both to what Tina risks and to what I see as a wound still bleeding in Albania.

First, on the nature of the wound: In January 2012, I visited a former prison camp, Fier Shtylle, in the south of Albania, near Lushnja. I went with a young man, Taulant Grabova, who was born in the camp and lived there until the communist government collapsed in 1991, when he was fourteen years old. In his early thirties now, Taulant is active with the Democratic Party and a primary organizer of an anticommunist club that wants, among other things, to remove all "communists" from power. Approximately one third of the people originally exiled to this camp still live there—including some of Taulant's cousins.

A particularly chilling scene from this visit remains with me and will not let me shake it. Taulant, who wanted me to see how small the living quarters were, how many people were crammed into one room, became increasingly angry at not being able to gain entry to an apartment in one of the boarded-up buildings. I followed him up to the top floor of one of these buildings, where I watched, silently, as he kicked in the door of the last apartment to the right of the stairs. We walked through the tiny kitchen, bathroom, living room, into the one tiny bedroom. Stepping over the debris of a building mostly abandoned—plaster, splinters of wooden rafters, the skins of walls and ceilings the building had been shedding—I focused primarily on the floor, cautious of the danger of falling through. Noticing the light streaming in from the collapsing roof, I looked up, and met the eyes of the rats, poised on the ceiling beams, looking down at me. Overcome with the convergence of Taulant's emotion and the threat of rats hovering above me, I led the way outside, into fresh air. Only on the descent did I notice the bodies of the dead rats littering the stairs. Once outside, we proceeded along the length of this building that had once been the camps' living quarters. In the last room on the ground floor, men were drinking beer and macchiatos and shooting pool on the billiards table occupying most of the room. The room was freshly painted, with music playing. Crumbling rafters, rats, a freshly painted billiards room. Music and macchiatos, the drive for life and pleasure in the very midst of a living, breathing wound.

In my family structure, I am the youngest of seven children. In a family system in which all of us were under the tyranny of a paranoid man, subject to his whims, violence was dispersed, differently, across the family. I was the baby, my father's favorite, and he seldom hit me. My father's violence toward me was camouflaged: under the cover of night, with presents, with rewards for being his "special" baby, the one who "understood" him.[1] To my siblings against whom my father directed both physical and sexual violence, I was "privileged." The "privilege" of not being hit cost me my mind and my body: my father took both when I was still a child, before I had language. I never thought of resisting. I was twenty-one years old before I could finally stand up to him, before I could tell him that what he had done was wrong and that he had caused great harm. This smallest of steps, my first act of "resistance," came only after four years of college, taking classes in philosophy and psychology, and meeting people who showed me a different way to live. If I had not had the benefits of education and distance from my father, I do not know if, or when, I could have taken even that first small step. My first language was the silence of complicity, and learning to speak was a long, slow process.

I am with Saadawi when she calls on us to "encourage dissidence and rebellion against injustice, oppression, and all forms of discrimination" (2006, 23). Frequently, though, it is not through open rebellion, but, rather, with trepidation, steps at times faltering, that we find our way through our own ignorance, our own submission, our acceptance of injustice. When we are born into the silence of complicity, dissidence, like learning how to speak, requires exposure to new people, new ideas, new ways of living. If our first language is the silence of complicity, we learn to speak through the creative activity of opening up to the world around us and reconstituting ourselves through the new knowledges to which we open, as a way of forging new knowledge to bring into the world. Frequently, new knowledge comes to us as a rupture, a breaking-open of the ideas, experiences, and beliefs upon which we have built our identities. Even when our identities have been forged through violence and tyranny, this breaking-open is never easy. Each step along this path is a creative act in a long process of remaking a broken-open self.

If—like Taulant, like my brothers and sisters who were beaten—the "self" is constituted, first, by holding together the body broken open by violence, what does it mean to reopen that self in a way that can see the multiple forms violence takes, the ways that it is dispersed, differently, throughout the totalitarian system?

It is in this sense of reconstituting a self that we want to think of friendship and dissidence. The cornerstones of dissident action—refusal of and resistance to exploitation, domination, and oppression—take different forms, work in multiple directions. The form our resistance takes will depend to some extent on our location within the violent system, on the ways we have held ourselves together or have been broken open. When the bleeding wounds of a past still not understood divide people and breed hatred, dissidence is a creative act that returns to the past, not simply to identify "perpetrators" and "victims," "good" and "evil," but, as importantly, to understand how violence is bred, lived, repeated. Tzvetan Todorov's analysis of the violence of totalitarianism gives us an important entry point for this work. As Todorov argues, the most extreme violences proceed, not simply through the horrific acts of extraordinary villains, but, rather, through the routine conscription and indoctrination of ordinary people into oppressive, violent, brutal systems. Brutal systems—the totalitarian state of the Hoxha regime, the global siege President George Bush began with his 2002 State of the Union address that divided the world into "good" and "evil"—breed fear and hatred, inculcate people to do terrible things, pervert the fabric of our sociality. We need a theory and practice of dissidence as a creative act, as the ground for transforming the social fabric. In order to really change the structures, forces, and dynamics that oppress us, we have to change the terms of our relations. Friendship—as a personal relation, as a political principle—is crucial to this process.

We write with the desire to remake this social fabric. And, as Todorov shows us, neither heroes nor saints are required for this work. Most of us are neither good nor evil, heroes nor cowards. To reshape our social fabric, we need not "imitate saints. Nor need we fear monsters; both the dangers and the means with which to neutralize them are all around us" (1997, 291). Brutal systems can function only to the extent that ordinary people serve them. We remake the social fabric when we extricate ourselves from service to our oppressors, when we dismantle the us/them, enemy/ally binaries through which brutal systems divide ordinary human beings and conscript them into extraordinary acts of violence. Albania's prison camps, America's Abu Ghraib . . . the worst forms of these violences were committed, not by the architects of brutal regimes, but by the ordinary people conscripted into their service. Todorov proposes a code of "ordinary moral values and virtues, one commensurate with our times" (291) through which ordinary people can take up the extraordinary work of social transformation. With Todorov, we propose, as part of the ordinary virtues for social transformation, friendship as the ground of democratic sociality and dissidence as a creative act of reshaping the social fabric. Through our friendship, we take up dissidence, not as a grand political act of revolution, not as a larger-than-life heroism, but as the daily labor of finding the language to speak our ways out of the silence of complicity.

Note

1. I am of course not making a one-to-one parallel between violence in my family and the totalitarian state of Albania. I do, however, think a family violence perspective can bring a deeper understanding of the nature of traumatic experience in Albania and its after-life in individuals and society. For a specifically political lens on traumatic history in Albania, see my "Totalitarian Legacies, Transitional Symptoms: Subjectivity, Memory, and Identity in Post-Communist Albania"; for more on the structure of family violence out of which I draw my analysis, see *The Wars We Inherit: Military Life, Gender Violence, and Memory*.

References

Amy, Lori. 2010a. "Re-Membering in Transition: The Trans-National Stakes of Violence and Denial in Post-Communist Albania." In *History of Communism in Europe, Vol. I, Politics of Memory in Post-Communist Europe*, edited by the Institute for the Investigation of the Communist Crimes and for the Memory of the Romanian Exhile, 205–222. Bucharest, Romania: Zeta Books.

———. 2010b. *The Wars We Inherit: Military Life, Gender Violence, and Memory*. Philadelphia, Pa.: Temple University Press.

———. 2010c. "The Impact of the Wars We Inherit." North Philly Notes (blog post). Accessed 29 January 2012.

———. 2011a. "Listening for the Elsewhere and the Not-Yet: Academic Labor as Matter of Ethical Relation." In *I, IR: Autobiographical International Relations*, edited by Naeem Inyatullah and Kiran Pervez, 103–118. New York: Routledge.

———. 2011b. "Totalitarian Legacies, Transitional Symptoms: Subjectivity, Memory, and Identity in Post-Communist Albania." NCEEER Working Paper. Washington, D.C.: National Council for Eurasian and East European Research.

Amy, Lori, and Eglantina Gjermeni. 2012. "Where Is the 'State' in Albania? The Unresolved Contradictions Confronting Civil Society in the 'Transition' from Communism to Free Markets." *Studies of Transition States and Societies* 5(17): 7–21.

Bertelsmann Stiftung's Transformation Index (BTI). 2012. *Albania Country Report*. Gütersloh, Germany: Bertelsmann Stiftung.

Chivers, C. J. 2008. "Supplier under Scrutiny on Arms for Afghans." *New York Times*, 27 March. Accessed 15 August 2012. http://www.nytimes.com/2008/03/27/world/asia/27ammo.html?pagewanted=all.

Chow, Rey. 2006. *The Age of the World Target: Self-Referentiality in War, Theory, and Comparative Work*. Durham, N.C.: Duke University Press.

Devere, Heather, and Graham M. Smith. 2010. "'Friendship': Descriptive, Analytic, Normative." *Political Studies Review* 8: 341–356.
Eyal, Gil. 2004. "Identity and Trauma: Two Forms of the Will to Memory." *History and Memory* 16(1): 5–36.
Freedom House. 2012. "Albania: Freedom in the World 2012." Accessed 29 January 2012. http://www.freedomhouse.org/report/freedom-world/2012/albania.
Gillis, John R., ed. 1996. *Commemorations: The Politics of National Identity*. Princeton, N.J.: Princeton University Press.
Gjipali, G. 2011. "Nations in Transit 2011: Albania." *Freedom House*. Accessed 29 January, 2012. http://www.freedomhouse.org/sites/default/files/inline_images/NIT-2011-Albania.pdf.
González-Enríquez, Carmen. 2001. "De-communization and Political Justice in Central and Eastern Europe." In *The Politics of Memory: Transitional Justice in Democratizing Societies*, edited by Alexandra Barahona de Brito, Carmen González-Enríquez, and Paloma Aguilar, 218–247. Oxford Studies in Democratization. Oxford: Oxford University Press.
"Index on Efraim Diveroli Reporting." 2012. *New York Times*, August. Accessed 15 August 2012. http://topics.nytimes.com/topics/reference/timestopics/people/d/efraim_e_diveroli/index.html.
Kajsiu, Blendi. 2010. "Down with Politics! The Crisis of Representation in Post-Communist Albania." *Eastern European Politics and Societies* 24(2): 229–253.
Korten, Tristram. 2009. "Playing with Fire." *Details*. Accessed 29 January 2012. http://www.details.com/culture-trends/news-and-politics/200902/arms-dealer-efraim-diveroli-and-his-contract-with-the-us-army?printable=trueandcurrentPage=4.
Krasniqi, Afrim. 2012. "Albania 'Civil'—An Infinite History of Transition." Unpublished manuscript. Univerisity Revista Illyrus. 165–183. KRISTALIANA—HK, nr.1/2012, ISSN 2225–2894. Romë / Tiranë, fq.
Likmeta, Besar. 2012. "Albania Blast Trial Sentences Disappoint Victims." *Balkan Insight,* 13 March. Accessed 15 August 2012. http://www.balkaninsight.com/en/article/light-sentences-in-albania-deadly-blast-trial.
Markus, David Oscar. 2011. "Efraim Diveroli Gets Four Years." *Southern District of Florida Blog*, 4 January. Accessed 15 August 2012. http://sdfla.blogspot.com/2011/01/efraim-diveroli-gets-4-years.html.
Saadawi, Nawal el. 2006. "The Seventh Annual AWSA Conference: Rationale and the Way Forward." *Meridians: Feminism, Race, Transnationalism* 6(2): 22–32.
Schwarzenbach, Sibyl A. 2005. "Democracy and Friendship." *Journal of Social Philosophy* 26(2): 233–254.
Stan, Lavinia. 2006. "The Vanishing Truth: Politics and Memory in Post-Communist Europe." *East European Quarterly* 4(4): 383–408.
Todorov, Tzvetan. 1997. *Facing the Extreme: Moral Life in the Concentration Camps*. New York: Henry Holt.

U.S. Attorney's Office (USAO), Southern District of Florida. 2010. "Munitions Supplier Convicted of Defense Procurement Fraud and Lying to Army on Government Munitions Contract," 17 December. Accessed 15 August 15 2012. http://www.justice.gov/usao/fls/PressReleases/101217-03.html.

U.S. Department of State (USDOS), Bureau of European and Asian Affairs. 2012. "Background Note Albania," 5 April. Accessed 15 August 2012. http://www.state.gov/r/pa/ei/bgn/3235.htm.

Young, Iris Marion. 2001. "Activist Challenges to Deliberative Democracy." *Political Theory* 29: 670–690.

Zarkov, D. 2008. *Gender, Conflict, Development: Challenges of Practice.* New Delhi: Zubaa.

Contributors

Dr. Lori E. Amy is Professor of Writing and Linguistics at Georgia Southern University, where she also served as Director of the Women's and Gender Studies Program from 2002 to 2009. She is currently working on her second book, *Re-Membering in Transition: Trajectories of Violence, Structures of Denial, and the Struggle for Meaning in Post-Communist Albania*. An analysis of traumatic memory and identity under communism and in transition, this book brings a global dimension to the analysis of cultural violence she undertook in her first book, *The Wars We Inherit: Military Life, Gender Violence, and Memory* (Temple University Press, 2010). With research specializations in narrative, memory, and trauma studies, she has published widely in the areas of violence, identity, and subjectivity and has received numerous research and project grants. She was a Fulbright Scholar in Albania 2009–2010 and a Research Fellow at the Woodrow Wilson International Center for Scholars 2014. Amy serves on the editorial board of the *Journal of Narrative Politics* and serves as an editorial reviewer for *Studies of Transition States and Societies*, *Feminist Formations*, and *History of Communism in Europe* and as a judge for the Department of State Fulbright and Humphrey Scholars programs.

    Azza Basarudin is a Research Scholar at the UCLA Center for the Study of Women. She received her PhD in Women's and Gender Studies from UCLA (2009). Her teaching and research interests include feminist studies in Islam, transnational and postcolonial feminist theories, and feminist ethnography. Azza held fellowships and visiting scholar positions at Harvard University,

Syracuse University, University Kebangsaan Malaysia, Universiti Sains Malaysia, and the American University of Cairo. She has received awards from the Wenner-Gren Foundation, the Social Science Research Council, and the National Science Foundation, among others. Her essays and creative writings have appeared in journals, edited anthologies, and online/popular forums. Azza is the author of *Humanizing the Sacred: Sisters in Islam and the Struggle for Gender Justice in Malaysia* (University of Washington Press, 2015).

Himika Bhattacharya is Assistant Professor of Women's and Gender Studies, and a faculty affiliate with South Asia Studies and the Department of Communication and Rhetorical Studies at Syracuse University. Her research and teaching interests include transnational and Dalit feminisms; gender and violence; and interpretive research methods. Upon completing her MSW from TISS Bombay, she worked as a community organizer in the Lahaul valley of Himachal Pradesh, India. This led to her doctoral work, a collaborative project based in Lahaul focusing on marriage practice and antiviolence organizing. Her next project is a critical performance ethnography, which centers on women's oral histories from Lahaul with a focus on violence and is based on fieldwork conducted in 2010–2011. Her writings on gender and caste violence, ethnography, and civil rights movements in India appear or are forthcoming in *Meridians, Qualitative Inquiry, Feminist Formations, The Handbook of Emergent Methods, The Encyclopedia of Qualitative Research,* and *Kafila*.

Kabita Chakma is a researcher, writer, and architect. Her research interests include conflict and peace building, and the history, culture, and architecture of disadvantaged communities, particularly the indigenous peoples of Chittagong Hill Tracts (CHT), Bangladesh. She is a Coordinator of the Chittagong Hill Tracts Indigenous Jumma Association Australia (CHTIJAA), a member of the International Council for the Indigenous Peoples of CHT (ICIP-CHT), and a community adviser to the charity BODHI Australia. She has tutored and lectured at the School of Design, University of Technology, Sydney. Her publications include "Politics of the Orphans of War: 72 Children's Journey from the Chittagong Hill Tracts of Bangladesh to the Suburbs of France," with Glen Hill in *Children, Politics and Violence in South Asia*, edited by Bina D'Costa (Cambridge University Press, 2016); "The Chittagong Hill Tracts (CHT): Diminishing Conflict or Violent Peace?" with Bina D'Costa in *Diminishing Conflicts in the Asia-Pacific: Why Some Subside and Others Don't*, edited by Edward Aspinall, Robin Jeffrey, and Anthony Regan; and "Building a Bamboo Mountain: The Chakma House and the Cosmology of Mount Meru," *Architectural Theory Review*.

Elora Halim Chowdhury is Associate Professor and Chair of Women's and Gender Studies Department at the University of Massachusetts Boston. Her research and teaching interests include critical development studies, transnational feminism, gender violence, and human rights narrative and advocacy. She is the author of *Transnationalism Reversed: Women Organizing against Gendered Violence in Bangladesh* (SUNY 2011), which was awarded the Gloria E. Anzaldúa Book Prize from the National Women's Studies Association (2012). Her work has appeared in journals such as *Meridians, Hypatia, Human Rights Quarterly, Women's Studies International Forum, Gender Place and Culture,* and *International Feminist Journal of Politics*. She has contributed chapters to anthologies on gender and development, religion and culture, violence, and Islam and politics. Her current work focuses on narratives of war, gender violence, and healing in South Asia.

Dr. Laurie R. Cohen is an historian and researcher who has taught history and gender courses for many years at the University of Innsbruck and the University of Klagenfurt as well as recently at the University of Salzburg. Her recent publications in English include *Germans in Smolensk: Everyday Life under Nazi Occupation* (University of Rochester Press 2013), "Transnational Feminist Pacifists, 1900 to the Present," in: Ana Carden-Coynes (ed.), *Gender and Conflict Since 1914* (Palgrave 2012), and "'Fighting for Peace amidst Paralyzed Popular Opinion': Bertha von Suttner's and Rosa Mayreder's Pacifist-Feminist Insights on Gender, War and Peace" in: Bruna Bianchi and Geraldine Ludbrook (eds.), *Living War: Thinking Peace (1914–1921)* (forthcoming 2016). Her research focuses on nineteenth- to twenty-first-century Eastern and Central European as well as U.S. social and gender history, especially women's and peace movements.

Yuanfang Dai received her PhD in philosophy from Michigan State University. She also holds a PhD in philosophy from Peking University, China. She teaches at Michigan State University and has published articles on feminist issues in journals such as *Asian Women*. She works primarily in feminist philosophy, ethics, and social and political philosophy, with a particular interest in women's identity, cultural dynamics, and women's solidarity across cultural differences.

Esha Niyogi De's current research interests lie in South Asian women's cinema, screendance and gender, and theories of postcoloniality and mobility. She is the author of *Empire, Media, and the Autonomous Woman* (Oxford University Press) and the coauthor and coeditor of *Trans-Status Subjects: Gender in the Globalization of South and Southeast Asia* (Duke University Press). Her articles have appeared in such leading journals as *Screen* and *Feminist Media Studies,* and in other scholarly venues in the United States, India, Bangladesh, and Australia. Recently, she completed a Senior Fulbright Multi-Country Research Fellowship in Pakistan, Bangladesh, and India. Based on this research, she is writing a new book tentatively titled *Women's Transborder Cinema: Authorship and Femininities across South Asia*. She holds a PhD in English and teaches at UCLA.

Eglantina Gjermeni, Minister of Urban Development, Republic of Albania, has always been fascinated by social issues. She received the title Associated Professor from the Department of Social Work, Faculty of Social Science, University of Tirana, Albania, in 2015. She worked as a Professor at the Faculty of Social Work from 1995 until September 2013. Fully dedicated to social research, Eglantina Gjermeni is author and coauthor of numerous articles, such as "Feminist Friendships and the Social fabric of Democracy: The Dissidence of Daily Life"; "Mapping Women's Representation in the Local Councils of Albania"; "Where Is the 'State' in Albania? The Unresolved Contradictions Confronting Civil Society in the 'Transition' from Communism to Free Markets," as well as studies and publications addressing social issues, mainstreaming gender in policy, and women empowerment as concepts strongly related to the social and economic development of the country.

Glen Hill is Associate Professor of architecture at the faculty of Architecture, Design, and Planning, University of Sydney. He currently coordinates the Sustainable Architecture Research Studio and teaches research methods for higher degree research students. His research interests span issues of human rights, ecological sustainability, and design philosophy. Recent publications include "The Aesthetics of Architectural Consumption" in *Aesthetics of Sustainable Architecture* edited by Sang Lee; "Indigenous Women and Culture in the Colonised Chittagong" in *Everyday Occupations: Experiencing Militarism in South Asia and the Middle East* with Kabita Chakma, edited by Kamala Visweswaran; and "Poetic Measures of Architecture: Martin Heidegger's '... Poetically Man Dwells ...,'" *ARQ Architecture Research Quarterly*.

Alka Kurian is a lecturer at the University of Washington Bothell where she teaches film studies, human rights, women's studies, and postcolonial literature. Prior to this, she taught at the University of Sunderland, England, from 1991 to 2006. Dr. Kurian published a single author book titled *Narrative of Gendered Dissent: South Asian Cinemas* (2012, Routledge: Taylor and Francis). She was the founding coeditor of the peer-reviewed journal *Studies in South Asian Film and Media* from 2006 to 2014. Dr. Kurian has presented papers on gender, human rights, and film studies at several national and international conferences. She is the Chair of Tasveer Board, a community-based organization on South Asian film and art, and regularly codirects the annual Seattle South Asian Film Festival. She is also faculty adviser to the Film Club at the University of Washington Bothell.

Meredith Madden is a program administrator and research assistant for The Democratizing Knowledge Project at Syracuse University. She holds a PhD in Cultural Foundations of Education from Syracuse University where she also earned a Certificate of Advanced Studies from the Women's and Gender Studies Department. Her research and teaching interests lie in gender and education, decolonial studies in education, women's studies, and sociology of education. Committed to social justice education research, her recent work has been published in Feminist Teacher and Equity and Excellence in Education.

Angie Mejia is a doctoral candidate in the department of sociology at Syracuse University. Her research encompasses immigration, mental health, ethnicity, bio/psychopolitics, and citizenship by looking specifically at U.S. Latinas' experiences with depression and depression treatment. As a critical theorist and public sociologist, she collaborates with other Chicanas and Latinas and shares (via performance and public presentations) their experiences of crossing (and surviving) the affective *fronteras* constituted by the interaction of neoliberal forces, subjectivities, U.S. cultural practices, and the availability of mental health treatment to minority women. Angie's work has appeared in *Action Research* and *Theory in Action*.

Chandra Talpade Mohanty is Distinguished Professor of Women's and Gender Studies and Dean's Professor of the Humanities at Syracuse University. She is author of *Feminism without Borders: Decolonizing Theory, Practicing Solidarity* (Duke University Press, 2003), and coeditor of *Third World Women and the Politics of Feminism* (Indiana University Press, 1991), *Feminist Genealogies, Colonial Legacies, Democratic Futures* (Routledge, 1997), *Feminism and War: Confronting U.S. Imperialism* (Zed Press, 2008), and *The Sage Handbook on Identities* (Sage Publications, 2010).

A. Wendy Nastasi is a PhD candidate in Cultural Foundations of Education at Syracuse University. As a philosopher of education and a dialogue practitioner, Wendy's research interests include developing social justice curriculum and pedagogy centered on race and ethnicity that facilitate young people's (high school and college) active engagement with multiple communities to construct meaning and to create understanding toward knowledge justice. Wendy extends her commitment to making knowledge with and for diverse communities in her work with Imagining America's CNY PAGE program; Wendy was CNY Regional Page Director from 2010 to 2012. In addition to cofacilitating Intergroup Dialogue on Race and Ethnicity at Syracuse University, Wendy cofacilitated a course-based and after-school dialogue centered on race and ethnicity at Nottingham High School in Syracuse, New York.

Nicole Nguyen is Assistant Professor of Social Foundations of Education at the University of Illinois—Chicago. Her research examines the relationships among national security, war, and public schooling. Her first book, *A Curriculum of Fear* (University of Minnesota Press, 2016), ethnographically examines the political, material, and affective implications of a specialized Homeland

Security program in a U.S. public high school. She also collaborates with youth who contribute to urban school reform efforts. Nicole's work has appeared in *Political Geography, Geopolitics,* and *The Feminist Wire.*

Liz Philipose researches the movement of consciousness and global social transformation through fields such as law, human rights, militarism, feminism, spiritual principle, and critical race theory. She develops frameworks of knowledge and embodied practices that clarify the nature of power, the human condition, and the experience of suffering and, thus, inform the creation of systems of equitable distribution, caring economies, and peace. She has taught in political science, human rights, international, and women's studies programs in Canada and the United States. She earned her PhD from York University. She has presented her work in the United States, Canada, Korea, Mexico, Switzerland, South Africa, Ireland, England, Hungary, and Spain. Her articles have appeared in leading journals, including *Hypatia, Signs, International Feminist Journal of Politics,* and *Works and Days,* and in edited collections on feminism, war, and global ethics.

Anya Stanger teaches Sociology at Sierra College in Rocklin, California, and is an affiliate of the Gender, Sexuality, and Women's Studies Department at UC Davis. Her research explores contemporary U.S. nonviolent activism for peace and justice within the context of ongoing legacies of inequality and specifically investigates issues around privilege and solidarity. She holds a PhD in Social Science from Syracuse University.

Shreerekha Subramanian is Associate Professor of Humanities and Chair of Department of Liberal Arts at the University of Houston—Clear Lake. Her teaching ranges across disciplines in the humanities from literature and Women's Studies to Cross-Cultural Studies. She is the first recipient of the Marilyn Mieszkuc Professorship in Women's Studies (2008) at the University of Houston—Clear Lake, and she published her monograph, *Women Writing Violence: The Novel and Radical Feminist Imaginaries* (SAGE 2013). She publishes articles on South Asian, African American, and Caribbean literature and media, and she edited the anthology *Home and the World: South Asia in Transition* (Cambridge Scholars Press, 2006). At present, she is working toward her next monograph on carceral imaginaries addressed through the contexts of late capitalism and new imperialism.

Index

ableism, 12, 19, 156–157
Abu-Lughod, Lila, 43, 46
academic-feminist, 66
academy: construction of global feminism in, 72; dissident friendships and, 12–14; oppression in, 16–17, 72; racism and sexism in, 16; transnational feminist friendships outside, 27–31; Transnational Feminist Theory and Practice graduate seminar (Syracuse University), 4, 12, 14–27, 30–31, 32–38; "women elsewhere" and, 76. *See also* education of women
access to sovereignty (Gopal), 148–149
accountability: in epistemic friendship, 17, 18, 26, 38, 39; in transnational feminist praxis, 43, 45, 59
acid attacks, 99, 105
activism: action projects, 37–38; in Albania, 7, 229–230, 233; development of graduate course module, 4, 12, 14–27, 30–31, 32–38; epistemic friendships and, 30, 31–32; feminist-activists, 13, 77; in feminist ethnography in Kuala Lumpur, Malaysia, 48–50; in feminist ethnography in Lahaul valley, India, 62–63; integrating feminist theory with, 27–28; in Naxalite movement in India, 125–127; peace activists, 6–7, 30, 203–218; political, 179; of women in Bangladesh, 98–110
Adams, Maurianne, 15
Addams, Jane, 208, 213, 215, 216
Adnan, Khader, 34
Adnan, Shapan, 94, 99–100
AEY, Inc., 224–225
affect: in employer-servant bond, 122, 147, 160–163, 165–180, 185–188, 196–197; in feminist ethnography, 44; film as veritable festival of affects (Heath), 145–146; in friendship, 3, 4–5, 145, 151–158, 190; reciprocity of, 156; and texture, 146, 148
Affective Communities (Gandhi), 122, 160
affective contact, 150
affective cosmopolitanism (Gandhi), 192–193
Afghanistan war, 224
African American feminism, 81
agency, 6; in becoming transnational feminists, 22; ethical agents, 122, 137; exercising, 176, 195–196; in feminist ethnography, 43, 58; indirect, 169, 171;

agency (*continued*): journey of, 189, 190; limits of, 179; as malignant, 178; in Naxalite movement in India, 127–137; oppositional, 135–136; role of oppression in undermining, 123; self-propelled agents, 144–145, 150; women's, 171, 179
Age of the World Target, The (Chow), 228
Ahmed, Hana Shams, 97–98
Ahmed, Leila, 48
Ahmed, Rahnuma, 112n25
Ahmed, Sara, 156
Ahuja, Shiney, 118
AIPP (Asia Indigenous Peoples Pact), 97
Akhter, N., 96
Albania, 221–240; activism in, 7, 229–230, 233; arms decommissioning explosion, 224–225; communism in, 221–223, 234, 235–236; prison camps, 235–236, 237
Alcoff, Linda M., 28
Alexander, M. Jacqui, 2–3, 4, 7, 11–14, 31, 43
Allen, Amy, 73, 74
alliance building, 44, 52
alliances, 3–4, 123–124; across differences, 163–164; in Bangladesh, 101–102; cross-cultural, 2–3, 13, 162–163, 164, 185; discrete categories and, 76; dissident feminist, 7, 135; in employer-servant bond, 122, 147, 160–163, 165–180, 185–188, 196–197; in feminist ethnography, 43–48; in gender-based oppression, 168; politics of, 66n1, 73; transnational feminist, 185; violent, 153
Alonso, Harriet Hyman, 207
Amy, Lori E., 7, 223–225, 227–238, 228, 230
Andrews, Charles Freer, 118–119, 192–193
anticapitalist, 39, 77, 199, 215–216
anticolonialist, 162, 192–193
anti-imperial, 39, 118–119, 135, 160, 199
antiracism, 5, 23, 39, 76, 77, 189
anti-Semitism, 189
Anzaldúa, Gloria, 52, 185
Appadurai, Arjun, 33
Aristotle, 233–234
armed resistance: in Bangladesh, 5, 93–94, 99–103, 105, 109; Naxalite movement in India, 124–127; war on terror, 1, 223–225, 227

arms trafficking, 224–225
Asian feminism, 81, 194
attachment: in friendship, 2–3; in research partnerships, 7
Augspurg, Anita, 207, 212–213, 216
Australia, 198
Austria-Hungary, 204, 208, 212, 214
Austrian Peace Society, 205

Bachchan, Amitabh, 151
Baer, Gertrude, 214
Baer, Lars-Anders, 93
Baier, Annette, 129
Bajpai, Manoj, 151
Balch, Emily Greene, 212, 216
Balkans. *See* Albania
Banerjee, Sumanta, 125
Bangladesh, 5, 91–110; creation of state, 91, 93; development in, 94–96, 98–99, 102–105, 108; Jumma and Bengali women's movement, 98–110
Bangladesh Mahila Parishad (BMP), 98, 107–108
Barlow, Tani R., 85
Barthes, Roland, 146
Bartky, Sandra L., 74, 89n1
Basarudin, Azza, 4–5, 43–68, 45, 46–47, 48–50, 52–59, 66
Bawarchi (film), 147
Behar, Ruth, 46
"believing women," 1–2
Bell, Lee A., 15
belonging, 2, 3, 147, 149, 192, 198–199
Berardi, Franco, 143
Bhatia, Bela, 128
Bhattacharya, Himika, 4–5, 43–68, 45, 47–48, 50–52, 59–65, 66
binaries: colonized/colonizer, 124, 160–161, 169, 183; fiction/non-fiction, 182; Global North/Global South, 5, 39, 46, 87, 182, 184, 187, 191; "good" and "evil," 237; insider/outsider, 45–48, 53, 133, 145, 198; One-Third World/Two-Thirds World, 77; oppressed/oppressor, 3–4, 6, 76–77, 124, 131, 135, 161–162, 164, 168; Sameness/Otherness, 206; self-Other, 6, 45–48, 53, 122–123, 163; West/non-West, 163
BIWN (Bangladesh Indigenous Women Network), 107–108

Blackmore, Jill, 13
Blackwell, Joyce, 207
BLAST (Bangladesh Legal Aid Services and Trust), 97
Bloem, M. W., 96
Bollywood, 118, 138n3, 145, 146, 148, 149, 152. *See also* Indian cinema
bonding, 143; affective, 157; in employer-servant relationship, 122, 147, 160–163, 165–180, 185–188, 196–197; in friendship, 3, 145, 162–163, 164; in friendship through difference, 151–158, 166–170; social, 157
border-crossing, 3, 12, 28, 144, 151; cross-border solidarity, 6–7, 12; Jumma and Bengali women's movement, 98–110; by peace activists, 203–218
Borderlands (Anzaldúa), 185
Bose, Rahul, 152
bourgeois hegemony (Williams), 187–188
Bunch, Charlotte, 74, 75
Bush, George W., 224, 237
Butler, Judith, 18

Campaign for World Government, 209
capital, 185–186; cultural, 17, 225; in free market, 190; in globalization process, 144–145; neoliberal, 150; social, 176, 225–226
capitalism, 12, 19, 21, 138n4; communism *versus,* 221; effects on women, 77–78, 86; exploitation in, 168; masquerading as democracy, 227; neoliberal, 28; struggle against, 77–78; transnational, 83
Carillo Rowe, Aimee, 43–45
caring: competing ideologies of, 169; ethic of care, 161, 169; in friendship, 2–3; transnational analytic of, 4
Case, Kim A., 15
caste, 152–158; in Indian cinema, 5–6, 152–155; in Lahaul valley, India, 51–52, 60, 63, 64
CEDAW (Convention on the Elimination of all forms of Discrimination against Women), 95, 96, 99
Chadha, Kalyani, 119
Chakma, Bartika, 111n15
Chakma, Bhumitra, 99–100
Chakma, Bidhan, 111n12

Chakma, Bithika, 104
Chakma, Dhiraj, 111n12
Chakma, Kabita, 5, 91–116, 111n11, 111n14
Chakma, Kalpana, 101–102, 106, 109–110
Chakma, Kanak Chanpa, 112n24
Chakma, Mangal Kumar, 111n9
Chakma, Nairanjana, 111–112n16
Chakma, Samari, 101
Chakma, Sugata, 92
Chakma, Sujata, 108
Chakma, Tandra, 108–109
Chakraborty, Eshani, 100
Chanan, Michael, 198
Chatman, Seymour, 146
Chelser, Mark, 15
Chen, Yan, 88
Cheney, Jean, 179
China: Albania and, 223; Chinese Revolution (1949), 125, 126; World Conference on Women, Beijing (1995), 88, 95, 99, 102, 104, 105, 107
Chinese women, 80, 83–88; education of, 87–88; foot binding, 84; global collaboration of women, 86–87; marginalization of, 84–85; one-child policy, 85–86
Ching, Ma Mya, 104
Chittagong Hill Tracts (CHT), 91–110; CHT Accord (1997), 93, 100, 102, 106, 107–110; education of women, 97, 100, 104, 109; food insecurity, 96–97, 109; health outcomes, 96–97, 109; history of, 92–94; militarization, 5, 93–94, 99–103, 105; political alliances, 101–102; violence against women, 97–98, 99, 100–101, 104–109
Chittagong Hill Tracts Hill Women's Federation (HWF, Bangladesh), 101–102, 104–106, 111n10
Chivers, C. J., 224
choice, 166–168, 176–178
Chopra, Yash, 146
Chow, Esther Ngan-ling, 88
Chow, Rey, 228
Chowdhury, Elora Halim, 1–7, 6, 43, 72, 74, 76–78, 83, 95, 102–103, 105, 118, 122–124, 160–181, 182
Chowdhury, Najma, 102
Chowpatty, 173
Chronicle of Higher Education, 20, 87–88

citizen/state relation, 209, 225
civic friendship, 233, 234
class: class-based networks in Bangladesh, 95, 107–110; in employer-servant relationship, 122, 147, 160–163, 165–180, 185–188, 196–197; impact of middle-class femininity, 6; in Indian cinema, 5–6, 125–136; in Kuala Lumpur, Malaysia, 49–50, 58; in Lahaul valley, India, 64; in Naxalite movement in India, 125–136; in peace movement, 206–207; solidarity across classes, 122, 160, 161, 165–180, 185–188, 196–197
class consciousness, 125, 197
class oppression, 132–133
Clavin, Patricia, 206
coalitional communicative gestures (Lugones), 183
coalitional limen (Gandhi), 185
coalitionary politics, 13–14, 73, 82, 87, 107–110, 129
cobelonging, 192, 198–199
Cohen, Laurie R., 6–7, 203–220, 204, 209
Colby, Ruth Gage, 217–218
Cold War, 7, 224–225, 227, 230
Cole, Elizabeth R., 32
collaboration: in coalitionary politics, 13–14; in feminist ethnography, 43–48; in Transnational Feminist Theory and Practice graduate seminar (Syracuse University), 4, 12, 14–27, 32–38; unity based on principles of, 80
collective consciousness, 73, 87, 136
collective memories (Gabriel), 147
Collins, Dana, 48
colonial encounter, 160, 162, 163
colonialism, 109, 162, 169, 185, 189
colonial modern gender system, 167, 177
colonial system: Israeli Occupation of Palestine, 4, 12, 15, 18, 27–28, 30–31, 32–38; postcolonial India, 6, 118, 144, 145, 151, 162, 184–185, 189, 191; in South Asia, 154, 156
colonization: of Bengal by British, 92–93; of Chittagong Hill Tracts by Bengalis, 99–110; in South Asia's history, 154, 156. *See also* colonial system
colonized, 124, 160–162, 169, 183

colonizer, 124, 160–161, 169, 183
commonality: relationship between diversity and, 75; of women's oppression, 77
common oppression, 5, 77, 132–133
communism: in Albania, 221–223, 234, 235–236; in India, 124–125
community, 189–190
compassion: in cross-class solidarity, 167–168; in friendship, 3; humanity based on, 163
complicity, 16, 129, 172, 229, 230, 236
connectivity: flexible, 144; in friendship, 2–3, 27, 144, 161; human, 144
consensual elements, 6, 171, 176
consent: and agency of women, 122, 160, 162, 165, 170, 176–177; to forced marriage, 60–62; and resistance, 170–171, 177
"Consent, Agency, and Rhetoric of Incitement" (Sangari), 122, 160, 165, 170, 176–177
contractual relationships, 167–168, 170–171, 175–178
contrapuntal perspective, 123, 161–162, 167–168
cooptation, 164
Cost of Living, The (Roy), 184
Council for Advancement of People's Action and Rural Technology (CAPART, India), 59
cronyism, 234
crossover cinema, 119–120. *See also* Indian cinema
cultural capital, 17, 225
cultural differences, 71–72, 81–82, 84, 89
Culture and Imperialism (Said), 162
Curtin, Nicola, 13, 21
Cytryon-Walker Adena, 15

Dai, Yuanfang, 5, 71–90
Das, Nandita, 6, 117–118, 120–124
Das, Veena, 185
Dastidar, Ranajit, 94, 99–100
De, Esha Niyogi, 6, 143–159, 145, 154
Dead Can Dance, 184
Dean, Jodi, 74
Deb, Basuli, 46

decolonial, 17, 162, 245
decolonial friendship, 162
decolonial praxis, 17
decolonization, 77–78, 125, 130
decolonizing knowledge, 4
decolonizing pedagogies, 13, 20
De Lauretis, Teresa, 146
Deleuze, Gilles, 143
deliberative democracy, 231–232
democracy, 72, 77, 223, 227, 228, 231–233
democratic sociality, 234–235, 237–238
demographic engineering (Adnan), 94
development: in Albania, 227–228; in Bangladesh, 94–96, 98–99, 102–105, 108
Devere, Heather, 233
Devi, Mahasweta, 125
Dholakia, Rahul, 119–120
diaspora, 64, 183, 188–190, 194
dictatorship, 207, 221–224, 229, 230, 232, 234, 237
difference: cultural, 71–72, 81–82, 84, 89; friendships through, 146–158, 166–170; politics of, 45, 80; relationships of women across, 71–75, 78–89, 161–168, 171, 173, 178–179
difference critique, 73–74, 82–84
disciplinary frameworks, 24–25
dissidence: classrooms as sites of, 13, 18, 23; in friendship, 229–231, 234–236 (*see also* dissident friendship); through solidarity, 121–124
dissident friendship: cross-cultural, 2–3, 13, 162–163, 164, 185; erasure of culture of, 125–126; examples in Indian cinema, 121–124; friendship through difference, 151–158; "hijab day," 1–2; as metaphor, 6; nature of, 3–4; transnational feminism and, 12–14, 122, 195–197
dissident transnational sisterhoods, 183
Diveroli, Efraim, 224–225
Diversi, Marcelo, 48, 63
diversity: feminist appreciation of, 75; relationship between commonality and, 75
divide: academy/community, 29; between women of color feminism and third world/transnational feminism, 71, 73–74, 82–83, 88–89
Dolma, Pema, 47

domestication, 169
domestic work market, 87
domination: class, 162–163, 164, 167; colonial, 109, 169; patriarchal, 101–102, 171
Dominguez, Virginia R., 48
Doty, Madeleine Zabriskie, 206, 211–216, 217
dowry practices, 99, 105
Dutta, Divya, 147
Dutta, Rajatabha, 156
duty, love and, 174–175
Duyker, Edward, 126

Early, Frances H., 207
education, epistemic friendship in urban school reform, 29–30
education of women: in China, 87–88; Chittagong Hill Tracts (CHT) of Bangladesh, 97, 100, 104, 109; family violence and, 225, 226, 236–237, 238n1; in India, 125–126, 171–172; Transnational Feminist Theory and Practice graduate seminar (Syracuse University), 4, 12, 14–27, 32–38. *See also* academy
emotions: in feminist ethnography, 43–44; in friendship, 2–3, 4–5, 52–53
empathy: in cross-class solidarity, 167–168; in friendship, 3, 127; humanity based on, 163; in research partnerships, 7
empire, 2–3, 77, 145, 146, 156
employment: of Chinese women, 85–87; employer-servant bond, 122, 147, 160–163, 165–180, 185–188, 196–197; gender inequities in Bangladesh, 98–99
epistemic friendship, 11–40; accountability in, 17, 18, 26, 38, 39; activism and, 30, 31–32; connecting through, 27; defined, 4, 11; importance of, 11–12; for Latina mothers and food access, 29; limitations of, 20–21; making meaning as a collective, 16–18; in peace activism, 6–7, 30, 203–218; possibilities of, 18–20; risk taking in, 24; in Transnational Feminist Theory and Practice graduate seminar (Syracuse University), 4, 12, 14–27, 32–38; in urban school reform, 29–30; value of, 25

epistemic privilege, 128–129, 133–135
epistemology, 4–5, 13–14, 18–19, 24–25, 28, 29
Eskildsen, Tom, 107
ethic of care, 161, 169
ethnographers, 4–5, 7, 43–67
ethnographic research. *See* feminist ethnography
ethos of friendship, 26
Evdin Ltd., 224
Eyal, Gil, 230

family systems, 236–237
family violence, 123, 225, 226, 236–237, 238n1
Felman, Shoshana, 52, 187, 196
feminism: Asian, 81, 194; as collective movement, 80; difference critique, 73–74, 82–84; hegemonic, 72, 76, 78; importance of solidarity in, 73–74, 75; Lesbian, 81; as philosophy (Mohanty), 134; postcolonial, 185, 189; postmodern, 73, 143–144; relationship with nationalism, 5; second wave, 74, 83, 194; third wave, 83; third world, 5, 71, 76, 77–78, 83, 84, 165, 194; transnational (*see* transnational feminism); Western, 72, 77–78, 83, 84–85; White, 72, 76–78, 194; without borders, 198–199; women of color, 71, 76, 77–78, 82, 83, 194
Feminism and Community (Weiss and Friedman), 179
feminist ethnography: agency in, 43, 58; friendship in, 4–5, 7, 43–67; in Kuala Lumpur, Malaysia, 45, 46–47, 48–50, 52–59; in Lahaul valley, India, 45, 47–48, 50–52, 59–65, 66; methodology, 43–48; positionality of ethnographers, 45–48, 53, 197; privilege in, 44, 46, 51–52, 60, 63, 64
feminist methodology, 43–48
Ferguson, Ann, 130, 134
Ferrer, Wilfredo A., 225
feudal power, 125, 137, 162–163, 172, 179
15 Park Avenue (film), 155
Final Solution (film), 119–120
Firaaq (film), 117–118, 119, 120–124, 133, 137
food justice, 29, 96–97, 109

foot binding, 84
Ford, Henry, 209, 210
Foster, Carrie A., 207
Freedom House, 234
Fregoso, Rosa Linda, 52
Freire, Paulo, 23
Freud, Sigmund, 187, 196
Fried, Alfred Hermann, 204
Friedman, Marilyn, 179, 180
friendship: affect in, 3, 4–5, 145, 151–158, 190; bonding in, 3, 145, 162–163, 164; as challenge to patriarchy, 144; characteristics of, 52–53; between Chinese and American women, 87–88; civic, 233, 234; defined, 204–205; emotions in, 2–3, 4–5, 52–53; in feminist ethnography, 4–5, 7, 43–67; "hijab day," 1–2; impact on women's solidarity, 80; importance to solidarity efforts, 1–2, 237; intimacy in, 2–3, 44, 46, 56, 163, 178; kin metaphor *versus*, 143; levels of, 50; liberatory, 162; logic of plural realities in, 164; love in, 2–3, 4–5; as metaphor for solidarity, 144–145; nature of, 2–3; *philia* of Aristotle, 233–234; as political act, 44–45, 161, 233–234. *See also* dissident friendship
Frye, Marilyn, 73–74

Gabriel, Teshome, 147
Gain, Philip, 97
Galpo Holeo Satti (film), 147
Gandhi, Leela, 3, 13, 118–120, 122–124, 127, 129–131, 134–137, 160–161, 162, 164, 182, 185, 192–193, 198–199
Gandhi, M. K., 192–193
Geiger, Susan, 45, 48, 66
gender oppression, 71, 72, 75, 81–82, 84
German Peace Society, 212–214
Ghosh, Robi, 147
Ghosh, Suniti Kumar, 137
Gillis, John R., 230
Giroux, Henry A., 28
Gjermeni, Eglantina, 7, 221–223, 226, 228, 229–231
Gjipali, G., 228, 234
Global Campaign for Women's Human Rights, 75

Global Feminisms Project, 13
globalization, 3, 6; capital in, 144–145; costs of, 183; exploitation in, 77–78; intersectional, 191–195; local processes and, 4
Global North, 5, 39, 46, 87, 182, 184, 191
global sisterhood (Morgan), 5, 74–75, 82
Global South, 5, 39, 46, 87, 182, 187
global war economy, 1, 223–225, 227
Glücklich, Vilma, 214–215
González-Enríquez, Carmen, 230
Gopal, Sangita, 148, 149
Gosh, Rituparna, 155
Grabova, Taulant, 235–237
Greenhalgh, Susan, 85–86
Grewal, Inderpal, 43, 183, 185
Griffin, Pat, 15
Guattari, Felix, 143
guerrilla organizations, 93, 126
Guhathakurata, Meghna, 106
Gustafson, Melanie, 209

Halim, Sadeka, 100, 105
Hall, Stuart, 144
Hasina, Sheikh, 96
Hazaar Chaurasi Ki Ma (*HCKM*, film), 6, 117, 126–137
Hazaaron Khawishein Aisi (*HKA*, film), 6, 117–119, 126–137, 138n6
Heath, Stephen, 145
hegemonic feminism, 72, 76, 78
Heinrich Thomet, 224
Helm, Bennett, 7, 204
Hertzka, Yella, 214, 215, 217
heteropatriarchy, 12, 19, 21, 130, 146
heterosexualism, 146–147, 167
Heyes, Cressida J., 73
Heymann, Lida Gustava, 212–216, 217
hierarchy, 45, 161, 176
"hijab day," 1–2
Hill, Glen, 5, 91–116
Hill People's Council (HPC, Bangladesh), 101
Hill Student's Council (HSC, Bangladesh), 101
Hill Women's Federation (HWF), 101–102, 104–106, 111n10
Hindu caste system, 5–6, 51–52, 60, 63, 64, 152–158

Hindu nationalism, 6, 144, 154
Hindutva hegemony, 119–124
Hitler, Adolf, 216
Hofer, Maria, 214
Holbrook, Florence, 209
Holocaust, 217
home, 194–195
hooks, bell, 13, 133
Hossain, Hameeda, 99
House of Memories/Paromitar Ek Din (film), 6, 145, 152, 155–158
Hoxha, Enver, 221–224, 234, 237
HSB (Health and Science Bulletin), 96
Huang, Ping, 86–87
human connection, 144
humanity, 120, 151, 161, 163, 169, 186
human rights, 5, 75–77, 223, 228
Hussain, Begum Rokeya Sakhawat, 98
Hussein, Saddam, 155
HWF (Hill Women's Federation, Bangladesh), 101–102, 104–106, 111n10

identity: experiences of, 52; lesbian, 81, 85; multiplicity of identities, 80, 185; in Western feminism, 84
identity markers, 48
identity politics, 73, 81–82
If Today Be Sweet (Umrigar), 183, 188–190
imaginary, literary, 183, 184, 198
immigrant women, 29, 87, 209
imperialism, 3; of India, 125; neoliberal, 145; privileges of, 160; reigning order of, 185; unchecked, 183
imperialist project, 160
incitement, 160, 165, 170, 177–178
indefinite detention, 19
India, 4–5; education of women, 125–126, 171–172; feminist ethnography in Lahaul valley, 45, 47–48, 50–52, 59–65, 66; Hindutva-led anti-Muslim violence in Gujarat, 119–124; marriage by abduction, 50–51, 60–65; Naxalite movement, 6, 117–118, 124–137, 138–139n7; partition in 1947, 93, 119; patriarchy in, 50–51, 121, 123, 129, 147, 155, 156–157, 165–180, 185–188, 196–197; postcolonial, 6, 118, 144, 145, 151, 162, 184–185, 189, 191

Indian cinema, 5–6, 117–139, 143–158; *Bawarchi*, 147; *15 Park Avenue*, 155; *Final Solution*, 119–120; *Firaaq*, 117–118, 119, 120–124, 133, 137; *Galpo Holeo Satti*, 147; *Hazaar Chaurasi Ki Ma (HCKM)*, 6, 117, 126–137; *Hazaaron Khawshiein Aisi (HKA)*, 6, 117–119, 126–137, 138n6; *House of Memories/Paromitar Ek Din*, 6, 145, 152, 155–158; *Mr. and Mrs. Iyer*, 6, 145, 152–155; *Parzania: Heaven and Hell on Earth*, 119–120; *Veer Zaara*, 6, 145, 146–152, 155, 158; *We*, 182–185
indirect agency, 169, 171
insider/outsider: oppression and, 133; positionality of ethnographer, 45–48, 53, 197; women's feelings for outsider, 145
institutionalized gender violence, 100–101, 104–105, 107
International Council of the Indigenous Peoples of CHT (ICIP-CHT), 100
International Council of Women, 206–207
internationalism, 207
International Monetary Fund (IMF), 95, 184, 228
International Women's Suffrage Association, 206–207
International Work Group for Indigenous Affairs (IWGIA), 93, 107
International Year of Women (1975), 95, 99
intersectionality theory, 76, 185, 191–195
intimacy, in friendship, 2–3, 44, 46, 56, 163, 178
Iraq war, 224
Islamaphobia, 1–2, 6, 117, 119–124, 152–155
Israeli Occupation of Palestine, 4, 12, 15, 18, 27–28, 30–31, 32–38
ivory tower, 20
IWGIA (International Work Group for Indigenous Affairs), 93, 107

James, Ada, 208–209
Jeffrey, Patricia, 137
Jha, Prakash, 138n3
Johnson-Reagon, Bernice, 32
Joseph, Suad, 58
Jum cultivation, 92
Jumma and Bengali women's movement, 98–110; activism after CHT Accord (1997), 107–109; differences in early movements, 102–103; future of, 109–110; pre-CHT Accord (1997), 98–102, 104–106
Jumma people, 92–94, 97–100
Jus Suffragii (journal), 208
justice. *See* social justice

Kajsiu, Blendi, 230
Kaplan, Caren, 12–13, 28, 43, 183, 185, 198
Kaplan, E. Ann, 154
Karim, Lamia, 95, 102–103
Kavoori, Anandam P., 119
Kellogg, Paul, 208
Khan, Ferdous Kaiser, 106
Khan, Shah Rukh, 146–147
Khanna, Rajesh, 147
Khanna, Ranjana, 183, 197
Khayyam, Omar, 188
Kher, Kiron, 148
Klapper, Melissa R., 207
Koopman, Sara, 30
Korten, Tristram, 224
Krasniqi, Afrim, 228, 232–233
Kristeva, Julia, 184, 195–196
Kuala Lumpur, Malaysia, 45, 46–47, 48–50, 52–59
Kurian, Alka, 5–6, 117–140

LaCapra, Dominick, 152
Lahaul valley, India, feminist ethnography in, 45, 47–48, 50–52, 59–65, 66
Lal, Jayati, 46
language, importance of, 22–23
Lawrence, Charles R., 184
Lawrence, Pethick, 213
Lay Down Your Arms! (Suttner), 204
League of Nations, 210
lesbian feminism, 81
lesbian identity, 81, 85
Levene, Mark, 99
Li, Xiaojiang, 87
liberatory friendship, 162
liberatory trajectory, 79
Liddington, Jill, 207
Light, Alison, 195
Likmeta, Besar, 224, 225
limen, 184–185
Listening to Grasshoppers (Roy), 184

Lloyd, Lola Maverick, 206, 209–211, 217
love: as counterpoint to hostility and ridicule, 205; cross-cultural, 79, 152–155; cross-racial, 79; defined, 44; duty and, 174–175; in feminist ethnography, 44; in friendship, 2–3, 4–5; in intellectual life, 48; in politics, 48; revolutionary, 134
lower class. *See* class
loyalty, 53, 121, 168, 174, 179–180, 185
Lugones, Maria C., 5, 6, 12–13, 72, 74, 78–80, 83, 143, 150, 164, 167, 183, 185, 198
Luna, Zakiya T., 32

Madden, Meredith, 11–42, 22, 38, 40
Madison, Soyini D., 43
Mahadevan, Ananth, 138n3
Malaysia, feminist ethnography in Kuala Lumpur, 45, 46–47, 48–50, 52–59
male supremacy, 74
Manges, Johanna, 204
Manning, Erin, 148–149
Mansbridge, Jane, 163
Marks, Laura, 148, 156
Markus, David Oscar, 224–225
marriage by abduction, 50–51, 60–65
Martin, Biddy, 189
McAdams, Dan P., 52
McCall, Leslie, 28
McFadden, Margaret H., 211
McGuire, Kristin, 13, 21
Mejia, Angie, 11–42, 29, 38, 40
Melia, 53–59
mentorship, 21–22, 54
Mernissi, Fatima, 15
Merrill, Ralph, 224–225
microcredit arrangements, 95, 99
middle class. *See* class
militarization: arms trafficking in Albania, 224–225; in Bangladesh, 5, 93–94, 99–103, 105, 109; Chittagong Hill Tracts (CHT) of Bangladesh, 5, 93–94, 99–103, 105; Naxalite movement in India, 124–127
Millennium Development Goals (2011), 96
minority: in Bangladesh, 96; in India, 117–119, 152; majority-minority communities, 123; in Malaysia, 48; Muslim, 119, 120, 152; in the U.S., 76; women as, 77
Mishra, Sudhir, 6, 117, 126, 127–128
Mitchell, Juliet, 187
modern China, 85, 88
modern gender system, 167, 177
modern imperialism, 185
modern oppressive states, 120
modern technologies, 207
Mohanty, Chandra Talpade, 4, 12, 13–18, 21–22, 27–28, 31, 38–40, 43, 74, 77–78, 83, 84, 130, 134, 189, 194–195, 198
Mohsin, Amena, 99–100
Moi, Toril, 197
Moraga, Cherrie, 52, 124, 165
Morales, Yoland, 29
Moreira, Claudio, 48, 63
Morgan, Robin, 74–75
Morrison, Toni, 39
Moya, Paula, 34
Mr. and Mrs. Iyer (film), 6, 145, 152–155
multiculturalism, 3, 73, 84
Muslim women: Bengali women's movement, 98–102; "hijab day," 1–2; Islamaphobia, 1–2, 6, 117, 119–124, 152–155; in Kuala Lumpur, Malaysia, 45, 46–47, 48–50, 52–59

Naficy, Hamid, 144
Nagar, Richa, 43, 45, 46, 48, 59, 66, 66n1
Nagda, Biren A., 15
Nandy, Ashis, 183
Naples, Nancy, 28
Narayan, Kirin, 46
Narayan, Uma, 84, 118, 128–130, 131, 133, 161, 163–164, 186, 206
Nasreen, Zobaida, 110
Nastasi, A. Wendy, 11–42, 16, 22–23, 38, 40
nationalism: Austrian-Hungarian, 204; Bengali, 5, 91–92; Hindu, 6, 144, 154; Pakistani, 146–147; relationship with feminism, 5
National Organization for Women, 232
National Socialism (Nazism), 207, 214
native: colonial subjects, 161, 183, 191; as description of ethnographer, 45–47; as term, 33
Naxalite movement, 6, 117–118, 124–137, 138–139n7

neocolonialism, 125, 183
neoliberal intellectual system, 18, 28
neoliberal shock therapy, 228, 229
neoliberal transnationalism, 3, 144–151
Nepstad, Sharon E., 30
Newman, A. Evelyn, 213
new woman (Barlow), 85
"New Women," 206
Nguyen, Nicole, 4, 11–42, 16, 38, 40
Nihalani, Govind, 6, 117, 126, 127
Nine Inch Nails, 184
Nobel Peace Prize, 204
nongovernmental organizations (NGOs): in Albania, 228; in Bangladesh, 95, 99, 100, 102–103, 104, 105, 106, 108–109; in China, 88, 95, 99, 102, 104, 105, 107; in Kuala Lumpur, Malaysia, 48–49; women as staff members, 99, 102–103

Oedipal drive, 146, 149–152
Oesch, Corinna, 214
Okazawa-Rey, Margo, 15, 18, 28
Oliver, Kelly, 195–196
one-child policy, 85–86
One-Third World, 77
oppositional agency, 135–136
oppressed, 3–4, 6, 76–77, 124, 131, 135, 161–162, 164, 168
oppression: in the academy, 16–17, 72; alliances of, 6; in Bangladesh, 105; categories of, 185; causal/structural analysis of, 133; common, 5, 77, 132–133; gender, 71, 72, 75, 81–82, 84; identity politics and, 81–82; in India, 50, 123; insider/outsider, 133; interlocking systems of, 129; intermeshedness of, 79–80; patterns of, 72; resisting, 79; role in undermining personal agency, 123; understanding, 164
oppressor, 3–4, 6, 124, 131, 135, 161–162, 164, 168
Other: empathy and, 163; friendship as vital relationship with, 143; in Indian cinema, 119–120; Jumma indigenous women as, 100; ontology of, 197; politics based on understanding of, 124; recognizing, 199; Sameness/Otherness, 206; self-Other, 6, 45–48, 53, 122–123, 163; subjective, 184–185

pacifism, 205–218
Packouz, David, 224–225
Pakistan: creation in 1947, 93, 119; nationalism, 146–147
Palestine, 4, 12, 15, 18, 27–28, 30–31, 32–38
Panagides, D., 96
Parbartya Chattagram Mahila Samity (Chittagong Hill Tracts Women's Association), 100
Parbattya Chattagram Jana Sanghati Samity (PCIJSS or JSS), 93, 100, 102
Paromitar Ek Din (film), 6, 145, 152, 155–158
Parsi, 120, 161, 166, 170, 183, 184, 186, 188
partisan politics, 91, 222, 227, 232–235
partnership, 31, 110
Parzania: Heaven and Hell on Earth (film), 119–120
paternalism, 161, 168–169
patriarchy: in Albania, 230, 232; in Bangladesh, 5, 99, 101–102; contractual relationships, 176; evolving structure of, 162–163; failure of, 122, 160, 161, 165–180, 185–188, 196–197; female maintenance of, 6, 170–171; friendship as challenge to, 144; heteropatriarchy, 12, 19, 21, 130, 146; "hijab day," 1–2; in India, 50–51, 121, 123, 129, 147, 155, 156–157, 165–180, 185–188, 196–197; observations concerning, 170–171; social structure based on, 196; as universal, 74
patronage, 167, 197
Paul, Alice, 209–210
Pax International (journal), 206, 212, 215–216
peace activists, 6–7, 30, 203–218
peasants. *See* class
pedagogy project, Transnational Feminist Theory and Practice graduate seminar (Syracuse University), 4, 12, 14–27, 32–38
Pee Sde, Ibrahim QIU, 96
peripheral, 138, 162
Permanent Forum on Indigenous Issues (UNPFII), 93
Pethick-Lawrence, Emmeline, 212
Pettman, Jan Jindy, 169
phallogocentric logic, 193–194, 197

philia, 233–234
Philipose, Liz, 1–7, 182
Photovoice, 29
Plowshares, 30
Podrizki, Alexander, 224–225
political persecution, 234
political resistance, 234–235
political structures, 3
political transformation, 124, 160, 163, 179, 234–235
politicization, 130, 134–135
politicized consciousness, 130–131, 134–135
politics: in Albania, 227, 232–233; of alliances, 66n1, 73; based on understanding of Other, 124; coalitionary, 13–14, 73, 82, 87, 107–110, 129; friendships as political acts, 44–45, 161, 233–234; identity, 73, 81–82; love in, 48; partisan, 91, 222, 227, 232–235; political friendship, 233–234; of solidarity, 5, 118; of women in Bangladesh, 98, 99, 100, 102–103, 104
politics of difference, 45, 80
politics of knowledge, 18–19
Politics of the Possible (Sangari), 161–162
Ponzanesi, Sandra, 145
positionality, 45–48, 53, 197
postcolonial feminism, 185, 189
postmodern feminism, 73, 143–144
Pötting, Hedwig von, 203–205, 209
poverty, 85, 87, 96–97, 109, 165, 175, 223, 234
Povinelli, Elizabeth A., 198, 199n3
power: colonizer/native subject, 183; consolidation in Bangladesh, 95, 102–103; dismantling power performances, 26; in feminist ethnography, 44, 45, 46, 49–50; feudal, 125, 137, 162–163, 172, 179; friendship and, 2–3; hierarchies of, 45, 130; in Kuala Lumpur, Malaysia, 58; resistance to (*see* resistance); understanding, 164
powerlessness, 182
Pratt, Minnie Bruce, 189
praxis: of feminist knowledge production, 4–5; transformative educational, 19. *See also* transnational feminist praxis

privatization, 184, 228
privilege: decentering different forms of, 26; epistemic, 128–129, 133–135; in feminist ethnography, 44, 46, 51–52, 60, 63, 64; of imperialism, 160
psychoanalysis, 146, 149–152, 187, 196
public sphere, 227

Qayum, Seemin, 162–163
Quakers, 208, 214
Quiroz, Olivia, 29

racism: in the academy, 16; sexism compared with, 161
radical vulnerability (Nagar), 59
Rahman, Sheikh Mujibur, 93
rape, 98, 99, 100–101, 104, 108
Ray, Raka, 162–163
Ray, Satyajit, 126, 138n3
Rege, S., 52
reproductive rights, 85–86
research dilemma, 46, 66
resistance: Chittagong Hill Tracts (CHT), Bangladesh, 91–110; consent and, 170–171, 177; Israeli Occupation of Palestine, 4, 12, 15, 18, 27–28, 30–31, 32–38; to male domination, 82, 236–237; Naxalite movement, 6, 117–118; nodes across patriarchal ossifications (Lugones), 185
revolutionary love, 134
Rich, Adrienne, 124, 163, 198
rights: of the colonized, 161–162, 169; consent and, 60–61, 170–171, 176–177; human, 5, 75–77, 223, 228; reproductive, 85–86; voting, 206–207, 208–209. *See also* women's rights
Rojas, Maythee, 183
Rosezelle, Pat Alake, 143, 150
Rowe, Aimee Carillo, 43–45
Roy, Arundhati, 133, 182–185, 198
Rozario, Shanti, 95
Rupp, Leila, 207, 212

Saadawi, Nawal, 230, 236
Said, Edward, 145, 162, 198
Sandoval, Chela, 48, 66
Sang, Tze-Ian D., 85

Sangari, Kumkum, 122, 160, 161–162, 165, 170, 176–177
Sanmilita Nari Samaj, 106
Sawant, Kshama, 126, 138n4
Scheu-Riesz, Helene, 214
Schott, Linda K., 207
Schwarzenbach, Sibyl A., 233–234
Schwimmer, Rosika, 206, 208–211, 212, 217
second wave feminism, 74, 83, 194
Sedgwick, Eve Kosofsky, 146, 153
Sehgal, Zohra, 147
self, 236–237
self-actualization, 164
self-determination: in Bangladesh, 101–102, 109; solidarity and, 118
self-Other, 6; political agency as "ethical agent," 122–123; positionality as "native" ethnographer, 45–48, 53; self- and-Other-perception, 163
self-propelled agents, 144–145, 150
self-reflexivity, 4, 7, 45, 124, 164, 198, 205
Sen, Aparna, 6, 145, 152, 153, 155–156
Sen, Mrinal, 126, 138n3
sensorium: familial, 149; Hindu, 154; human, 145; normative, 147, 149
sexism: in the academy, 16; racism compared with, 161
sexual violence, 98–101, 104, 108, 136–137, 196, 236
Shalabi, Hanaa, 34
Shanti Bahini (peace force), 93–94
Sharma, Konkona Sen, 152
Sharma, Rakesh, 119–120
Sheehan, Cindy, 191
Sheepshanks, Mary, 216
Sinha Roy, Mallarika, 126, 137, 138–139n7
Sippy, Mabel, 209
sisterhood: dissident transnational, 183; global, 5, 74–75, 82; solidarity with, 194; as term, 12–13
Sisterhood Is Global (Morgan), 74–75
Sisters in Islam (SIS), 48
Smith, Dorothy, 130
Smith, Graham M., 233
social capital, 176, 225–226
socialists, 209, 211, 217, 227, 232
social justice: activism committed to, 22; in Albania, 225; in Bangladesh, 95–99, 108; creating and increasing, 23, 28, 31–32; in employer-servant relationship, 167, 176–178, 183; epistemic, 14, 18, 30; food insecurity, 29, 96–97, 109, 213, 223; in India, 125; for Muslim women, 48, 49, 59; peace activism and, 206, 213; political work aimed at, 31–32; in transnational feminism, 197–198; vision of, 11, 230–231
social transformation, 95, 128, 130, 179, 237–238
Soja, Edward, 15
solidarity: across classes, 122, 160, 161, 165–180, 185–188, 196–197; among peace activists, 6–7, 30, 203–218; among women in India, 50, 125–127; approaches to, 74–78; in coalitionary politics, 13–14; cross-border, 6–7, 12; defined, 122; dissidence through, 121–124; feminist transcultural, 77–78; friendship as metaphor for, 144–145; "hijab day," 1–2; impact of friendship on, 80; importance in feminism, 73–74, 75; importance of friendship in, 1–2, 237; in Indian cinema, 5–6; nature of, 72; perspectives on, 71; politics of, 5, 118; in transnational feminist praxis, 44, 77, 83; as vehicle for transformation, 5; in Western feminism, 84. *See also* transcultural feminist solidarity
South Africa, 192–193
Space Between Us, The (Umrigar), 122, 160, 161, 165–180, 183, 184, 185–188, 196–197
Spencer, Anna Garlin, 209
Spivak, Gayatri Chakravorty, 125, 154, 189
Stacey, Judith, 46
Stallkamp, G., 96
Stan, Lavinia, 232
Stanger, Anya, 11–42, 18, 23, 38, 40
Stanley, Liz, 203, 210
Stewart, Abigail J., 13, 21
Stöcker, Helene, 211, 217–218
Stone-Mediatore, Shari, 12, 164–165
structural violence, 16, 185
struggle: in female friendship, 161, 164–165, 179; for social transformation, 179–180; toward liberation, 5–6, 12–13
struggle toward liberation, 39, 77

subaltern, 135, 136, 184, 187
Subramanian, Shreerekha, 6, 182–200
Sudbury, Julia, 15, 18, 19, 28
Suriano, Maria Grazia, 207
Suttner, Bertha von, 203–205, 208, 209, 217, 218
Swarr, Amanda Lock, 43

Teng, Jinhua Emma, 84
terrorism, 1, 184, 223–225, 227
texture, 146, 148
third wave feminism, 83
third world feminism, 5, 71, 76, 77–78, 83, 84, 165, 194
This Bridge Called My Back (Moraga et al.), 165
Thomet, Heinrich, 224
Three Guineas, The (Woolf), 225
Tobin, Amon, 184
Todorov, Tzvetan, 237–238
Torlesse, H., 96
totalitarianism, 207, 221–224, 229, 230, 232, 234, 237
trafficking of women, 75, 99
transcultural approach: in feminist political movement, 80–81; problem of difference in, 78–80
transcultural feminist solidarity, 5, 71–89; approaches to solidarity, 74–78; imagining, 81–83; "world"-traveling and, 72, 78–81, 83
transculturalism, 82
transculture, 82–83
transdisciplinary approach (Soja), 15
transformation: in education, 19, 21–27; in feminist ethnography, 43; in friendship, 3, 13–14; political, 124, 160, 163, 179, 234–235; social, 95, 128, 130, 179, 237–238
transition doctrine, 228, 230
transmigration, 91–94, 101
transnational capitalism, 83
transnational feminism, 6–7, 77, 183–185, 195–197; defining, 164–165; and dissident friendships, 12–14, 122, 195–197; friendships within, 195–197, 216–218; outside the academy, 27–31; transformative process in, 21–23

transnational feminist analysis, 122, 160, 164
transnational feminist praxis: accountability in, 43, 45, 59; friendship and alliances in, 43–48; in Kuala Lumpur, Malaysia, 45, 46–47, 48–50; in Lahaul valley, India, 45, 47–48, 50–52, 59–65; peace activists, 7, 205–218; solidarity in, 44, 77, 83; Transnational Feminist Theory and Practice graduate seminar (Syracuse University), 4, 12, 14–27, 30–31, 32–38
transnational feminist solidarity, 44, 77, 83
transnationalism, 3, 144–151, 206, 217
Two-Thirds World, 77

Umrigar, Thrity, 6, 122, 160, 161, 165–180, 183, 184, 185–198
United Nations (UN): charter conference (1945), 218; Convention on the Elimination of all forms of Discrimination against Women (CEDAW), 95, 96, 99; Decade of Women and Development, 95; International Women's Day, 104; International Year of Women (1975), 95, 99; IRIN, 96; Millennium Development Goals (2011), 96; Office of Geneva archives, 204; Permanent Forum on Indigenous Issues (UNPFII), 93; Women in Development program, 94–95; world conference on women, Beijing (1995), 88, 95, 99, 102, 104, 105, 107; world conference on women, Copenhagen (1980), 95; world conference on women, Mexico (1975), 95; world conference on women, Nairobi (1985), 95
United Nations Development Programme (UNDP), 94, 96–97
United States: Chinese women and, 83–88; food justice in, 29; global feminism in political strategy, 77; immigrants in domestic work market, 87; Israeli Occupation of Palestine, 4, 12, 15, 18, 27–28, 30–31, 32–38; as paradise, 223; peace activism, 30; urban school reform, 29–30; war on terror, 1, 223–225, 227
U.S. Attorney's Office (USAO), 224–225
U.S. Department of State (USDOS), 224
U.S. National Women's Party, 209–210

Veer Zaara (film), 6, 145, 146–152, 155, 158
"the veil," 1–2
Villard, Fanny Garrison, 210
violence against women (VAW): Chinese foot binding, 84; Chittagong Hill Tracts (CHT), Bangladesh, 97–98, 99, 100–101, 104–109; commonality of women's oppression, 75; family violence, 123, 225, 226, 236–237, 238n1; in India, 50–51, 60–65, 123, 136–137; institutionalized, 100–101, 104–105, 107; marriage by abduction, 50–51, 60–65; phallogocentric logic and, 193–194; sexual violence, 98–101, 104, 108, 136–137, 196, 236; trafficking, 75, 99
Visweswaran, Kamala, 43
voting rights, 206–207, 208–209

Die Waffen nieder! (monthly), 204
Waller, Marguerite, 145
Wang, Zheng, 88
war on terror, 1, 223–225, 227
Wars We Inherit, The (Amy), 223
We (film), 182–185
Weight of Heaven, The (Umrigar), 183, 184, 191–195, 196–198
Weiss, Penny, 179
Welland, Sasha Su-Ling, 88
Western feminism, 72, 77–78, 83, 84–85
White feminism, 72, 76–78, 194
"white man's burden," 161
white supremacism, 12, 19, 21
Williams, Raymond, 187–188
Wilmers, Annika, 213
Wilpfers, 7, 205–218. *See also* Women's International League for Peace and Freedom (WILPF)
Wilson, Robin, 20
women of color feminism, 71, 76, 77–78, 82, 83, 194
women's agency, 171, 179
Women's Bell, The, 88
Women's (Peace) Conference (1915), 209, 211, 212–213, 216

women's group identity, 72, 81, 89
Women's International League for Peace and Freedom (WILPF), 7, 205–218; Madeleine Zabriskie Doty, 206, 211–216, 217; International Executive Board, 214–215, 216–217; Lola Maverick Lloyd, 206, 209–211, 217; origins, 206–208; resignations, 210–211; Rosika Schwimmer, 206, 208–211, 212, 217; transnational female friendships and, 216–218
Women's Peace Party, 209, 211
Women's Peace Society, 210
women's rights: advocacy for, 99, 102–103; consent and, 60–61, 170–171, 176–177; as human rights, 5, 75–77, 223, 228; in Islam, 49, 53–54 (*see also* Muslim women); and origins of WILPF, 206; reproductive, 85–86; voting, 206–207, 208–209; "women's rights activism," 77
women's solidarity. *See* solidarity
Woolf, Virginia, 190, 225
World Bank, 95, 184
World Citizenship for the Stateless, 209
World Conferences on Women: Beijing, 1995, 88, 95, 99, 102, 104, 105, 107; Copenhagen, 1980, 95; Mexico, 1975, 95; Nairobi, 1985, 95
World Peace Prize, 210–211
World Trade Organization, 184
"world"-traveling (Lugones), 72, 78–81, 83
World War I, 206–208, 216–217
World War II, 211, 216, 217
Wynner, Edith, 209

Yashodha, 59–65
Young, Iris Marion, 13, 229, 231

Zarkov, D., 228
Zhang, Hong, 86
Zinta, Pretty, 146–147
Zuniga, Ximena, 15
Zweig, Stefan, 205, 217

DISSIDENT FEMINISMS

Hear Our Truths: The Creative Potential of Black Girlhood   *Ruth Nicole Brown*
Muddying the Waters: Coauthoring Feminisms across Scholarship and Activism
   Richa Nagar
Beyond Partition: Gender, Violence, and Representation in Postcolonial India
   Deepti Misri
Feminist and Human Rights Struggles in Peru: Decolonizing Transitional Justice
   Pascha Bueno-Hansen
Against Citizenship: The Violence of the Normative   *Amy L. Brandzel*
Dissident Friendships: Feminism, Imperialism, and Transnational Solidarity
   Edited by Elora Halim Chowdhury and Liz Philipose

The University of Illinois Press
is a founding member of the
Association of American University Presses.

Composed in 10.25/13 Marat Pro
by Kirsten Dennison
at the University of Illinois Press
Cover designed by Jennifer S. Holzner
Cover illustration: Ambreen Butt

University of Illinois Press
1325 South Oak Street
Champaign, IL 61820-6903
www.press.uillinois.edu